Participatory Networks and the Environment

Seeking innovative answers to global sustainability challenges has become an urgent need with the onslaught of environmental and ecological degradation that surrounds us today. More than ever, there is a need to carve new ways for citizens and different industries and institutions to unite – to cooperate, communicate and collaborate to address growing global sustainability concerns.

This book examines one such global collaboration called The BGreen Project (BGreen): a transnational participatory action research project that spans the United States and Bangladesh with the aim of addressing environmental issues via academic–community engagement. By analysing and unpacking the architecture of BGreen, Hasan teases out the key factors that are required for the continued momentum of environmentally focused, academic–community partnership projects in order to present a workable model that could be applied elsewhere. This model is based around a unique conceptual framework developed by the author – "transnational participatory networks" – which is drawn from participatory action research and actor network theory, with the specific aim of addressing the common challenge of building evolving, stable and sustainable networks.

This book will be of great interest to students and scholars of environmental communication, citizen participation, environmental politics, environmental sociology and sustainable development.

Fadia Hasan is a Visiting Assistant Professor at the Urban Studies Program in Trinity College, Hartford, CT, USA.

Routledge Studies in Environmental Communication and Media

Environmental Advertising in China and the USA
The Desire to Go Green
Xinghua Li

Public Perception of Climate Change
Policy and Communication
Bjoern Hagen

Environmental Communication and Community
Constructive and Destructive Dynamics of Social Transformation
Tarla Rai Peterson, Hanna Ljunggren Bergeå, Andrea M. Feldpausch-Parker and Kaisa Raitio

Environmental Communication Pedagogy and Practice
Edited by Tema Milstein, Mairi Pileggi and Eric Morgan

Environmental Pollution and the Media
Political Discourses of Risk and Responsibility in Australia, China and Japan
Glenn D. Hook, Libby Lester, Meng Ji, Kingsley Edney and Chris G. Pope
with contributions from Luli van der Does-Ishikawa

Environmental Communication and Critical Coastal Policy
Communities, Culture and Nature
Kerrie Foxwell-Norton

Climate Change and Post-Political Communication
Media, Emotion and Environmental Advocacy
Philip Hammond

The Discourses of Environmental Collapse
Imagining the End
Edited by Alison E. Vogelaar, Brack W. Hale and Alexandra Peat

Environmental Management of the Media
Policy, Industry, Practice
Pietari Kääpä

Participatory Networks and the Environment
The BGreen Project in the US and Bangladesh
Fadia Hasan

For more information about this series, please visit: https://www.routledge.com/Routledge-Studies-in-Environmental-Communication-and-Media/book-series/RSECM

Participatory Networks and the Environment

The BGreen Project in the US and Bangladesh

Fadia Hasan

LONDON AND NEW YORK

First published 2019
by Routledge
2 Park Square, Milton Park, Abingdon, Oxon OX14 4RN

and by Routledge
52 Vanderbilt Avenue, New York, NY 10017

First issued in paperback 2020

Routledge is an imprint of the Taylor & Francis Group, an informa business

British Library Cataloguing-in-Publication Data
A catalogue record for this book is available from the British Library

Library of Congress Cataloging-in-Publication Data
Names: Hasan, Fadia, author.
Title: Participatory networks and the environment : the BGreen Project
in the US and Bangladesh / Fadia Hasan.
Description: Abingdon, Oxon ; New York, NY : Routledge, 2018.
Series: Routledge studies in environmental communication and media |
Includes bibliographical references and index.
Identifiers: LCCN 2018008877| ISBN 9781138234734 (hardback :
alk. paper) | ISBN 9781315306230 (ebook)
Subjects: LCSH: BGreen Project. | Communication in the
environmental sciences. | Environmental protection—International
cooperation. | Environmental protection—United States. |
Environmental protection—Bangladesh. | Action research.
Classification: LCC GE25 .H37 2018 | DDC 363.7/0525—dc23
LC record available at https://lccn.loc.gov/2018008877

ISBN 13: 978-0-367-58755-0 (pbk)
ISBN 13: 978-1-138-23473-4 (hbk)

Typeset in Perpetua
by Florence Production Ltd, Stoodleigh, Devon

Contents

Foreword   ix

1 Introduction   1

2 Theory and methods   16

3 Transnational political economic realities and their impacts
   on social transformation   66

4 The networked architecture of the BGreen experience   86

5 Multi-media amplification of the BGreen Project   114

6 Youth reflections, growth and sustenance of BGreen
   participatory network   169

7 Conclusion   192

Index   211

Foreword

I met Fadia Hasan during a time in higher education in which there was growing concern over civic engagement and community-based research taking place locally across the United States and around the globe. The concern centered on the necessity to develop community–university partnerships that did not treat communities as laboratories but were in fact, equal partners in the development of participatory action research and community engagement projects in which the needs and voices of community participants (as opposed to the desires of academic researchers) led the way, and discussions over limited economic, educational, political and environmental resources took place. From the first time I met Fadia Hasan, she exuded an energy that telegraphed a commitment to social justice, community engagement, and participatory-based research that was sorely needed in the academic conversations about globally and transnationally located community–university partnerships. During her time at graduate school in the Department of Communication at the University of Massachusetts Amherst, it was clear she had a vision of the type of scholar-activist she wanted to become particularly within the context of the global south.

Her book not only speaks to this vision but provides a model for the type of reciprocal and impactful community–academic (research) partnerships that are possible and increasingly necessary. The BGreen Project (BGreen) began through a desire to create deliberate, participatory interventions that brought together students, business leaders, policymakers, academics and activists to collaboratively address pressing, locally-based environmental questions that are affecting populations across the world. What began as something local, grew into a transnational movement through which the concerns over the geo-politics of sustainability could cut across nation, language, race, class and location differences and bring together globally disparate subjects in a conversation about why the environment matters and what can be done to create sustainable responses to environmental challenges. As Fadia Hasan notes in her introduction, BGreen and the transnational youth activists involved in the project aimed to develop meaningful reciprocal partnerships that were rooted in a commitment toward social change, inclusivity, and the contestation of power dynamics that often leave community voices out of the important conversations regarding the intersections of economic structures, environmental conditions, educational access and sustainability approaches.

The significance of this monograph is that it takes seriously the interrogation of civic engagement praxis in the context of a global academic–community project while also pointing to potential lessons that participatory action research, in conjunction with participatory actor networks and technological support, can provide for the development of conscientious counter-narratives regarding ethical collaborations and the "architecture of participation" across (neo-liberal) multi-institutional contexts. Over the course of seven chapters, this book explores the transnational creation of a collectively-formed, youth-led organization and the challenges as well as opportunities that forward-looking academic–community partnerships can produce for social justice-oriented civic engagement across global settings, networks and institutions which assiduously address the challenges of not only the environment, economy and education, but also the voices of communities which are often silenced and unheard. Fadia Hasan is meticulous in this transnational endeavor and successfully maps a framework that can be adapted and transformed in a variety of ways to engage with other global academic–community partnerships. Dear reader, you will not be disappointed with the story you are about to delve into, and in fact, I hope you become inspired to cultivate collaborative social change in your community. It's more important than ever!

Mari Castañeda, Amherst, MA

1 Introduction

Seeking innovative answers to global sustainability challenges has become an urgent need with the onslaught of environmental and ecological degradation that surrounds us today. More than ever, there is a need to carve new ways for citizens and different industries and institutions to unite—to cooperate, communicate and collaborate to address growing global sustainability concerns. Through the lens of a transnational participatory action research project that I founded, called *The BGreen Project (BGreen)*, multi-industry, political and economic network connections were developed. The formation of these connections into a transnational academic–community platform spanning the US and Bangladesh is analyzed here. The connections between multi-institutions, culture, and politics from a US and Bangladeshi perspective is explored, as well as how such intersections impact development and sustenance of academic–community partnerships, models, and frameworks globally. It is not so much a comparative analysis of the two geopolitical locations, but more an analysis of the transnational continuum that illuminates the complex interweaving of diverse global, regional, and local policies as they play out in these disparate locations in the creation, implementation, and operationalization of transnational academic–community partnerships such as BGreen.

The main goal of the formation of BGreen was to create new ways of organized participation of global youth, community, and academia towards inclusive and sustained social change. The very different roles of youth in both countries, the US and Bangladesh, will be explored in this book and how it has shaped the experience of BGreen and its global proliferation (Kabir, 2010; Giroux, 2002, 2005, 2013; Tuck, 2009; Cammarota & Fine, 2008; Khaleduzzaman, 2014). In brief, BGreen is a participatory action research platform that had its roots in Western Massachusetts, USA and Dhaka, Bangladesh. As a scholar interested in connecting community with academia, I wanted to create a trans-local and transnational academic–community platform in Dhaka, Bangladesh and Western Massachusetts, USA that merged youth with academic and non-academic organizations to bring about sustained social change in the fields of education, environment, and sustainability. Upon its creation, the platform mobilized global high school, college, and university youth in an assortment of participatory/ deliberative activities in the fields of education, environment, and sustainability in both geopolitical locations in and out of the classroom.

Via BGreen, global youth have negotiated their affiliation to diverse political economic structures (for example, their educational institutions) in creative ways and developed innovative methods of public engagement and participation as a means for potentially deep, sustained, and long-term social change. The nature of participation and academic community engagement took different shapes in the two locations due to the differing contexts creating a nuanced and complex transnational network; these issues will be analyzed in the following chapters. Combining the theoretical paradigms of Actor Network Theory (ANT) and Participatory Action Research (PAR), I argue for the development of what I call the BGreen *participatory network* (to be defined later) that is informed by the democratic inclusion of multi actors/actants to address the challenges at hand. The BGreen participatory network builds on the frame of an "architecture of participation" (Harvey, 2014) that involves the contribution of human and non-human actors/actants to gain network stability. The onset of climate change calls for new, humane, and inclusive frameworks. These frameworks, combining economy, ecology and education, can effectively address environmental issues by creating trans-local and transnational spaces. BGreen aims to be such a space, purposefully constructed for optimal emergence of solutions.

Freire's call for the emergence of "critical consciousness" or *conscientização* (1970a, 1970b, 1973) is a desired goal for BGreen that can potentially transform the way in which youth, community and academic institutions relate to one another. The complex and sometimes contrasting understanding and application of *conscientização* as a working concept of the youth from the two locations is also explored in this book. When explaining the concept of *conscientização*, Freire (1970a) writes, "Humankind *emerge* from their *submersion* and acquire the ability to *intervene* in reality as it is unveiled. *Intervention* in reality—historical awareness it self—thus represents a step forward from *emergence,* and results from the *conscientização* of the situation. *Conscientização* is the deepening of the attitude of awareness characteristic of all emergence" (p. 109). Building the collaborative architectural process of a platform like BGreen holds the potential to the emergence of "new epistemologies that celebrate, rather than suppress, alternative ways of knowing" (Shabazz & Cooks, 2014, p. 27). *Conscientização* (critical consciousness) is key to the networked political economic process of BGreen. This is because the different stages of this idea (magical, naïve and critical) are necessary to build a participatory process that engages multiple institutions and youth. These participatory processes, where all members are actively making sense of and engaging with their social and political realities, is capable of generating action and social change (Freire, 1970a, 1970b).

The youth is the thread that connects multi-industries and institutions, potentially creating *conscientização* that addresses the pressing issues of education, environment, human rights, citizen participation and deliberation. All of this is key to a balanced and well-functioning society, as the well-being of a few cannot come at the expense of tragedy, loss and displacement of many. Such inclusive solution building of communities directly counters the "damage-centered" (Tuck, 2009) perspective of interacting and working with communities from the borderlands (Anzaldua, 1999) as being broken, damaged, deranged, or dysfunctional. More specifically, my research interrogates the tensions *and* potentials of hybrid, in-between spaces that exist between political economic structures and networked, youth-led academic–community connections. Political economic analysis of the different actors/actants can be referred to as "the social relations, particularly the power relations, that mutually constitute the production, distribution, and consumption of resources" (Mosco, 1996, p. 24). This analysis, a focal point of my research, examines youth-led action alternatives on the ground that complicate the way in which both ends of the power spectrum operate. To study this transnational networked academic–community project, I use and extend what Busch and Juska (1997) call the *political economy of networks*. This concept focuses on "the relationships among people, things, institutions and ideas [that] are created, maintained and changed through time" (p. 701) by taking into account the role of human *and* non-human actors/actants in the analytic process.

Academic–community partnerships have many names, including the following: community–university partnerships, community service learning, civic engagement, scholarship of engagement, community-based research, citizen science, public engagement, to name just a few. While it has varied names, "the landscape of community-university partnerships include service-learning, community-based participatory research and partnerships focused on solving a particular problem or achieving a particular goal (i.e., neighborhood economic development, workforce development), among other approaches" (Holland et al., 2003). Reflecting on their long engagement with community-engaged work, Cooks and Scharrer (2006) write, "by situating learning in the relational and contextual processes through which people make meaning, we also are able to situate community service-learning as engaged practice – a practice that offers learning in situ through challenges to notions of power, identities, cultures, community and change" (p. 2).

The relationships between pedagogy and institutions and the mechanisms that are in place to facilitate and maintain such processes need to be mapped. Doing so will aid understanding of the complexities of northern and southern educational systems as part of global policy and funding shifts around education. Numerous studies have been done in analyzing the networked political economy of such academic–community partnerships mainly in the global north, all of which will form a general backbone of this research. However, my project takes this investigation further by looking at the development of one such PAR-ANT based project in *both* the global north and the global south, providing a fresh comparative narrative. Perhaps lessons from such global academic–community projects hold the potential to redefine the way in which youth can engage with academia and community organizations to address these pertinent social issues and build a newer, better, fairer "architecture of participation". As a generative and transformative space built on the foundations of *conscientização*, BGreen complicates the outmoded binary of "core" and "periphery" developed as a result of the critical political economic lineage (Wallerstein, 1974). BGreen has the potential to unsettle and reconfigure such divisive, asymmetrical power constructs by creating hybrid spaces that combine citizens, institutions and technology for social change, although as the chapters will delineate, the project played out differently in the two geopolitical locations.

Using participatory action research (PAR) as a tool for "fundamental, critical strategy for youth development, youth based policymaking and organizing and education" (Cammarota & Fine, 2008, p. 7), the youth are consciously and unconsciously navigating academic–community partnerships like BGreen for the realization, sustenance and application of Freire's concept of *conscientização,* which is designed to complicate epistemic communities as a theoretical and institutional project. Reid and Frisby's (2008) work on critical participatory action research well articulated the theoretical knowledge that backed the practical design of this PAR project, one that calls for "accounting for intersectionality, honoring voice and differences through participatory research processes, exploring new forms of representation, reflexivity, and honoring many forms of action." PAR as a field has its direct origins in Freire's idea of *conscientização*, and PAR has been theorized in a multitude of different ways (among others Sparks, 2007; Servaes & Malikhao, 2008; Jacobsen & Kolluri, 1999; Gibson-Graham, 2005; Escobar, 2008; Cammarota & Fine, 2008; Tuck, 2009; Stoval, 2006; Patel, 2012), most of which have been used in different ways in the field of communication. While there are nuanced differences in all approaches, they all work with the central theme of *conscientização* as defining a starting point, even though the term and its applications have been interpreted in a variety of different ways and have found unique meanings in different parts of the world while forming heterogeneous participatory forms.

In my research, the goal is to combine critical PAR with Actor Network Theory (ANT) (Latour, 1987, 2004; Hassard & Law, 1999; Callon, 1987; Cressman, 2009), which is a constructivist theory that has its roots in complexity theory, or as Latour calls an "infra-language" (Latour & Crawford, 1993) used to explore and analyze the relational ties within an emerging network, where the "socionatural relations are multiple, messy and complex" (Castree & MacMillan, 2001). ANT takes a performative approach to tracing the networks through which multifarious entities are scripted, fabricated, and transformed and the concept is explored in all its complexity and not simply reduced to "an actor alone nor to a network . . . an actor-network is simultaneously an actor whose activity is networking heterogeneous elements and a network that is able to redefine and transform what it is made of" (Callon, 1987, p. 93). While PAR was used to develop BGreen on the ground, I use ANT to analyze the process of developing this participatory network. PAR in collaboration with ANT aids in the development of a participatory mechanism for working with the human actors/actants on the ground that helped build this "architecture of participation" (Harvey, 2014). However, ANT's other critical contribution to this research process is its inclusion of studying non-human actors/actants that helped build the "architecture of participation", such as technological and multi-media innovations, which subsequently led to the process of building a stable, global participatory network for BGreen.

"Architecture of participation" as a concept is defined as being a process that uses ICT-mediated environments and relationships to democratize any collective, political process that creates new possibilities of participation and openness within the power dynamics that frame new media processes (Harvey, 2014). To develop this robust architecture via PAR and ANT, the project deals with the relational dynamics and the resulting, evolving, and ever-changing outcomes of human and non-human actors/actants that inform the growth of participatory actor networks, with a special emphasis of course on the role of communication technological innovations. Hence, the infralanguage or theory of ANT (barring some modifications, which will be addressed in the literature review) is used extensively alongside PAR to address the research process. Merging the two complementary approaches of PAR and ANT allows for the creation of what I call participatory networks (in our case, the BGreen participatory network), one which works based on the synthesis of these two complementary approaches of working with human and non-human actors/actants and participatory processes.

With the coining of participatory networks as an interdisciplinary concept, I am referring to the way in which elements of the two theoretical frameworks of PAR and ANT can be combined to work together to create an architecture of participation amongst multi-actors/actants across institutions and industries that can be sustained. At its best, participatory networks will challenge the concept of epistemic communities and instead create a deep, engaged, complex and open participatory network that addresses issues of power (institutional, cultural, locational, vocational, individual, etc). In addressing issues of power, creating relationships to the realization of participation and engagement in an organic, meaningful way, there exists potential to impact the ways in which education, environment, sustainability and economy relate to one another. Inspired by ANT, a participatory network is comprised of human actors and non-human actors/actants that are relationally related to one another, such as technology, organizations, ideologies, cultural attitudes (to name just a few) in the development of the project.

ANT is a complex theoretical framework with roots in complexity theory. In applying it to my research, I am following what Castree and MacMillan (2001) call for, which is a weak version of ANT, in combination with the PAR approach to make the theoretical frame of the project. Why such a theoretical decision is required to form a participatory network is explained in detail in the next chapter. In the way that I have envisioned a well-functioning participatory network, Freire's *conscientização* is at the core of the synthesis of PAR and ANT. Freire (1970a) reflects on the importance of the emergence of *conscientização* and how the pursuit of it can truly connect theory and praxis. He writes, "human activity consists of action and reflection: it is praxis; it is transformation of the world. And as praxis, it requires theory to illuminate it. Human activity is theory and practice; it is reflection and action" (p. 25). The formation of such participatory networks ideally connects these different theories or "infralanguages" of participation and social change that can guide the search, exploration, participation, and creation of praxis close to the way in which Freire had envisioned it. The idea of participatory networks and the way in which I developed it in conjunction with PAR and ANT will be elaborated further in the following chapters and its potential relevance to the formation of multi-industry and institutional networks in this context.

It is my hope that the critical performative participation of the global youth in the creation of the architecture of the BGreen participatory network would result in the creation of alternative discourses and practices around the ways in which multi-actors/actants can combine forces to design a collaborative process for social change that is directly triggered by academic engagement. The relationship between national and international community organizations, academic institutions and youth collaborating together to design the BGreen experience in Dhaka, Bangladesh and Western Massachusetts, USA (and beyond) is an important story to map and narrate since it provides insights from the under-documented periphery (youth cultures) from both the global north and south on alliances and networks that are intentionally built towards sustained social change. This narrative provides a glimpse into the endless possibilities and potentials for a society in which academic institutions provide the initial foundation to promising social change ideas and initiatives such as BGreen. One of the goals of this project was to provide youth action plans with the most sound institutional support, via the academic and civil society partnerships and see the ways in which such intentionally built networks of alliance can transform isolated industries into more collaborative ones.

Research questions

Participatory academic–community counter-narratives such as BGreen carve out examples of how the power and resources of the academy can indeed be used to mobilize, engage and unite other non-academic social actors and organizations towards inclusive social change. The extent to which heterogeneous, complex and hybrid participatory networks are formed by way of an academic–community movement that is triggered by global youth is guided by the exploration of these research questions:

1. By utilizing and building on the concept of *conscientização* and merging *PAR and ANT,* how are *participatory networks* like BGreen created in the midst of the current de-politicized higher educational system in Bangladesh and the United States, one that challenges the apolitical, disengaged, neoliberal set-up of education today?
2. How did the human and non-human actors/actants contribute to the emergence of the BGreen participatory network? What do such participatory networks like BGreen look like on the ground and how do they recruit "allies" and acquire a modified notion of ANT's "black box"?
3. How can citizen science initiatives such as BGreen influence/alter/ transform/redefine multi-institutional relationships by building sustained networks of communication, cooperation and collaboration? How can PAR and ANT work together in fruitful ways such as BGreen to gain momentum to form larger, more sustained reach and results?

BGreen: content and its relationship to the "architecture of participation"

The need to build a new form of architecture of participation was the vision behind the development of this counter-cultural academic activist platform that encourages the development and use of citizen science discourses, which rely on the "direct participation by lay people in citizen science and community-based research" (Worthington, Cavalier et al., 2012, p. v). The convergence of different institutional strengths and visions, as they impacted the formation of this BGreen participatory network to develop this architecture of participation, is important to analyze as it contributes to the destabilization of "core" and "periphery" as fixed, irrevocable categories that perpetuate binarism. "Core" and "periphery" will be re-negotiated in this project in more ways than one, because of the direct involvement of youth *and* marginalized peoples (both groups that are most often excluded from "important" decision-making) to solution-build together, challenging a "damage-centered" framework which is often used in interventionist research.

This destabilization will make way for youth to examine "the historical and social contexts and contingencies of scientific knowledge and technology. In doing so, they are explicitly rejecting a linear model of scientific and technical change and with it any hint of social, technical or scientific determinism, reductionism or autonomy" (Cressman, 2009, p. 3), which is in alignment with the "messy, complex, hybrid, chimeric and entangled" approach of ANT (Castree & MacMillan, 2001). As the following chapters will delineate, the action research content in both the US and in Bangladesh was generated in consultation with the youth groups and individuals I worked with to build this participatory network, consistent with the goals of creating an "architecture of participation" that is democratic, inclusive, engaged and following a participatory model.

After searching for an appropriate name that pays homage to the idea of *conscientização* in relation to how human and non-human actors/actants like environment, education, youth, and action can connect globally, "BGreen" was collectively generated by the core group of community partners. This name was coined with the consultation of the youth groups and individuals who were on the ground as community partners for the project. We wanted to find a name that focused on at least three of the four most important parts of developing the project. We came up with *BGreen: (Youth. Environment. Action.)* that included all but education in the title. While we all wanted to use the word education in the title, at the given time of finalizing this name, we were unable to come up with a catchy title that attracted the urban youth but still stayed true to the goals of the project. In the name, B signifies the idea of *"being"* in motion, action and bringing about potential and sustained change. Green signifies one of the main themes that connect the desired audience in their discussions and deliberations of developing a new global youth community that is green, sustainability focused and environmentally conscious.

BGreen seeks to support youth in developing the empowering citizen science paradigms of thought and praxis and claiming the highest meaning of knowledge according to Freire, one which leads to "a deepened consciousness of their situation [that] leads [individuals as well as organizations] to apprehend their situation as a historical reality susceptible of trans-formation" (Freire 1985, p. 253). Hence praxis, which Freire (1970a, 1970b) refers to as "reflection combined with action" in a participatory setting will ideally and consciously result in social transformation led by the synthesis of global youth and community–academic partnerships in the US and Bangladesh.

Isolated institutions and industries, be they academic, governmental, activist, or otherwise, all have their unique ways of engaging with social challenges, often having expertise in some aspects of developing solution-building strategies to address a social issue at hand. However, as often happens, each industry perspective comes with its limitations and suffers from what is called organizational tunnel vision. Building networks across industries that result in communication, cooperation and collaboration could potentially overcome some of these exclusionary challenges for a greater overall impact. As explained earlier, the combination of PAR, ANT and Freire's *conscientização* that forms the basis of participatory networks as a concept guides this research exploration and addresses the way in which power plays into the formation of such networks. I hope to engage with the ways in which perhaps, small global movements like BGreen, can develop creative ways to benefit from external institutional power to use to their advantage, to support the growth of such youth-engaged PAR projects that use academia as a driving force towards social change.

Increasingly within academia, there is a shift towards embracing the strength in the interdisciplinarity of different departments and schools of thought. This is leading to the creation of many creative centers within academic institutions that combine scholars and research stemming from various disciplines. My idea is to take such interdisciplinarity beyond the academy and to apply it to the merging of diverse industries, to create more of an opportunity for inter-mingling of the perspectives of multi-industries and multi-actors, often ones that do not speak to one another. The goal is to concoct creative combinations of actors/actants to work together for the realization of *conscientização,* a journey, which does not necessarily have an end, but instead functions as a constant form of reflection and action, which has the potential for bigger social impact (Straubhaar, 2014).

In a global context of the exclusivity in the structures of how educational institutions function and operate, there is more than ever a need to support and nurture the growth of academic–community partnerships to bring back a more politicized, community- and civically-engaged approach to education. Higher education and its relationship to politics has a complex history in Bangladesh as well as the United States. Both countries share some contextual similarities but just as many stark differences in terms of the way in which education, politics, activism, economics, and youth intersect. As my research will delineate, the United States educational traditions have significantly affected Bangladeshi educational models as they stand today. Hence, the project of BGreen directly advocates for a new kind of community-engaged, politically- and socially-relevant form of research—one that directly challenges the intentionally apolitical neoliberal set-up of education today in Bangladesh and the US (Kabir, 2011; Muhammad, 2003; Buckland, 2005). The current apolitical and socially divorced form of education perpetuates a form of mechanical knowledge building devoid of critical thinking, one that does not encourage the formation of new knowledges and fresh discourses. Creative connections that can be made from having multiple industries work together have potentially far-reaching, positive results and consequences. The implementation of citizen science and community engagement programs in educational institutions and classrooms, may be an important innovation in the higher educational context, to lead the way for more socially engaged, critical thinking youth that participate in collaboration with organizational structures to achieve their localized version of *conscientização*.

I will provide a breakdown of my book chapters in the following paragraphs, giving a summary of each, and how they address the main questions that are guiding my research. Following the introduction is theory and methods chapter that maps and expands the theoretical contributions that frame this research project and subsequently the methods used to collect data for this PAR-ANT project. This is followed by the five main analysis chapters of this comparative research project, which were organized to address and answer the three main research questions that were laid out earlier in this section. In all four main analysis chapters, I address my research questions thematically and in combination with one another, rather than in neat, isolated sections.

The main analysis chapters are as follows:

The first analysis chapter (Chapter 4) consists of the important social and historical themes that provide the backbone and context for my research and findings. It provides the historical overview and political economic analysis of both the US and Bangladeshi higher educational systems and how politics and academic–community partnerships, models and frameworks have played out in the past before the transition of the economy into a hyper-capitalist, neo-liberal system. Political economic realities of both nations and their relationships to education and social change are discussed, as are the differences and the similarities in the ways in which networks are built based on the complex intertwining of various social, cultural, economic factors in the contest of global north and south. Investigation and analysis of the major actors in the local and global levels that structurally impact the development and sustenance of such collaborative academic–community engaged projects is highlighted.

This chapter also provides insight into the influence of US policies on privatization and education and how it impacts the formation of academic–community networks within the US as well as countries as geographically far away as Bangladesh. In the specific context of the global south, literature focused on the Bangladeshi higher educational system and its contested relationship to politics, youth and social change is explored that creates barriers to apply Freire's approach to developing an educational project that is community engaged and geared towards social inclusion, innovation and transformation. I investigate how such an economic system controls the funding, structure and curriculum goals of dominantly privatized education in both Bangladesh and the US. Privatization of education and how it has negatively impacted the scope of developing an educational project with *conscientização* as the central driving force is addressed in this section. The chapter also provides direct commentary and analysis about the state of academic–community partnerships in both US and Bangladesh today, and establishes the need for projects like BGreen to challenge the current educational and youth engagement challenges, one that dismisses "damage-centered" discourses.

In the second analysis chapter (Chapter 5), the larger frame that drives the creation of this concept is the relational dynamics between transnational political economic systems and participatory action initiatives (on the ground and online) to create transnational participatory networks, in this specific case, the BGreen participatory network contributes to the transformation of academic–community partnerships that connect Bangladesh and the US. This chapter is divided into two major sections, each section focusing on the concurrent and connected development of BGreen in Bangladesh and the US. Questions addressed and explored include: What are the shared similarities and what are the striking differences in developing such academic community projects in the US and in Bangladesh? How do existing discourses of environment and education frame the experience of developing such an academic community action network? How are these discourses different from and/or similar to the two diverse geopolitical locations and how does that affect the way in which BGreen operates in these two distinct (yet interconnected) spaces?

The strategies undertaken by the institutional and independent actors working as a team towards a common goal are investigated and how those decisions are reflective of a participatory process like BGreen. The importance of having academic roots for this youth engagement project of this nature, one which de-centers, ideas of "core" and "periphery" will be the key points of discussion and analysis in this chapter. This will shed light on the endless possibilities and potentials for a society in which academic institutions provide the initial foundation to innovative social change ideas and initiatives such as BGreen.

The next analysis chapter (Chapter 6) specifically traces the academic–community partnerships and networks (online and offline) that were established with national and international organizations to make BGreen possible in the US and Bangladesh. I engage with PAR, ANT and application of Freire's *conscientização* in the development of the participatory networks on the ground and online in the formation and proliferation of BGreen. More specifically the specific contribution of media institutions in the development of the architecture of BGreen is explored. It is important that the nature of the media exposure (mainstream and alternative) and amplification for a non-commercial academic–community engaged project like BGreen is explored; it provides insights on how commercially driven enterprises, such as the different media industries in Bangladesh and the US hold the power to significantly contribute to the organizing efforts of less-institutionally powerful groups, such as youth, civil society and community organizations.

Chapter 6 both narrates and analyzes the media (digital and new media) networks (radio, television, print and new media outlets) that contributed to the flourishing of the participatory action research project. The actors involved in the process of developing media participatory networks and the extent to which these multi-media networks helped in amplifying the goals of such an academic–community engaged environmental mission such as BGreen is studied. The structural significance of media support for projects like these is interrogated and analyzed to understand the flourishing of such projects to gain network stability. How did the media support vary in the two geopolitical locations and what are the reasons for these differences and/or similarities, and to what ends? Ultimately, the question that is posed is what stream of media goes the farthest and deepest to sustain movements like BGreen that are noncommercial and constantly evolving and why perhaps some media streams may be better than others to contribute significantly to the development of such a participatory network.

This chapter will look at the political economy of the media and the importance of such media exposure and amplification for a project, especially considering that BGreen has non-commercial academic–community origins. Media is an important industry perspective to add to the collaborative mix for environmental youth engagement work. The way in which BGreen was represented in the media in Bangladesh versus that of the US is an important point of inquiry to understand the larger discourses that frame such an academic–community partnership in the two nations. The participatory network building capacity via the proliferation of the movement through transnational media networks points to the potentials of youth to navigate an unlikely space for the realization, sustenance and application of Freire's *conscientização* to create new discourses and bring about lasting environmental change. What is the impact of on-ground and e-activism? The latter is a route that especially Bangladeshi youth have found to voice their opinions on environmental social justice that bypasses institutional structures of universities and civil society organizations. Is this phenomenon creating a community of idea exchange, action and change using the multi-media outlets such as print, radio, television and internet as a space for social transformation?

The final analysis chapter (Chapter 7) narrates this environmental academic–community engaged project from the perspective of the affiliated youth. It explores global youth community organizers as agents of action, addressing how their identities are negotiated when attaching themselves to academic–community movements such as BGreen as independent and key stakeholders. The chapter takes a comparative approach on how the nature of the youth involvement, initiatives and aspirations are different and similar across the two geopolitical locations in study. This chapter brings the discussion full circle, as it puts forth the voices and perspectives of the youth who are participating in this academic–community project, which was designed to provide an alternative to the way in which Bangladeshi and US youth could navigate the educational and community organizations that they are affiliated with. There is a need in both the US and Bangladesh for a shift in the educational model to one that puts student needs, ideas, and aspirations at the core of their goals and makes youth participation, engagement, and deliberation a center piece that can benefit from the established structural and political economic strengths of multi-institutions and industries as explored in the different chapters that came before this.

Can academic–community partnership models bring to the forefront newer forms of politicized student engagement tradition in Bangladesh and the US that is a departure from the older forms of political affiliations and controversies of public universities and student bodies of the past, considering the market-based funding structure of higher-education institutions in Bangladesh and the US? Despite the market limitations, how can youth, universities and community organizations achieve *conscientização* as an institutional goal, one that holds transformative potential for society? How can citizen science initiatives such as BGreen influence/alter/transform/redefine multi-industry relationships by building sustained networks of communication, cooperation, and collaboration amongst them?

Bibliography

Alam, M., Haque, M. S. & Siddique, S. F. (2007). *Private higher education in Bangladesh*. N. V. Varghese (ed.). Bangladesh: International Institute for Educational Planning.

Anzaldua, G. (1999). *Borderlands/La frontera: The new mestiza*. San Francisco: Aunt Lute Books.

Buckland, P. (2005). *Reshaping the future: Education and postconflict reconstruction*. Washington, DC: World Bank Publications.

Busch, L. & Juska, A. (1997). Beyond political economy: actor networks and the globalization of agriculture. *Review of International Political Economy*, 4(4): 688–708.

Callon, M. (1987). Society in the making: The study of technology as a tool for sociological analysis. In W. E. Bijker, T. P. Hughes and T. Pinch (eds) *The social construction of technological systems: New directions in the sociology and history of technology*. Cambridge, MA: The MIT Press, pp. 83–103.

Cammarota, J. & Fine, M. (2008). *Revolutionizing education: Youth participatory action research in motion*. New York: Routledge.

Castree, N. & MacMillan, T. (2001). Dissolving dualisms: Actor-networks and the reimagination of nature. In N. Castree and B. Braun (eds) *Social nature: Theory, practice, and politics*. Malden, MA: Blackwell Publishers, pp. 208–224.

Cooks, L. & Scharrer, E. (2006). Assessing learning in community service learning: A social approach. *Michigan Journal of Community Service Learning*, 13(1): 44–55.

Cressman, D. (2009). *A brief overview of actor-network theory: Punctualization, heterogeneous engineering & translation*. Burnaby, BC: Centre for Policy Research on Science and Technology.

Escobar, A. (2008). *Territories of difference: Place, movements, life, redes*. Durham: Duke University Press.

Freire, P. (1985). *The politics of education: Culture, power, and liberation*. Santa Barbara, CA: Greenwood Publishing Group.

Freire, P. (1970a). *Pedagogy of the oppressed*. New York: Continuum.

Freire, P. (1970b). *Cultural action for freedom*. Cambridge, MA: Center for the Study of Development and Social Change.

Freire, P. (1973). *Education for critical consciousness*. New York: Continuum.

Gibson-Graham, J. K. (2006). *A postcapitalist politics*. Minneapolis: University of Minnesota Press.

Gibson-Graham, J. K. (2006). *The end of capitalism (as we knew it): A feminist critique of political economy*. Minneapolis: University of Minnesota Press, pp.1–23.

Giroux, H. A. (2002). Neoliberalism, corporate culture, and the promise of higher education: The University as a democratic public sphere. *Harvard Educational Review, 72*(4): 425–463.

Giroux, H. A. (2005). The terror of neoliberalism: Rethinking the significance of cultural politics. *College Literature, 32*(1): 1–19.

Giroux, H. A. (2013). *Youth in revolt: Reclaiming a democratic future*. Boulder: Paradigm.

Harvey, B. (2014). Negotiating openness across science, ICTs, and participatory development: Lessons from the AfricaAdapt network. *Information Technologies and International Development, 7*, 19.

Hassard, J. & Law, J. (1999). *Actor network theory and after*. Hoboken, NJ: Wiley-Blackwell.

Holland, B. A., Gelmon, S., Green, L., Greene-Moton, E. & Stanton, T. K. (2003). *Community-university partnerships: What do we know?* National Symposium on Community-University Partnerships, April 2003. San Diego, CA.

Jacobson, T. L. & Kolluri, S. (1999). Participatory communication as communicative action. *Theoretical Approaches to Participatory Communication*, 265–280.

Kabir, A. H. (2010). Neoliberal policy in the higher education sector in Bangladesh: Autonomy of public universities and the role of the state. *Policy Futures in Education, 8*(6), 619–631.

Kabir, A. H. (2011). A new discourse of 'international understanding': Nothing but 'Americanism'. *Critical Literacy: Theories and Practices, 5*(1): 38–50.

Khaleduzzaman, M. (2014). Students unrest in higher education level in Bangladesh: A study on Dhaka and Rajshahi University. *IOSR Journal of Research & Method in Education, 4*(2): 6–16.

Latour, B. (1987). *Science in action: How to follow scientists and engineers through society*. Cambridge, MA: Harvard University Press.

Latour, B. (2004). *Politics of nature*. Cambridge, MA: Harvard University Press.

Latour, B. & Crawford, T. H. (1993). An interview with Bruno Latour. *Configurations, 1*(2): 247–268.

López, A. (2010). Defusing the cannon/canon: An organic media approach to environmental communication. *Environmental Communication, 4*(1): 99–108.

Manzo, L. C. & Brightbill, N. (2007). Toward a participatory ethics. In S. Kindon, R. Pain & M, Kesby (eds) *Participatory action research approaches and methods: Connecting people, participation and place*. London: Routledge.

Mosco, V. (1996). *The political economy of communication: Rethinking and renewal*. London: SAGE Publications.

Muhammad, A. (2003). Bangladesh's integration into global capitalist system: Policy direction and the role of global institutions. In M. Rahman (ed.) *Globalisation, environmental crisis and social change in Bangladesh*. Dhaka: University Press, pp. 113–126.

Patel, L. (. (2012). Contact zones, problem posing and critical consciousness. *Pedagogies: An International Journal*, 7(4): 333–346.

Reid, C. & Frisby, W. (2008). Continuing the journey: Articulating dimensions of feminist participatory action research (FPAR). In P. Reason & H. Bradbury (eds) *Sage handbook of action research: Participative inquiry and practice*. London: SAGE Publications, pp. 93–105.

Servaes, J. & Malikhao, P. (2008). Development communication approaches in an international perspective. In J. Servaes (ed.) *Communication for development and social change*. New Delhi: SAGE Publications, p. 158.

Shabazz, D. R. & Cooks, L. M. (2014). The pedagogy of community service-learning discourse: From deficit to asset mapping in the re-envisioning media project. *Journal of Community Engagement and Scholarship*, 7(1): 71.

Sparks, C. (2007). *Globalization, development and the mass media*. London: SAGE Publications.

Stovall, D. (2006). Forging community in race and class: Critical race theory and the quest for social justice in education. *Race Ethnicity and Education*, 9(3): 243–259.

Straubhaar, R. (2014). A place for organisational critical consciousness: Comparing two case studies of Freirean nonprofits. *Comparative Education*, 50(4): 433–447.

Tuck, E. (2009). Suspending damage: A letter to communities. *Harvard Educational Review*, 79(3): 409–428.

Wallerstein, I. (1974). The rise and future demise of the world capitalist system: concepts for comparative analysis. *Comparative studies in society and history*, 16(04): 387–415.

Worthington, R., Cavalier, D., Farooque, M., Gano, G., Geddes, H., Sander, S., Sittenfeld, D. & Tomblin, D. (2012) Technology assessment and public participation: From TA to pTA, *Expert and Citizen Assessment of Science and Technology (eCAST)*.

2 Theory and methods

The theoretical frameworks that form the foundation of this research encompass the fields of communication, science and technology studies, education, critical geography, political science, and political economy. While some of these theories are shared within these distinct fields, my research creates pathways for new theoretical innovations by connecting different ideas that have not been used together before to create intersections that address a common, shared challenge. The larger frame that drives my research questions is the relational dynamics between transnational political economic systems and participatory action initiatives (on-ground and online) to create transnational *participatory networks*, in this specific case, the BGreen participatory network that contributes to the transformation of academic–community partnerships as it flows through transnational spaces.

The theoretical background is set up in the following way:

1. Individual overviews of PAR and ANT are followed by an analysis of how these two frames were used in complement to develop the concept of participatory networks.
2. The way in which PAR and ANT was specifically integrated to fulfill the research goals is delineated. The challenges and advantages of using these theories in integration to develop participatory networks is also laid out.
3. This is followed by an overview of how aspects of political economic theory can inform the deficiencies of PAR and ANT as frameworks, a conversation that is crucial to the development of participatory networks.
4. A synthesis of the contribution of each theoretical concept as used in this research, to expand on what a participatory network is meant to be, how it can gain network stability and the justification for building such a transnational participatory network in the US and Bangladesh in light of the current contextual realities.
5. Finally, the way in which the PAR-ANT methodology is operationalized on the ground in the form of a *multimethod* qualitative research design is explored.

Project orientation

The central theoretical aim of the project is to make the diverse theories from these various fields connect with Freire's notion of "critical consciousness" or *conscientização* (1970a, 1970b, 1973), which through the BGreen participatory network will re-define the relationship between youth and multi-institutions in imagining and forging a different educational-environmental future for the US and Bangladesh. Straubhaar (2014) applies *conscientização* in navigating diverse institutions and writes that this term takes different shapes as it navigates through different entities. He says that it is necessary to be aware that "consciousness comes through participation in an iterative process of reflecting upon one's social reality and taking action to improve it" (Straubhaar, 2014), irrespective of the shape *organizational conscientização* takes in diverse institutions. Before *organizational conscientização* is achieved, it is necessary to understand the three stages of consciousness that Freire talks about in the context of education, community, and social change, which applies to this project.

Freire's three stages are *magical consciousness*, *naïve consciousness* and finally *critical consciousness*. Magical consciousness is referred to as being in a state of silence, disengagement, and inaction to one's social and political realities, where one adapts to the status quo without being conscious of the oppressive elements in society that are being used to structurally disempower certain actors. Naïve consciousness is acknowledging the existence of a problem or a situation that needs changing, but on an individual level, rather than being able to connect it to a structural level. Critical consciousness, or *conscientização*, takes the process to its highest level of consciousness where individuals start looking beyond the personal to start connecting it to structural processes and problems. In this stage, the individuals forge important connections between their own lived realities and larger structural trends and issues that often are designed to silence and omit the under-class (Freire, 1970a, 1970b).

Hence, at its best, the emergence of such critical consciousness will lead to politically motivated behavior in the individuals, where they can use this shift to form a collective or a communion. As Freire (1970a) writes, "Nobody liberates nobody, nobody liberates themselves alone: human beings liberate themselves in communion". Hence, the participation from human and non-human actors/ actants—individuals who work within and between organizations—have the power to transform larger political economic structures by using *conscientização* as an effective social tool, that can change individual and organizational futures. Straubhaar (2014) also points out that each organization's path to seeking *organizational conscientização* will be unique and complex in an aim to transform the structure, goals and ideals of each entity from inside out based on specific geopolitical realities (Straubhaar, 2014).

Using multi-theoretical frames, this research project explores the potentials of the interconnectivity of youth and multi-institutions in creating and utilizing *conscientização* to address issues of environment, education, sustainability and citizen participation. Such inclusive solution building of communities counters the standard approach of big institutions that adhere to a closed, insular system of governance following the political scientific concept of *epistemic communities* that help sustain political economic structures. Epistemic communities are referred to as a "network of professionals with recognized expertise and competence in a particular domain and an authoritative claim to policy-relevant knowledge within that domain or issue-area" (Haas, 1992, p. 3). The aim of using participatory action research (PAR) in combination with actor network theory (ANT) is to develop a "fundamental, critical strategy for youth development, youth based policymaking and organizing and education" (Cammarota & Fine, 2008, p.7). This can be made possible by navigating transnational academic–community partnerships like BGreen for the realization, sustenance, and application of Freire's concept of conscientização, which is designed to complicate epistemic communities as a theoretical and institutional project.

This is where the importance of the concept of participatory networks emerges—I am proposing that elements of the two theoretical frameworks of PAR and ANT can be combined to work together to build an "architecture of participation" (Harvey, 2014) that leads to the formation of a sustained BGreen participatory network.

I'm using the term "participatory networks" as a theoretical frame for this project. As a concept, it brings together Freire's notion of *conscientização* with human and non-human actors/actants in complex emerging networks. Adapting ANT's idea of a classic black box, my notion of participatory network is challenging power and binarism, which often work together to limit the scope and stability of actor networks. This adaption to forming participatory networks instead of black boxes re-theorizes the way actors/actants navigate and negotiate emerging networks that have *conscientização* as the binding force.

Figure 2.1 visually explains participatory networks.

Through the merging of participatory methods, actor networks and political economy, I am treading on the tension of in-between spaces where political economic theories end and community-engaged theories start. The theoretical exploration of this tension forms the central point of analysis in the later part of the literature review, after laying out each theoretical trajectory and its contribution to this project. My goal is to understand this in-between, hybrid space that is creatively trying to develop its own path through the narrow cavities of these seemingly disparate and incompatible actors/actants that do not want to interact with one another. In this project, I have tried to address this in-between space, albeit from a ground-up, participatory perspective, where the role of larger,

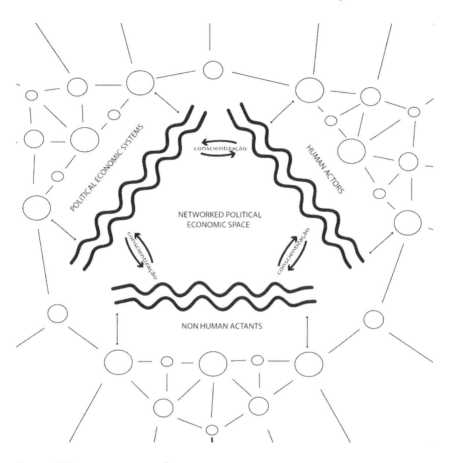

Figure 2.1 Participatory network.

institutional bodies is incorporated into the way in which we relate to the construction and development of small projects such as BGreen. Ultimately, through the synthesis and merging of large and small, as ANT would have it, some of the salient outcomes of this participatory network building process show that larger, political economic entities like universities and media houses, did not stay untouched and unchanged through the formation of participatory networks. It brings into the forefront, the power of small in redefining the ways in which insular, institutional structures operate when they are touched by open, fluid, participatory networks.

At its best, participatory networks will challenge the concept of epistemic communities within political economic structures and instead create an inclusive, democratic network that addresses issues of power (institutional, cultural, locational, vocational, individual, etc) and its relationship to the realization of participation and engagement in a deep, meaningful way, that has the potential to impact the ways in which education, environment and economy relate to one another. Through the investigation and analysis of participatory networks that emerged out of the youth citizen science action research project, perhaps a more inclusive, localized definition of epistemic communities can be developed—one that contributes to the proliferation of such participatory networks. Based on the principles of PAR, citizen science projects attempt to engage "common" people in the process of developing informed scientific discourses and developing a democratic mechanism of reaching policymakers with this participatory approach towards dealing with "hard" science (Worthington, Cavalier et al., 2012).

The participatory citizen science approach is invested in "institutionalizing of a practice that had been proven viable as a way of mobilizing citizen views on global issues" (Worthington, Cavalier et al., 2012) that changes the divisive ways in which epistemic communities operate in keeping the public out of important, scientific discourse building and decision making. The extent to which academic–community networks are developed can be a game-changer in the way in which the youth can create a new "architecture of participation" (Harvey, 2014). This network building aids in realizing solution and environmental social change, perhaps transforming the power relations within and between organizational structures. Through investigating the aforementioned processes, I hope to identify the historical and present cultural scenarios in the US and Bangladesh that have resulted in a certain kind of education and community engagement culture and what the youth are doing actively to change their situations, from inside out.

History and application of participatory action research (PAR) in BGreen

There are nuanced differences in the many iterations of PAR, but all approaches work with the central theme of *conscientização* as defining starting point, even though the term and its applications have been interpreted in a variety of different ways and found unique meanings in different parts of the world while forming heterogeneous networks (among others Sparks, 2007; Servaes & Malikhao, 2008; Jacobson & Servaes, 1999 ; Jacobson & Kolluri, 1999; Gibson-Graham, 2006; Escobar, 2008; Cammarota & Fine, 2008; Tuck, 2009; Stovall, 2006; Patel, 2012). Citizen-science projects such as BGreen are an example of one kind of a PAR project with very specific goals for community transformation. Cammarota and Fine (2008) write:

> PAR is intimately concerned with extending the notion of the so-called "expert" to encompass a wider range of stakeholders. At its very best, PAR opens up a space for a critical, multi-generational dialogue about research

itself—one that looks beyond rarified university walls. This is a fundamental challenge to the ways that research is traditionally conducted and knowledge is traditionally stratified. It too is necessary for universities to meaningfully engage in democratic dialogue in these new and uncertain times.

(Cammarota & Fine, 2008, p. viii)

Cammarota and Fine (2008) advocate for the PAR process in academic–community settings, as they really challenge teachers, students, and administrators to ask hard questions about the true goals of education and how it relates the people it is designed for. Reid and Frisby's (2008) work on critical participatory action research well-articulated the theoretical knowledge that backed the practical design of this PAR project, one that calls for "accounting for intersectionality, honoring voice and differences through participatory research processes, exploring new forms of representation, reflexivity, and honoring many forms of action." In recent years, participatory development projects in the global scene have garnered widespread attention and successful projects have been implemented which target local issues by citizen participation. While there are many expressions of the participatory paradigm, all the emerging traditions in development communication consider the criticisms of the traditional notions of unidirectional communication and modernization development model (among others Sparks, 2007; Servaes & Malikhao, 2008; Jacobson & Kolluri, 1999; Gibson-Graham, 2006; Escobar, 2008). In all the theoretical expressions of participatory research, there is an emphasis on ethical community building and how citizens can, should (and of course, be systematically allowed to) effectively engage in such decision-making: one that is not exclusive, hierarchical, ethno-centric, classist and racist. Recognizing this crucial interdependence allows for re-thinking and redefining economic (and environmental) discourse and decision making to center on potential well-being for all (Gibson-Graham, 2006).

Moving away from damage-centric research projects, this process of bringing together the youth, civil society members and other "experts", is not about telling people how to live or to identify to them what they need. Instead this project is actively designed to build on the participation and needs of the youth themselves that they articulate on their own as they move through the different stages of Freirean consciousness. This project is designed to potentially generate new spaces to create new knowledges, which creates a disruption to status quo that ultimately has the potential to impact the way in which political economic institutions and actor/actant networks relate to one another (Cressman, 2009). As Oberhauser and Kountoupes (2012) write, "from a scientific perspective, public involvement has expanded scientific capabilities and applications". In line with various citizen science projects around the world, BGreen is designed to target environmental questions using community and academia as engaged allies and participants, in this case, specifically the youth to generate innovative solutions for environmental health and well-being for a larger population.

Since PAR forms an important part of this project, it is important to locate the roots of the field of participatory politics within diverse communication and development literature. To explore and fully understand why PAR came into being as a theoretical concept and tool, it is important to know the development agendas that preceded it—modernization and dependency, in order to identify the shortcomings and challenges that were overcome by the creation and adoption of a participatory paradigm. The modernization paradigm had its roots in the 1940s with prominent scholars like Daniel Lerner, Wilbur Schramm and Everett Rogers leading the way. The modernization paradigm of the 1940s had a Western/ Northern origin which emphasized linear economic growth by the adoption of "modern" practices of Western, industrialized, First World Nations. This model separated societies into "traditional" and "modern" and advocated for top-down, positivistic, ethnocentric, interventionist projects to reform the "indigenous, poor, backward and uncivilized" societies.

Such a model was very close to the imperialist, colonialist vision of transforming "other" societies and transplanting European/Anglo/Northern/Western/North American local historical models as if they were a logical, natural and obvious fit. The problematic assumptions of this paradigm were that growth, progress and innovation (technological and otherwise) are equivalent concepts stemming exclusively from a fixed geographical location, namely Western Europe and North America. Also, this paradigm perceived development and progress as unidirectional processes through which underdeveloped nations evolve and advance to become closer to the so-called "core"—the wealthy and industrialized West/North. Within this modernization paradigm, there is one objective reality and the "under-developed" world is incapable of charting its own development and determining its own economic future (Wildemeersh in Jacobson & Servaes, 1999).

The dependency paradigm was a raging reaction from the so-called "periphery"— the poor, the despondent and the so-called underdeveloped and passive global south. It was a theoretical paradigm born out of the Latin-American critical communication and development studies tradition with scholars such as Luis Ramiro Beltran and Juan Diaz Bordenave challenging and rejecting the modernization paradigm as an inclusive and effective method for bringing about sustainable social change. However, dependency was initially theorized by other social science traditions by key figures such as Raul Prebisch, Fernando Cardoso and Anibal Quijano and it was initially influenced by European social science traditions, partly Marxism. This wave of theoretical framework spanned from the 1960s to early 1980s and it produced new critical epistemologies outside of Euro-centric forms of knowledge production for imagining, understanding, and encountering development from a very different vantage point. It drew attention to resist and challenge the historically uneven power relations between developed and less developed regions and the way in which this power differential resulted in the construction of unfair, exploitative systems (Jacobson & Kolluri in Jacobson & Servaes, 1999).

This reaction is entrenched in neo-Marxist and structuralist discourses that describe underdevelopment as a product of historically exploitative, uneven, and imperialistic global economic and political processes. Dependency Theory also considers development to be a uni-directional and linear process that focuses on external transfers (North–South/East–West) rather than internal processes of community building and sustenance (Servaes, 2002). There are different critiques to the dependency theory, where different limitations are identified. Scholar duo, Servaes and Malikhao (2008) add that even though this theory is useful in identifying global inequality on the macro-level, it fails to recognize the stark inconsistencies and disparities that exist on the local and national scale, within both the "core" and the "periphery", the "First World" and the "Third World."

According to them, the necessary complexities within these "peripheral" and "core" spaces of social movements and rebellion are not represented and accounted for, ones that challenge exploitation, cultural imperialism and more generally, western hegemony (Servaes and Malikhao, 2008). However, other analysis on the framework of dependency, points to the diversity of this theory and how scholar and politicians like Fernando Cardoso (1979, 2001) were really invested in the internal social dynamics within these postcolonial nation states such as class, social movements, and cultural politics, however, addressing international relations and how that is negotiated was still underdeveloped and desired stronger theorization.

Overall one of the stark limitations of the dependency paradigm was how the "periphery" is positioned to be a "passive" victim of the unidirectional, oppressive domination by the core (Wildemeersch in Jacobsen & Servaes, 1999). This is based on the old concept of communication, where the centralized "core" is the active sender and the periphery is a passive receiver, without any agency. This view has been criticized for overstating the strength of structures and understating the role of localized agency and autonomy (Servaes and Malikhao, 2008), much like the way it has been analyzed in the new left, cultural studies interpretation of critical Marxist theory (Morley & Chen, 1996). Even though dependency theory provides an insightful understanding of the macro-level of the world order, its limitation is in its exclusion and representations of counter movements from the "borderlands" (Anzaldua, 1999) in the "core" as well as the "periphery" in most of the seminal works of the theory.

This process, like many others, decenters power relations and the so-called "natural" dominance of the "core", redefining the terms of development and social change. With the proliferation of the modernization paradigm and then its backlash, the dependency paradigm, there was growing dissatisfaction about the extremities and inadequacies of these theories to provide a comprehensive and nuanced understanding of the world system. The core–periphery, north–south, east–west model is also heavily contested territory, as local opinion leaders (innovators) emerge from all geo-political regions, promoting development from the many "borderlands". During the 1970s and 1980s, as criticisms of the modernization theory and dissatisfaction with dependency theory reached their peak, new epistemological paradigms were required to address issues of sustainable development and social change. There was an emergence and adoption of participatory research and paradigms in the development of communication models.

With the inclusion of participatory models, the terms of conversation were changed: there was focus on horizontal, indigenous projects, rather than north–south, unidirectional vertical transfers of information and innovations. This line of thought focuses on connecting the local, national, regional and the global by emphasizing localized, culture-based participatory approaches that yield sustainable results. All participatory approaches emphasize that interaction must be dialogic, interactive, and sustained to create fair and sustainable communities, even if the process is laden with complexity and unpredictability (among others Servaes, 1996; Gibson-Graham, 2006; Escobar, 2008; Sparks, 2007). Local issues and stakeholders are at the core of all the different versions of the participatory paradigms, where there is an emphasis on changing the way in which the blueprint for social change is envisioned, designed, constructed, and implemented, that honor the complexity and dynamism in community economies.

With the emergence of the participatory paradigm, a new theoretical framework emerged that made internal, bottom-up, grassroots processes the central point, rather than solely focusing on the transfer of power, knowledge and innovations from external sources (Dervin & Huesca in Jacobsen & Servaes, 1999). The participatory approaches can aid in building linguistic and cultural defense for marginalized communities one that relies on community participation and bottom-up movements from the grassroots to action, rather than having top-down, vertical, external direction, which follow the traditional modernizing, diffusion of innovations model (Escobar, 2008; Gibson-Graham, 2005; Servaes, 1996; Sparks, 2007).

One such paradigm within the participatory tradition is the multiplicity paradigm where *interdependence* is emphasized between and among external and internal sources (Wildemeersch in Jacobsen & Servaes 1999) and targets development processes from post-structuralist and postmodernist frameworks, which highlights that there is no objective reality, no universal formula, "no universal path to development" (Servaes & Malikhao, 2008, p. 163). Central to the dialogical approach to development is the strong emphasis on participatory communication where people are the very nucleus of development and the controlling actors, with strong emphasis on the local community and culture who are actively working towards the decentering of and redistribution of power (Servaes, 1989). Jacobson and Kolluri (1999) also echo similar ideas where they mention that participatory approaches in the multiplicity paradigm tend to highlight "small rather than large media, horizontal rather than vertical communication, collective self-reliance rather than dependence on outside experts (p. 268)."

Then, Arturo Escobar's modernity/coloniality/decoloniality (MCD) framework based on a tradition of post-development emphasizes the importance of working in alliance with local people, by paying heed to the knowledge and insights that they have developed by being part of the place. According to Escobar, MCD is touched by many of the revolutionary ideas that have stemmed from that part of the world such as dependency theory, PAR (participatory action research) and liberation theology—all ideas that have changed the face of international social science inquiry. The MCD framework is also constructed as a decolonizing, participatory paradigm, which embraces difference and diversity, instead of a Eurocentric modernization project of creating hierarchies of cultures and practices that serve to only reinforce outmoded binary constructions instead of meaningfully addressing local problems.

Another expression of participatory politics and processes is scholar duo J. K. Gibson-Graham's feminist economic research of diverse economies. Gibson-Graham's work has been involved in theorizing, mapping, and performing community economies, and challenges the "capitalocentrism" (Gibson-Graham, 2006) of traditional political economic approaches to development. Their research consciously steers away from capilatocentrism, and instead focuses on remapping, representing, and developing other under-explored community economic approaches that constitute unfixed, ever-changing economies. Their work maps and establishes the economy as a discursive space by prioritizing it "as the only place from where they know how to start" (Gibson-Graham, 2006, p.27) to bring about new epistemologies and lasting changes. *Postcapitalist politics* (2006) explores the potentials of developing such ethical, inclusive community economies, by addressing different issues surrounding transparency and communal cooperation for the realization of such a communal vision and its relationship to expanding trade.

Pertaining to my discussion, scholar duo Gibson-Graham in *Postcapitalist Politics* create a discourse of community economy based on the idea of interdependence and active participation: both community and economy are constituted by social relations that are intertwined with one another, which leads to our inter (intra)-reliance and co-dependence. They emphasize the importance of ethical community building and how citizens can, (and of course, should be) allowed to effectively engage in such decision-making, one that is not exclusive and hierarchical. Recognizing this crucial interdependence allows for re-thinking and re-defining economic discourse and decision making to center on a potential well-being for all. Ontologically reframing the economy as a diversity of class processes and subjectivities in a continual process of *becoming* (Agamben, 1993) and generating community practices that charts the possibility for new imaginary and desires seems to be "one way to enact a counter-hegemonic project" (Gibson-Graham, 2006, p. 78) and a new way of envisioning and implementing social, political and development agendas.

All the above three versions of PAR stemming from different geopolitical locations are influenced by Paolo Freire's (1970b) work on critical pedagogy and his insistence in the emergence of *conscientização*. His work has been one of the principle building blocks of PAR models that all the theorists above work with in different capacities. As developed by Freire (1970a), PAR methods emerged in the global south to challenge the hierarchal knowledge production and development projects stemming from institutions operated by the global north. Colombian sociologist Orlando Eals Borda and other notable PAR scholars, practitioners, and advocates organized the first explicitly PA conference in Cartagena, Colombia in 1977. Freire (1970a), in his work, challenged the fixed notion of linear, top-down transfers of knowledge from teacher to student, a dominant model of pedagogy that has globally sustained itself over time. In terms of knowledge production, Freire urged for a model that integrates horizontal and dialogical processes that challenge the fixed power dynamics that are inherent to a vertical, interventionalist, unidirectional, de-contextualized approach. He urged for a participatory process that moves away from what he calls the "banking" approach to education, one where the teacher is described as "depositing" knowledge that the student passively accepts (Freire, 1970a, 1970b).

PAR applies these Freirean critical pedagogy models of horizontal communication and dialogue in the context of development and sustainable social change (Huesca in Servaes 2008). A multitude of research practices and designs co-exist under the labels participatory action research (PAR) (Reason & Bradbury, 2008). While there is some diversity in its expression and details, shared themes under the PAR umbrella are associations across usual subject–object divides, acknowledgement of participant empowerment, and a plan for potential social change. When coupled with a critical performative approach, as per the critical feminist tradition of Gibson-Graham, PAR projects allow for deep engagement with power *and* research through every stage of designing, conducting, writing, and representing a study (Hemment, 2007; Cameron and Gibson, 2005).

The rich, complex, and useful theoretical frameworks as developed by the different participatory methods outlined above and the intersecting literature on participatory action research add multiple, complementary elements to the theoretical backbone of my work. Escobar (1992, 2008) and Gibson-Graham (2006) propose to view economy and social systems as dynamic, discursive spaces, and something that is not fixed or pre-determined. They push for difference rather than dominance and take the asset-based, local approach to development, one that involves the participation of local communities, civilians, activists, and governments to develop frameworks that are suitable for the community at hand. This reduces the possibility of creating a linear narrative of community economies and instead reminds us that "complexity and development could be brought together because human cultural settings and institutions as related to development efforts are complex and dynamic by nature" (Nordtveit, 2005, p. 111).

Gibson-Graham advocate for a performative approach to participatory processes, defined by Cameron & Hicks (2014) in this mode of inquiry as a tool to "bring into being" the world that we want to construct and live in. Viewing a space as not being "deficient", which is the way in which the traditional modernization paradigm has viewed the global south or "depressed" areas within the global north, is empowering and transformative. Gibson-Graham being critical feminist, economic geographers extend Butler's (1988) idea on performativity and apply their disciplinary context in doing PAR work. Butler's idea on performativity deals with the idea of language and social practices resulting in the subject formation. Gibson-Graham et al., extend this idea in their PAR work, by counter-mapping deficient, damage-centric discourses and realities and instead creating new realities, by focusing on the unique assets that each region or community possesses and the subsequent possibilities that come along with it. The complex design and lofty goals of performative, participatory action research projects such as mine test the rigor and commitment of all involved in community development and sustainable social change. Due to the complicated and often unpredictable nature of the design, the process is a much riskier undertaking, as it is never possible to predict the outcome. However, the rewards are often much greater, in developing solutions that incorporate the complex needs of transnational communities, that can only be effectively decided with the direct involvement of people who live and participate in it—by engaging, discussing, and deliberating.

Another unifying argument of all the three traditions of participatory development mentioned above is the idea of "place". All the models critique the way in which place and the value of place-based cultures, knowledges and traditions have been undermined by the invasive processes of mainstream, modernizing globalization discourses. These authors are persistent in their advocacy of bringing place back into the conversation of globalization and development. They are aware that globalization is inevitable. They are strong advocates for changing "the terms of this conversation and not only the content itself" (Escobar, 2008) and bringing forth what the MCD calls *mundialization* or a more inclusive, just, holistic, and democratic globalization that pays homage to *pluriversality* of processes. Escobar also urges for performativity in his decolonial research agenda that replaces the transplanting of Eurocentric discourses, practices, and models with a pluriversal approach which prioritizes local history, politics and cultures of places in question.

Creating space for what the MCD calls "radical alterity" would make spaces for different processes and different assets, rather than imposing dominant and inadequate systems of operation that are designed and built for different (often, northern/western) geopolitical realities.

Latour, one of the icons of ANT, in his book, *The politics of nature* (2004) also grapples with the importance of pluriversality and how citizens must engage in practices that enable them to break away from outdated "isms" and "ologies". This must be done to beckon a new way of democratic collective action, which breaks away from what he refers to as the *politics of the cave*. Latour echoes the importance of pluriversality as well, by urging us to change the way in which science is defined, which allows for the outmoded, tightly knit knowledge and expert communities, called epistemic communities to thrive. Latour (2004) points to a different approach, one that embraces the pluriversality of this world, where we change the terms of conversation altogether by coming out of the "cave" or the "old regime", which is defined by him as the systemic, spatial, and ideological barriers that allow for the sustenance of tightly guarded, knowledge and expert and epistemic communities, where Science (with a capital S) resides.

He says, "we cannot settle for it without maintaining the politics of the cave, since doing so would amount to distancing ourselves still further from the reality of things themselves left intact in the hands of Science" (p. 232). The idea of this reconfiguration based on the inclusion of non-human actors/actants, on what he calls "sciences" rather than "Science" in building networks and impacting politics is explored in further detail in the following section that deals with the use of ANT in this research project as a main theoretical tool. Participatory citizen-science projects are one of the deliberate attempts in developing this idea of pluralistic sciences that is invested in a very inclusive approach towards developing scientific discourses.

Actor network theory in BGreen: history and application

Another theoretical root of the project is actor network theory (ANT) which is a constructivist theory stemming from complexity theory, that is used to explore and analyze the relational ties within an emerging network (Latour, 1987, 2004; Hassard & Law, 1999; Callon, 1987; Cressman, 2009). The theory's main goal is to describe social processes as being comprised of a variety of human/non-human, material/social actors that are equally contributing and tied to the network process of attaining a concrete target, which in this case is BGreen. Cressman (2009) writes, "ANT attempts to 'open the black box' of science and technology by tracing the complex relationships that exist between governments, technologies, knowledge, texts, money and people" (p. 3), much like the way in which I am exploring these relational dynamics between and within institutions and industries in the development of BGreen.

> An actor-network is composed of many entities or actants that enter into an alliance to satisfy their diverse aims. Each actant enrolls the others, that is, finds ways to convince the others to support its own aims. The longer these networks are, the more entities that are enrolled in them, the stronger and more durable they become. An actor-network is spliced; the actants intersect.
>
> (Spinuzzi, 2008)

This definition points to some of the key elements that make up this process, while alluding to some others that I will discuss in the following paragraphs. The meaning of actants and/or actors, needs clarification in the ANT process, since its holds very specific meaning that contradicts some generic definitions of actors that are used in other theorizing. Conventionally, "actors" are used to define human entities while "actants" are used to define non-human entities and the interactive and intersecting capacity of the two terms are used to define any human and/or non-human, social or natural entity that makes the network (Callon, 1987).

These actors/actants comprise an interaction between material and human factors in any process and ANT advocates of an "amodern" ontology, where there is attention on the "hybrids" and "quasi objects" that are comprised of the heterogeneous world that is constructed around us (Castree & Macmillan, 2001). This is a departure from the conventional definition of actors, which always takes an anthropocentric stance, of defining the term as a human or an organizational entity comprising of actors (Wasserman & Faust, 1994, p. 17). The means and actual products of these actor networks are never pure, since purity is not a goal of the ANT project, and instead they are "hybrids" comprising of three distinctly different categories: nature, society and language (Latour, 1987). Emergent, complex, actor networks gain stability through the process of *translation*, which in ANT is understood to go through four stages called 1. *problematization* (defining the problem and identifying key, indispensable actors); 2. *interessement* (recruiting subsidiary actors to fulfill the needs of the network); 3. *enrollment* (when every actor's role is defined and accepted as being functional and operative); 4. *mobilization* (moving all actors, human/non-human, social/natural into action by the primary actors/OPP). The translation process, which is sometimes also referred to as the sociology of translation, was developed to help with setting a common meaning/understanding of any project that has actors/actants involved in building this complex actor network.

At its best, an actor network, through the process of translation, gains what ANT calls *network stability* or *instability,* which is defined as being in the continuous process of evolution and re-evolution. This constant state of becoming, is something actor networks need to undergo to maintain themselves, which may ultimately lead to sustenance and hence the formation of a *black box* or possible dissolution. While each of the different stages of this translation process is certainly important to navigate, enrollment may rise to the top for this research, since this term implies that actors/actants are enrolled in a process when the choice offered to them is better than other choices available at any given moment (Latour, 1987) (Busch & Juska, 1997). This is important to note in the context of BGreen, since as the principle researcher, the goal was to develop an alternative space that would ideally generate interest among youth and organizational partners to enroll in the BGreen process.

Black box as a concept in ANT is adopted from the field of informational science, which refers to closed black boxes or processes that depend on "techniques, materials, thought processes and behavior" (Cressman, 2009, p. 7). It is explained that looking inside or opening up a "black box of technology leads the way to an investigation of the ways in which a variety of social aspects and technical elements are associated and come together as a durable whole, or black box" (Cressman, 2009, p. 7), one which is the most advanced sign of an evolving, yet stable actor network. Black box originally is a technical term, for any device, system, or object when it is viewed in terms of its input, output and transfer characteristics without any knowledge required of its internal workings (Cressman, 2009). However, the idea of black box as it operates in ANT is viewed as being a closed system, whose ability to flourish and keep its identity requires it to remain closed (Cressman, 2009). Hence, the blacker the box, the more "automatic" the process becomes, which presumably results in the attainment of more network stability.

In the context of ANT, BGreen is a black box, as it went through the various steps in the process of translation combined with the community building processes of PAR to build its identity and form the participatory networks. However, the idea of the black box, while useful in many regards, needs to be modified for my vision of attaining participatory networks. One of the key contributions of ANT is the emphasis on thinking relationally, hence, opposing binaries that are constructed between categories, such as nature/social, core/periphery. ANT argues that "things (including humans) are only definable *in relation to* other things" (Castree & Macmillan, 2001, p. 211), which is very aligned to the PAR approach taken by this project of combining multi-actors/actants in the collaborative process of BGreen which results in the creation of actor networks. This approach also is consistent with challenging the power hierarchies inherent to the binarism of dividing spaces and narratives into reductive categories of "core" versus "periphery" as it necessitates a more complex world view, that debunks the pervasive attempts to "illicitly compartmentalize a messy, impure, heterogenous world" (Castree & Macmillan, 2001, p. 211).

Despite the benefits of a decentralized approach of power to make way for the performative power of small, one of the weaknesses of the strong version of ANT is the romanticization and under-theorizing of power and its connection of binarism in its understanding of actor/actant networks. The way it is theorized is inadequate in its interrogation of how power contributes to the upholding of systematic processes that maintain an asymmetrical, binary worldview. The under-theorization of the connection between heterogeneity, difference, power and binarism is a significant limitation of the ANT framework, which required me to develop participatory network as a concept, which addresses some of these key weaknesses of ANT despite its many contributions in other aspects of interrogating and in many ways operationalizing complexity theory.

One of ANT's biggest contributions is its ability to go beyond the anthropocentric focus and instead look at complex dialectics and processes that involve human and non-human actors/actants. Latour (2004) talks about the importance of merging the human and non-human actors in the building of networks, which is an important point to emphasize to change the way in which practice and policies around collective action and democracy can be addressed. He writes:

> Seeking to forbid the exploration of new speech prostheses to take into account all the nonhumans whom, in any event, we already cause to speak in countless ways would amount, on the contrary, to abandoning the old tradition and becoming savage for real. The barbarian is indeed, as Aristotle claimed, someone who is ignorant of representative assemblies . . . . Far from calling this acquisition into question, I claim on the contrary to be extending it, naming the extension of speech to nonhumans Civilization, and finally solving the problem of representation that rendered democracy powerless as soon as it was invented, because of the counter invention of Science.
>
> (Latour, 2004, p. 71)

This powerful analysis speaks to the importance of paying attention to the contribution of non-human actants in the process of building actor networks that may or may not become a black box (Callon, 1987) and the architecture of participation that is constructed using one of the key non-human actants, technology. Harvey (2014) does not develop this term using ANT as the framework, however, he uses the term to challenge the idea of epistemic communities, as they exist in perpetuating asymmetrical structures and points to the potential of ICTs and technological innovations where, "ICTs and other mediating technologies play an influential role, both in the negotiation of meaning, and in determining how we move from meaning to action" (Harvey, 2011, p. 29).

For example, the use of technological innovations (social media, TV, radio, print) to garner this "architecture of participation" of Bangladeshi youth's creativity and ideas in the making of BGreen experience, are key points of analysis as important actors/actants that made the actor network into the complex, webbed, deep form that it is constantly shaping and reshaping into. Also, the themes of education and environment are key actants in this analysis and how they intersect with other non-human and human actants are explored in the narration and analysis. Hence, taking an anthropocentric approach, which focuses only on the institutional human and organizational actors is not a complete analysis of the making of a project like BGreen. Doing incomplete analysis that only focuses on human actors, reinforces binaries, which is about understanding the world in terms of conceptual dichotomies (Castree & Macmillan, 2001), rather than understanding how "the social and the technical co-constitute each other" (Latour, 1991, Callon & Latour, 1992). A complete analysis of social processes can only happen when technology and human actions are seen to be co-constitutive and deeply bound here "to read the social from the technical is similarly to read the technical from the social" (Latour, 1991, 1992; Cressman, 2009, p. 10).

ANT is designed to provide a more complete picture of the hybridity of this world where "such hybrids are ubiquitous rather than rare—as the modern imagination would have us believe" (Roberts, 1995, p. 211). Hence, ANT urges us to think about the world and processes as being complicated, complex hybrids always in the process of becoming and shifting. This hybridity of processes is evident through many phases of my study that is continuously looking at the role of non-human actants, such as technology, environment, education, politics (but not limited to these), in working with human actors in every stage of the process of developing BGreen. This reflection, connection and analysis of hybridity is important, since, non-human actants in a networked process cannot "be presupposed as an autonomous thing that exists outside of the social world" since they "contain a variety of political, social and economic elements" (Cressman, 2009, p. 9).

Additionally, as Latour (2004) insists in his ongoing work, the re-theorization and understanding of non-human actants like technology is crucial to the redefinition of "Science" to what he urges as being "sciences", since failing to do so supports the flawed binary of excluding local, "common" actors from attaining common good. In his book, *The politics of nature* (2004), he points to the necessity of connecting non-human actants such as objects, devices and technologies to the process of democracy, and how its absence only leads to the upholding of Science (with a capital S), rather than the sciences. Instead he urges for the need to develop a "new 'collective' that is no longer surrounded by a single nature and other cultures, but that is capable of initiating, in civil fashion, experimentation on the progressive composition of the common world" (Latour, 2004, p. 210). He further writes how the discourse and praxis around Science needs to shift:

I contrast Science, defined as the politicization of the sciences by (political) epistemology in order to make public life impotent by bringing to bear on it the threat of salvation by an already unified nature, with the sciences, in the plural and lowercase; their practice is defined as one of the five essential skills of the collective in search of propositions with which it is to constitute the common world and take responsibility for maintaining the plurality of external realities.

(p. 213)

Here, Latour is advocating for a definition of science that includes the reconfiguration of systems where the voices and knowledge of non-traditional scientific communities, human and non-human, are accounted for in the development of a new discursive space that does away with the "old regime", since all concentrated power centers are also complex points that are constructed of human and non-human actors/actants. Cooks (2001) reflects on the changing shape of power with the emergence of new media technologies and writes, "Indeed, power has never been contained or possessed simply in people, objects or spaces, but in the interactions that produced perceptions of and consequences for their value. And, as new articulations of power produce new (in)visibilities, identities shift and morph" (p. 487). The complex interplay between human and non-human actors/actants is a key analytical point that may help us address the nuances of how actants like new media technologies re-define the way in which power, people, democracy, and social change relate to one another.

Even though non-human actants are still working within larger political economic power systems where the "broader dynamics of power and authority of a given setting or epistemic community" does point to a "complex relationship between openness and the democratization of knowledge" (Harvey, 2014, p. 29). But attention and analysis to these same non-human actors/actants with human actors can potentially re-constitute the way in which binarism and power mutually reinforce, maintain and sustain one another. This is important to do to debunk the mythical construct of non-inclusive, erudite, epistemic communities and what Latour calls "divine Science" (Latour, 2004), which ultimately has profound effects in the way political economic structures are reorganized and reinstated.

Ethics, benefits, and challenges of integration

Combining performative models like PAR and ANT, this research project is a conscious departure from "damage-centered" (Tuck, 2009) discourses that are often produced by researchers who are interacting, studying, and working with communities from the borderlands (Anzaldua, 1999). Researchers using damage-centered frames often represent their "samples" from the borderlands as being broken, damaged, deranged, dysfunctional and in need of external assistance and solutions. Instead, I engage in a performative project that "goes beyond the traditional pathological or patronizing view by asserting that young people have the capacity and agency to analyze their social context, to engage in critical research collectively, and to challenge and resist the forces impeding their possibilities for liberation" (Cammarota & Fine, 2008, p. 4).

Tuck (2009) warns well-meaning researchers who are working with urban youth communities to not add to the pre-existing surveillance on them. She says, "the lives of city youth—already under the watchful eyes of police and school security officers, already tracked by video cameras in their schools, on the streets, and in subways—are [being] pursued by (well-intentioned) researchers whose work functions as yet another layer of surveillance" (p. 410). Hence, as a researcher working with global youth, I have to be mindful of such problematic ethical challenges that Tuck describes investigators often fall trap to which leads to the production of damaged-centered research. If done without consciousness, research becomes as a means of documenting deficit processes of individuals, entities, nations, etc from the periphery and/or borderlands, instead of producing and propagating processes and narratives that are uplifting and hence laden with positive potential to identify and tackle problems, but also engage communities and their voices to transform situations.

Tuck's ethical parameters that define damage-centered research and the role and power of the researcher in the process, are consistent with a PAR project design's ethical concerns; however, it is different from the way in which ANT approaches the role of the researcher in the medley of actors/actants of the network. For example, in PAR, one of the key issues that are mindfully grappled with is the power of the researcher in shaping the outcome of a process that involves so many actors/actant/entities. Knowing that the process of PAR is a very political, engaged, value-driven project, one that constantly requires reflection and monitoring, its larger (sometimes unprecedented) effects must be assessed frequently by the researcher(s)(Wadsworth, 1998). Researcher(s)/Initiators have an interesting and de-emphasized place in ANT. They are referred to as *obligatory points of passage (OPP)* who are essential network channels, since they are placed in a position where they are indispensable to the development and flourishing of the network, as all information must be filtered through them, hence placing them in a position of power.

However, in ANT, since there is an emphasis on difference and dispersed power, the OPP, while acknowledged as the starting point, is not theorized as being any different from all the other actors/actants and as the actor network grows it is normal for it to have multiple key OPPs. In fact, for the sustenance of an actor network, it is necessary that a network assumes multiple OPPs, to disperse the way in which power operates and functions. This is quite a contestable point in ANT, since power is theorized to be "flattened" in the process, where it is believed that the number of actors/actants in a network dilute the process and hold of power (Castree & Macmillan, 2001). ANT's stance on power is something that is quite controversial. It says that to view power as being

> concentrated rather than dispersed is, therefore, to be deceived. It is also to overstate the power of power. Once power is seen as a relational achievement—not a capacity subject to monopoly, radiating from a single center or social system—then it becomes possible to identify multiple points (neither social or natural but both simultaneously) at which network stability can be contested.
>
> (Castree & Macmillan, 2001, p. 214)

I approach this perspective as being a double-edged sword, since, while there is immense promise in seeing each small and/or big actor/actant in having transformative potential, it is important to also be aware of how some entities in a network exercise gain greater control of how the participatory network can/should progress. Often the principle researcher(s) or as ANT calls it, the OPP, holds a great deal of power in deciding the course of even the participatory action research process. Hence, the ethics of the researcher is of paramount importance in this PAR-ANT process, since the ramifications of their decisions and actions will be felt by larger groups of actors. Tuck also insists on changing the terms of research in whichever community we are trying to study and represent, "whether participatory or not", to "not fetishize damage but, rather, celebrate our *surviv-vance*." (Cammarota & Fine, 2008, p. 3). The former is a debilitating frame, which I reject very deliberately in conducting my performative research and in analyzing and representing the global south, urban, youth communities that I am in contact with through my work.

Hence taking this *survi-vance* approach that Tuck refers to is complementary to the performative approach of PAR, through which BGreen hopes to reconfigure and re-define the traditional constructs of "core" and "periphery" in addressing the environmental challenges of Bangladesh and the US, through the perspective of youth. BGreen destabilizes the power of representation of the youth, national and international community organizations, academic institutions from both the global north and south that collaborated to design the BGreen experience in Dhaka, Bangladesh and in Western Massachusetts, USA. This is because it provides insights from the under-documented periphery that represents the economy as an unbound system that works in complement to addressing ANT's attempts to deal with the futility of binary approaches of looking at complex, hybrid processes. Identifying, analyzing, and meaningfully engaging with the varied narratives that stem out of different vantage points of North American and Bangladeshi youth (from their inherently disadvantaged social contexts such as age, class, gender, education, nature and environmentalism) is key to understanding the alliances and networks that are intentionally built towards sustained social change, to change their reality from inside-out.

This kind of youth citizen science project will make way for the youth to examine "the historical and social contexts and contingencies of scientific knowledge and technology. In doing so, they are explicitly rejecting a linear model of scientific and technical change and with it "any hint of social, technical or scientific determinism, reductionism or autonomy" (Cressman, 2009, p. 3) and instead building a more democratic, inclusive, engaged and participatory model. Using the global youth's voice, strategies, and vision to address diverse environmental issues is an unconventional route, as youth are often simply reduced to being insignificant and invisible (Giroux, 2013). So, even though the urban youth affiliated with educational institutions hold relatively privileged positions in society, they themselves occupy a peripheral position in the context of larger society in decision-making for "important" issues such as any nation's environmental and educational future.

In *Borderlands* (1999), feminist Chicana scholar Anzaldúa expresses the complexities of speaking from the peripheral borderlands to the Euro-centric/ Western/Northern core and how this conversation as difficult as it is, must be made possible to create radically different value and knowledge systems that benefit more than a small, elite group of people. Taking this unconventional participatory path can be difficult, but necessary to create such alternative epistemologies and methodologies and it will require the shifting from the comfort zone of both the researcher and the "subjects". She writes that these spaces cannot be created without "a tolerance for contradictions, a tolerance for ambiguity" (Anzaldua, 1999, p. 101) and BGreen hopes for complex and useful organized dialogue and communication between groups in that vein where it engages those who are typically placed in the periphery to re-define the core.

Political economic complexity

While I am taking a PAR-ANT approach in investigating the BGreen participatory network, as I mentioned earlier, it is necessary to re-theorize power and binarism as it operates within political economic structures that interplay with the process of developing actor/actant networks. This is one of the key shortcomings of ANT, which forms the basic framework that I use to address the research questions. One of the main reasons for the need to develop the concept of participatory networks was to address this limitation, because it is not possible to look at the formation of networked multi-institutional, political economic processes, without grappling with the issues of power and binarism, which are at the core of it.

Political economy can be understood as a study of the relationship between politics and the economy and how structures maintain and sustain themselves through the process of globalization and social power enacted through economic and political institutions (Mosco, 1996; Busch & Juska, 1997; McChesney, 2008; Couldry, 2012, 2009). There are two mainstream wings within the large field of political economy that have been co-opted by various fields in understanding the ways in which institutions and power interplay. One of those wings fall under a classical political economic perspective, developed by Smith (1976) that divides the world into neat categories of micro and macro where the two are neatly separated and do not have any chance of interacting with one another (Mosco, 1996; Busch & Juska, 1997).

The other wing is the critical political economic approach based on Marx (1970) that focus on larger, macro level structural processes, which gave birth to Wallerstein's (1974) World Systems Theory, with seemingly inflexible, stable and closed categories of "core" and "periphery" at the center. In both iterations, however, there is no room for human actors/actants to enter the conversation and analysis (Busch & Juska, 1997). This lack of analysis points to the failure and futility of the concept of *functionalism* that dominates political economic theories and understanding of large structural processes (Couldry, 2012). Functionalism as a concept in political economic theory is explained by Couldry (2012) as being "an idea that large regions of human activity ("societies", "cultures", etc.) can best be understood as if they were self-sufficient, complex, functioning systems" (p. 124).

While functionalism acknowledges complexity to a degree, it fails to acknowledge the role of relational dynamics between human and non-human actors/actants that engage in the perpetuation and stabilization of these supposedly "stable" and "functioning" structures that are impervious and in some ways automatic. Hence, an anti-functional approach which Couldry (2012) advocates embraces the "multi-dimensionality of social and cultural practice" (p. 124) and the "openness to the variable and complex organisation of practice, and a concern to understand the principles whereby, and the mechanisms through which, practices are ordered" (p. 123).

Busch and Juska (1997) echo similar ideas, albeit urging for the merging of actor network theory to political economic analysis to provide a more in-depth and complete analysis of a networked yet structural process. I am doing this in my study too, to address the major limitations within the diversity of ways (classical and/or critical) in which functionalism in political economy is theorized and applied. They write, "approaches concentrate on describing conditions that explain why globalization occurs, while telling little about how this process actually takes place. Thus, from the macro perspective, globalization is understood to be an extension of the immutable and potent logic of the capitalist treadmill of production" (p. 690). This is the key contribution of the participatory networked approach, using ANT-PAR to work with political economic theories to balance the deficits of both ends of the spectrum. However, there is a difference between my use of participatory actor networked approaches and the way in which Busch and Juska (1997) use it: I am looking at the potentiality of the hybrid space that exists in between organizations, that space where small, alternative, multi-institutional, academic–community partnerships can emerge from the perspective of networks that are amorphous, looking into political economic structures. However, I am also adding participation to the mix, and analyzing how it relates to issues of power, binarism, structures and the eventual formation of participatory networks.

It is necessary to really connect the theorizing between these two paradigms, in a way that helps overcome the limitations of each and addresses the hybridity, complexity and fluidity of these spaces where we address what Busch and Juska (1997) call the *political economy of networks*, which focuses on "the relationships among people, things, institutions and ideas [that] are created, maintained and changed through time. The political economy of networks then becomes centered on the question: who or what, by using policies, inventing new technologies, modifying or creating institutions, is able to position him/her/itself in a strategic position so as to provide for his/her/its best interests?" (p. 701). This allows for investigating these hybrid in-between spaces that have the potential to create new participatory networks that allow for the navigation of structures from inside and outside and be involved in the constant process of negotiating how democratic spaces and processes can get institutions and practices to engage in social justice and transformation (McChesney, 2008).

Towards the building of participatory networks

In this section, I will explore the specific ways in which PAR and ANT is integrated into the process that supports the theoretical needs of the project and how this combination results in the development and definition of the concept of participatory networks. It is my hope that the critical performative participation and enrollment of US and Bangladeshi youth in the BGreen project would result in the creation of alternative discourses and practices around global and local environmental woes from fresh, under-researched perspectives that will bring about a political economic shift in the way in which academic–community partnerships are formed in Bangladesh. Perhaps projects like BGreen could be essential case studies for the development of a new vision where localized realities would inform the formation of a strategy to really address the global and local educational needs.

In general terms, PAR was integral to the success of small-scale community-based processes like BGreen that are looking at the ways in which human actors can work together to form new, innovative ways of relating to the world. Complementing it with ANT allows for a more complete picture of the development of a participatory process. The development of BGreen needs to make sense of non-human actants and their role in collaborating with human actors in developing an architecture of participation, that through a process of complex translation, can reach the status of a modified black box. Merging the two complementary approaches of PAR and ANT allows for the creation of what I have called a *participatory network*, the BGreen participatory network, which is explored in all its complexity and not simply reduced to "an actor alone nor to a network. . . . An actor-network is simultaneously an actor whose activity is networking heterogeneous elements and a network that is able to redefine and transform what it is made of" (Callon 1987, p. 93).

The flexibility of both the approaches, PAR and ANT, make it possible and useful for the two to be used together, albeit with some negotiations. The negotiations and/or changes that I am proposing to make these two work together are consistent with the ways in which Castree and Macmillan (2001) advocate for a weak version of ANT and subsequently combining it with the PAR approach to make the theoretical frame of the project. A weak version of ANT is defined by the scholar duo as one in which the strengths of social constructivism are not completely undermined, which I agree with. Despite my modifications, I see the benefits in the strong version of ANT, which really focuses on the world as being multiple, messy and complex, which Castree and Macmillan (2001) point out as being one of its core strengths. According to them (and I am in agreement with their critique), the strong version of ANT: 1. leads to the flattening of the process (ANT) and obscures the differences between being different; 2. there is an ontological challenge of each actor network being considered completely different, rather than focusing on/perhaps highlighting some trends that define similarities as well as differences; 3. also the way in which networks are theorized as a process is problematic since the focus is on description rather than having a political agenda (p.221–222).

To add to this interpretation of the limitations of a strong version of ANT, I am adding the challenges of viewing ANT as an infralanguage, which de-emphasizes the scientist/researcher who initiates the project. This does not pay attention to the "possibility that some actants 'marshall' the power of many others" (Castree & Macmillan, 2001. p. 223) and the level of power the OPP can really exercise in controlling the process of developing networks and in this case participatory networks. This is where the strength of performative PAR shines, where, the process being a value-driven one, seriously considers the role of the researcher in setting up a project that is shaped and originated from their positionality. All three versions of PAR (Servaes et al., Gibson-Graham and Escobar et al.) that I discussed above follow the performative approach to participatory project design and implementation, which makes it an ideal complement to the weak version of ANT as incorporated in this project.

Also, a weak version of ANT problematizes the way in which the concept of black box is theorized, understood and applied. Black box is understood in ANT traditionally to be a closed system and in order to operate and grow it must remain closed to reach network stability—this allows for that actor network to persist despite the changes, evolution and growth and becomes an automatic, common-sense process that runs itself in an evolving, dynamic fashion. This idea of black box is paradoxical to me, which necessitates the need for developing a modified black box that justifies the weak version of ANT that I am incorporating with PAR, which results in the creation of the concept of participatory networks. For participatory networks to strive, it cannot be predicted what actors/actants you will pick up along the way to make the actor networks stable, and this idea extends to the formation of participatory networks also. In strong ANT's black box, "the more automatic and the blacker the box is, the more it has to be accompanied by people" (Latour, 1987 p. 137).

However, for participatory networks to form and flourish in the way I have envisioned it (i.e. using PAR and a weak version of ANT), it needs to be an open process, unlike that of a classic, closed black box. I am modifying the way in which black box is traditionally understood in ANT, where power is theorized in a different way that differs from the traditional ANT approach. In the classic, strong ANT approach, power is under-theorized and the focus is on the diversity and difference of the actors/actants rather than the dominance of any one of them. While, there are merits of thinking in terms of "soft power" or "dispersed power" and how it has transformed the way in which we allow for potential of many small actors in contributing to a larger shift, I am uneasy like many other scholars who critique this aspect of strong ANT (Murdoch, 1995; Castree & Macmillan, 2001; Couldry, 2012). As Murdoch (1995) writes, "those who are powerful are not those who 'hold' power but those who are able to enroll, convince, and enlist others on terms which allow the initial actors to 'represent' the others" (p. 748).

Idealizing this flattened approach where the clear political economic control and power of some actants/actors, such as OPP is ignored, overlooks the dominance of certain actors/actants in any actor network that defines the flow and course of it. I am also aware of my role as OPP and principle researcher in this project, who has the power to interpret, represent and write about the entire participatory action research process, hence complicating the way in which subjective realities are ultimately created from my vantage point. As researchers, we have the power of representing, constructing and performing new discourses and realities. Denzin (2001) points out, "as researchers, we belong to a moral community" (p. 44). Hence conscious awareness about roles as critical, reflexive researchers who are actively channeling our subjective biases in developing performative research narratives is necessary to defy damage-centric research agendas.

"Given these premises, reflexivity is intended here as being inherently connected to action and as a part of the sense-making process in which both participants and the researcher are engaged" (Colombo, 2003, p. 12), but ultimately my written word as the researcher is an interpretation of a much larger, complex, multi-actor/actant process, which needs to be done with care and hence the "the task of researchers therefore becomes to acknowledge and even to work with their own intrinsic involvement in the research process and the part this plays in the results that are produced" (Burr, 1995, p. 160). Mindfully engaging with the issue of power and maintaining the balance between these two is what I am urging for in my interpretation of it in the form of a participatory network. Also in a well-functioning participatory network, the contribution of human and non-human actors/actants in deepening and reconstituting the network, forms a "sociotechnical network" that is central to the sustenance of the process (Cressman, 2009, p. 9).

This does not mean that PAR does not have its challenges: not all types of participatory action research are ethically oriented, which scholars Manzo and Brightbill (2007) write about. They say, "participation will not, in and of itself, make research 'ethical'; the approach can be deployed to support a researcher's pre-existing agenda, or to further the interests of a particular group" (p. 39). They instead propose that PAR project researchers really incorporate what they call participatory ethics, which is a commitment to the moral compass of the researcher and urges them towards accountability in representations of participants and/as the community. The participatory element of the process is often idealized and often not monitored closely enough, hence really doing a disservice to developing an ethical, morally sound research framework that serves the participants *and* the researcher engaged in the process.

Also, another consistent critique against participatory action research is that it lacks scientific rigor due to the messiness and complexity of multi-modal project design (Kemmis & McTaggart, 2000). Some of the existing definitions are not clear since there are many scholarly traditions that have co-opted this process and have created many versions of PAR. I do not necessarily see this as a bad thing, since the ambiguity of a theory, hence a "weak" version of any theory, allows for easier merging to other theories to form new theoretical paradigms, for example the formation of participatory networks by the combination of PAR and ANT. Despite the limitations of both the theories of PAR and ANT, the two approaches are still good complements, since I am using elements of both theories to make a new whole to reach the research goals. The use of PAR is championed in smaller processes and ANT has the potential to fill the gaps that are inherent in PAR projects to expand it into a larger scale that connects ground-up, community based initiatives to larger political economic approaches. This allows me to overcome one of PAR's most potent critiques of scale and perhaps embrace the foil of ANT to overcome the pitfalls that may act as a challenge to developing participatory networks.

Also, the core of such a participatory network is Freire's *conscientização*. Freire (1970b) reflects on the importance of the emergence of *conscientização* and how the pursuit of it, can truly connect theory and praxis. He writes, "human activity consists of action and reflection: it is praxis; it is transformation of the world. And as praxis, it requires theory to illuminate it. Human activity is theory and practice; it is reflection and action" (p. 25). Critical consciousness is a thread that runs through the participatory network and at its best, will have the power change the way non-human and human actors/actants relate to one another to form individual and *organizational conscientização* (Straubhaar, 2014).

The specific details and full scope of participatory networks in the context of BGreen is understood only when all human and non-human factors that contributed to its development and amplification are accounted for. Hence, each analysis chapter, in theory and praxis, unfolds the multi-layered complexity of the diverse actors/actants in this process that contributed to the development of participatory networks that are always in the process of becoming and cannot function in any other static, fixed, controlled ways. The formation of such participatory networks ideally connects these different theories or "infralanguages" of participation and social change that can guide the search, exploration, participation and creation of praxis close to the way in which Freire had envisioned it. Hence the BGreen participatory network needs to enroll all its human and non-human actors/actants to undergo ANT's complex stages of translation to gain network stability. Also, since a participatory network is defined as being an open, participatory and fluid process, it has the power to enlist human and non-human actors from within and outside its own network to be able to be in the continuous process of redefining and reconstituting itself, till it gains network stability, though never closure.

Justification and contribution

In the best version of the desired participatory network, BGreen may spark a sustained youth environmental movement in both countries, a sustained participatory network, based on both nations' divergent history in youth movements. While Bangladesh has a very rich history in youth movements, as recent as the Shahbagh Movement in February 2013), the US youth movements are few and far between. This is a rare opportunity for everyone involved to build and be part of an emerging participatory network where "we are not primarily concerned with mapping interactions between individuals . . . we are concerned to map the way in which they [actors] define and distribute roles, and mobilize or invent others to play these roles" (Law & Callon, 1986, p. 285). Therefore, participatory networks like BGreen can potentially help merge science and citizen-action (in this case youth-action) to create youth citizen science and to influence/alter/transform public environmental citizen science discourses. Through the synthesis of a few complementary theoretical tools and paradigms I plan to put political economic institutions in conversation with individuals and communities and witness how education, environment and communities are transformed as a result.

The architecture of participation that is at the core of the networked PAR processes that contribute to the development BGreen, hold the potential of contributing directly to taking steps in developing an alternative kind of educational experience in both nations. Castree and Macmillan (2001) write, "all forms of political thinking and action must have an environmental dimension, for the spaces of nature cannot be confined to a few fast shrinking areas" (p. 221). This indeed brings together the impetus for embarking on this project, where the goal is to use grassroots/community knowledge, educational institutions and engaged pedagogy as a vehicle to address the issues of environment and how they connect with global youth citizens future.

By engaging in research that steers away from being damage-centric and instead adopts a performative PAR-ANT approach, BGreen has the potential to create a safe platform for marginalized voices from the "periphery" to be heard by the privileged "core". The development of such participatory networks is an example of how active engagement and powerful possibilities are generated by selected methodological choices that were chosen to conduct the research. My research looks at the relational dynamics within the participatory networks, which upon narration and analysis will present examples from both the global north and south on how such youth engaged transnational academic–community partnerships are created and how they have the potential to redefine the way in which a new architecture of participation can be used to really engage youth in environmental solution building.

The profit-driven state of higher educational sector in both the US and Bangladesh feeds urgency to the need to create a new space for global youth using the support of already established networks of educational and community organizations. The relationship between national and international community organizations, academic institutions and youth collaborating together to design the BGreen experience is an important story to map and narrate, since it provides insights from the under-documented periphery on developing alternative educational futures for both US and Bangladesh. The main analysis of the study will be of the complex participatory networks that were developed as a result of the creation of the architecture of BGreen, which has youth participation at its core. The creation of such alternative discourses and practices around global educational-environmental challenges from a fresh, under-researched perspective holds the potential to help the youth in re-visualizing their roles in re-creating the multi-institutional structural realities in both countries through their participation.

This claim is supported by the narration and analysis of the diversity of the youth's active role in negotiating diverse political economic structures in the building of the BGreen participatory network, through their direct roles in mobilizing multi-institutions in adding complexity to the emerging participatory network via a myriad of different ways as analyzed in detail via the following chapters. As a result, the hope is to bring into the forefront the importance of youth in reviving and/or applying the concept of *conscientização* that can contribute to the process of building new, collaborative educational and environmental futures for both countries and contexts. As the youth undergo the different stages of critical consciousness (magical, naïve and critical), the hope is that such an iterative process will result in political manifestations and the emergence of new structural discourses.

The natural sciences and most projects affiliated to that general field have always distanced themselves from inclusion or community voice, and instead privileged distance, objectivity and authority, which are the defining points of expert epistemic communities (Harvey, 2014). This is a model of education that higher educational institutions in Bangladesh have internalized across all academic disciplines (Harvey, 2014). Hence collaborative citizen-science projects like BGreen can be game changers in the way in which multi-industries and institutions join forces towards socially engaged knowledge production that complicates the ideas of epistemic communities and the way in which it organizationally plays out in the higher educational sector in both nations.

Approach to inquiry and analysis

My research looks at the relational dynamics between two separate processes, one which is the political economic network that is formed via the multi-institutional collaboration and the emergent narratives and discourses that emerge as a result of creating the architecture of the BGreen participatory network. The gaining of network stability for the BGreen participatory network could become a new model of academic–community partnerships and participation for social change. My research questions require me to deal with two large issues: 1. To study and analyze the state of the larger political economic processes of higher educational institutions in the US and Bangladesh and their contested relationship to academic–community action projects like BGreen; 2. To study the ways in which BGreen was developed on the ground by combining visions, voices and actions of the actors and stakeholders on the ground, what kinds of discourses emerged as a result of it and how they can be applied to the future of higher education in the US and Bangladesh.

A project that has PAR and ANT as the theoretical frames necessitates the development of a complex, *multimethod* qualitative research design, since addressing the different research questions required different methods of data collection (Morgan, 1997). Projects that apply participatory research methods are:

> Geared towards planning and conducting the research process *with* those people whose life-world and meaningful actions are under study. Consequently, this means that the aim of the inquiry and the research questions develop out of the convergence of two perspectives—that of science *and* of practice.
>
> (Bergold & Thomas, 2012)

While this is a challenging process, it is ultimately rewarding, since all the actors/actants that are involved contribute to the participatory action research process because they seek answers that will benefit the community and presumably improve the quality of life for all involved. The involvement and utilization of community actors/actants into the research process is regarded as methodology on its own in PAR and the methodological tools used are not at odds from standard empirical social science research tools such as qualitative research processes, like interviews, focus groups, to name the most widely used processes (Bergold, 2007).

Bergold further writes:

> In our view, in order to gain a deeper insight into the contextual structuredness of meaning and the dynamism inherent in social action, it is worthwhile considering the inclusion of participatory research elements in research designs. Moreover, we believe that—precisely because the participation of all research partners is the fundamental guiding principle for this research approach—a methodological design that can be classified as a *participatory design process* in the narrower sense, represents an attractive and fruitful knowledge-generating option when it comes to researching the social world in the sense of habitualized practice.
>
> (2007, p. 3).

Therefore, the participatory design process combined with the strength of ANT are important contributors to the goals of BGreen in becoming a participatory network, where the actors/actants are not only involved in designing a participatory event, instead they actively contribute to a collaborative *process*, that goes beyond the actual event. From a methodological perspective, the multi-actor/actant involvement as co-researchers can be a cumbersome process also, since a consensus must be reached amongst community partners at each step in the organization, design and research process. However, one of the big advantages of this collaborative, participatory approach, especially with local community partners, is their familiarity about the topic and context, which overall adds to the quality of facilitating the participatory experience. This is exactly what happened in BGreen, as the community partners who co-designed the project with me, really paid attention to what my initial goal was to do with this project, which upon discussion, dialogue, and consultation of the core group of community actors, we adapted to the needs and feasibility on the ground.

The way in which the architecture for the core-community partnerships of BGreen was initiated is explored shortly, which provides details on how the initial connections to collaborate were made. The scope, nature and reach of action research was very different in the US and in Bangladesh. The intricate details of building the core partnerships on the ground and how ANT-PAR was applied for participatory network building is more fully analyzed in Chapter 5, as the complex relationships that developed as a result of these organizational alliances is one of the most important points of investigation and analysis to answer my research questions.

Due to the enthusiasm that the idea had generated among our community partners, which included higher educational institutions, community youth organizations, international non-profits, think tanks and independent university affiliated youth (all of which will be described in detail in Chapter 4), we had originally envisioned that both the locations would have similar ways of conducting participatory action research. While there were some general similarities in both country's adaptations and implementation of the BGreen process, there were some stark differences. A brief outline is provided below. All tropes will be extended and elaborated on in the subsequent analysis chapters.

The main similarities can be outlined below:

1. The acceptance, cooperation, engagement and implementation of BGreen projects in non-academic community organizations/partners in both nations was quick, fast and accepting. The structural processes of these organizations and partners were flexible and allowed for much needed fluidity in the creation of the BGreen participatory network.

2. The acceptance, cooperation, engagement and implementation of BGreen projects in academic partner organizations in both nations was generally slow and cumbersome, albeit respectful, curious and encouraging. The more fixed structural processes of these organizations and partners often created the need to adapt ideas and plans to revolve around their institutional needs.

3. The on-ground action research of BGreen took shape with much strength largely outside of traditional classrooms in the form of classroom workshops, seminars, trainings and conferences in both countries. However, in the US

the flexibility of the pedagogical space in the college classrooms was much more, which allowed for much more systematic inclusion of participatory action research in developing the curriculum for the classes that I was leading/teaching in different academic institutions in the US. In Bangladesh, the participatory action research was conducted outside of the "traditional" classroom in spaces that resembled seminars, workshops, trainings, and conferences that are housed within and/or outside educational experiences.

The main differences can be outlined below:

1. The interest and contextual relevance of participatory action research as a tool of liberation was perceived very differently by the youth participants of both nations.
2. The participation, access, and support of media organizations in both nations was radically different leading to wildly different results in project scope, reach and implementation.
3. The funding process for the two nations was contrasting. The financial support of projects to be conducted in Bangladesh was much higher than for projects to be conducted in the US.
4. The political scenario of the nations had starkly different effects on the scope and implementation of the participatory action projects.

Data collection

The sample for this action research project emerged through the entire process of conducting my fieldwork, as deeper and more complex actor networks were built over time to form the transnational BGreen participatory network. Using the process of translation in ANT, the participatory network grew in size and in depth, adding new and heterogeneous actors/actants of local, national, regional and international scope. It is important to lay out the initial sample that eventually flourished into these complex transnational participatory networks as the source of a process is always an important thing to trace and map, to really understand the politics of a project.

My position as a researcher in this process was complicated: being a Bangladeshi American was a double-edged sword in many respects, which led to the nature of my initial sample of participants. I had a global perspective—I was based at a North American university considering the Bangladeshi higher educational system from the outside. I saw a larger picture from the US, looking at Bangladesh, my previous home. However, the power dynamics of that gaze was problematic to an extent, since I had to be mindful of respecting what is unique and important to people in Bangladesh, who I would be working with because of my research and action plans. Maxwell (2004) writes, "The term 'sampling' is problematic for qualitative research, because it implies the purpose of 'representing' the population sampled", however, for qualitative projects like these, it is impossible to shy away from such limitations. I relied on snowball sampling (Lindlof & Taylor, 2010) for making the initial contacts via new media networks—email, phone and Skype.

This network that was sparked initially by my snowball sampling was global in reach because I was fortunate enough to know faculty members and community practitioners that are prominent in diverse fields of education, environment, sustainability, and communications from both academic, governmental and industry backgrounds. In the case of the United States, I reached out to my academic and community organizations contacts in the Pioneer Valley and introduced them to my idea and research, which led to my enlisting them in the building of the BGreen participatory network in different capacities. The action project implementation started in Dhaka, Bangladesh, hence the discussion will be initially dominated by the Bangladeshi context and experiences of building the transnational BGreen participatory networks.

In the context of Bangladesh, I wondered if I would be taken seriously since I was an outsider who had not worked in community engaged projects in the sustainability and academic sector in the recent past, with no record of recent previous work in Bangladesh in the field of higher education. Even though I am Bangladeshi-American and can speak fluently in both languages (having lived in the US and Bangladesh for almost equal number of years), my positioning as a graduate student at that time based in the US and having lived there for the past 15 years placed me as an outsider in the eyes of most people who are Bangladeshi living in Bangladesh. At the same time, my identity as a woman of color in the US conducting international research of this scope often created confusion about my abilities in the global north context.

Affiliations with northern/western universities are sought after in the emerging higher-educational sector of Bangladesh and so my appointment at the time as a doctoral student in a privileged North American university provided a relatively easy access into the institutions that I was seeking out. As problematic as this assumption was, I used that slant to gain entrance into a university work system in Bangladesh that I was completely unfamiliar with. It is interesting to note that foreign nationals who are working in Bangladesh in different relevant fields were the first people to respond and offer to support the project, as they were more familiar with the vision of a developing an academic–community engaged movement in Bangladesh, since some of these professionals have seen such projects being operationalized in their work in higher-educational institutions in the global north. My foreign university affiliation, especially, the link to a US institution, was an integral factor in validating my claims for doing this project in Bangladesh involving Bangladeshi youth, academic and community organizations.

It was an idea that excited them as it has not been done before in Bangladesh and provided them with the legitimacy they needed, since I, the principle researcher or according to ANT, the OPP, was affiliated with a renowned department and institution in the United States. My vision of combining theoretical paradigms of PAR and ANT to alter Bangladeshi and US academic–community engagements and having the youth as the centerpiece in creating a viable and applied educational alternative resonated to some of my contacts who were leading academic and civil society programs in Bangladesh (as well as in the US). I got together an initial proposal with ideas on what my specific vision of the project was and then sent it around to everyone I knew (professional as well as personal contacts) via email and phone with links to issues of sustainable social development and change. This list comprised of professors, scholars, practitioners, and students from my various multi-industry national and international networks. I had emailed most people my initial proposal and a personalized message on whether they were interested in getting involved with a project of this nature or knew of an individual or an organization who is interested in collaborating on this PAR project that will actively construct and generate counter narratives of global youth from two diverse geopolitical locations with similar goals of working on the educational-environmental futures of their communities.

I received a range of responses from people around the world. Most people, irrespective of country and origin were very encouraging about the idea and responded with enthusiasm and curiosity. They showed support by pointing out the need for developing a project like this that counter-maps global youth activism and hence results in innovative organizational connections that debunk the artificial binaries that are often constructed to separate the academy and non-academic sectors of an economy. This group of people wanted the full details on the project, why I was invested in it and why I think there is a need for this project in the context of both the countries, which was provided to them in the form of extended project visions that I shared with them via phone, emails or Skype. To make a collaborative PAR project like this successful I knew the importance of connecting with academic, civil society organizations and citizens in Bangladesh and beyond that are working in the field of education and sustainable development.

Even though the initial process of finding committed project partners—the initial key actors/actants—was slow and somewhat confusing, after e-connecting with various relevant people and groups (which eventually led to the many phone, Skype and face-to-face interviews), surely and steadily I found a group of reliable actors/actants who were committed to developing my idea into a contextually relevant event, which really connected to the core goals of the project, which is higher educational reform in both Bangladesh and the US. Organizations (NGOs, schools, universities, think-tanks, youth coalitions, media houses) and individuals from Bangladesh, Australia, and the United States (details provided in Chapter 5) were committed co-partners in the planning and progress of the academic–community partnership project based on my email, phone and/or skype conversations with them. Hence, these conversations (mainly emails, but also skype, phone conversations) became important actors/actants in developing the project.

Throughout the process of interacting with possible co-partners, I clearly pointed out to them that I am engaging in PAR while doing the research project, hence, I may be using all/part of our conversations and interactions as data to be later analyzed. At this stage, the IRB process was not approved, because I was still trying to navigate the research possibilities, however, none of the people showed any resistance in doing that. These initial conversations were key and led me to the on-ground, IRB approved interviews that I had with the final partners of the BGreen action research project once I was physically present for the fieldwork in Dhaka, Bangladesh as well as in the US. During my fieldwork period in Dhaka, Bangladesh, one-on-one, semi-structured interviews turned out to be the tool of choice as it allowed the actors involved to meet me at their convenience, given the political challenges that were faced during the time I conducted my research in Dhaka, Bangladesh. During my fieldwork in the US, a combination of one-on-one interviews, participant observation and focus groups became the modes of data collection.

The premises for the interviews were fluid and variable, since some one-on-one meetings happened in the middle of a group setting, where all the core community actors of this participatory network were meeting to organize and plan the different action research processes in both Bangladesh and the US. Most of my interviews with the participants were characterized by this fluidity and interactivity, and some of them generated long discussions on the state of academic–community partnerships and how a platform like BGreen is the new, desired direction for the public and private higher educational sectors of Bangladesh and the US today. In the context of BGreen in the US, minus the political chaos as experienced in conducting the ongoing project in Bangladesh, all the same principles of data collection were followed. The lack of political instability really helped shape the predictability of the data collection in the US, which was a luxury simply not available in the Bangladeshi version of the project. Because I am a resident of Western Massachusetts, my own time was much more available to deepen the work over longer periods of time in the US, by often meeting/interviewing/brainstorming/collaborating with community partners over a longer period, which contributed to participatory network stability.

Developing the messy PAR process as research design

To design an effective and relevant participatory action project, the needs of the site of inquiry and the actors involved in the process, in this case, Western

Massachusetts, USA and Dhaka, Bangladesh, the youth and institutional community actors are of prime importance (Gibson-Graham, 2006) (Escobar, 2008). The challenge is to develop a larger participatory network, which is ideally a product of truly a participatory research processes. The goal for this participatory research was to have the community build the architecture of participation, so that it avoids the limitations and barriers of building inclusive processes of social change (Lassen et al., 2011). Hence, the participatory design and content that the core community actors constructed has considered the critique of other participatory efforts that have been tried in the field of citizen participation and deliberation (Lassen et al., 2011). The consistent critique of citizen participatory action projects have been the weakness in explicitly explaining the exact role (and the extent of involvement) of the participants in the process of deliberation.

Citizen participation is a matter of much debate, and according to some researchers the practical application of citizen participation is often limited as "citizens are neither addressed nor implicitly called upon to act, and in most of the texts there are very few examples of citizens referred to as potential actors" (Lassen et al., 2011, p. 417). Lassen et al. (2011) point to the issues of coming up with a truly inclusive participatory action design, where the citizen responsibilities and expectations are clearly delineated and where the voices are clearly put in the core of the problem-solving design, as well as bringing about a change in the isolating and ambiguous language used to design such citizen participation. They talk about the ambiguity in the concept of participant citizen action in relation to the challenges in designing and implementing truly participatory action and deliberative processes for a variety of different reasons. Conflicting program structures, bureaucratic set-ups, and linguistic vagueness about citizen roles are often pointed out as being causes of an underdeveloped participatory process, all of which the BGreen team had to consciously consider while developing the architecture of participation combining multi-actors/actants.

According to Lassen et al. (2011):

> Dealing with these tensions more explicitly would be an opportunity for improving the practical application of citizen participation, for example, a clear identification and interpellation of the persons responsible for taking action and a clear identification of the types of action needed.
>
> (p. 425)

In order to increase citizen participation, in this case, youth participation, with regard to education and environmental crisis, there seems to be a need for more explicit and specific communication to actors about actions on both a global and a local level (p. 425). This is an important critique to pay attention to, because youth citizen participation is key to the path that BGreen is committed to, where educational and community organizations work with the youth to achieve collective *conscientização* on solving the educational and environmental challenges of the time.

To create an engaged academic experience with a special focus on education and environment, a great deal of attention was given to the construction of innovative and diverse, youth engaged workshops for the event that used a variety of participatory methodologies in working with the youth in developing democratic societies. The focus was on the innovative idea of using knowledge engagement as a form of developing informed youth citizens, who are able to connect academic ideas with on-ground challenges. As a PAR-based citizen-science initiative, the goals of the workshops were to translate institution specific, "expert" knowledge to a version that is accessible and understood by citizens, in this case the youth, and aid them in developing strategies to apply it in the larger communities.

Following the messy methodological processes of PAR observation occurred in the meetings that we had with the entire group of actors and stakeholders during the planning process of the action research initiative as well as during the days of the actual action research. In many ways, these collective community partners meetings mimicked focus groups, where the meta-discussion of the meetings not only became texts that I was recording, but it also allowed for group interaction and conversations which are crucial to the formation of sustained participatory networks.

As Morgan (1997) writes "the hallmark of focus groups is their explicit use of group interaction to produce data that would be less accessible without the interaction found in a group" (p. 2), which is key to understanding a participatory process, since the project's practical success and analysis depended on the relational dynamics and interactions among the actors/actants present in the meetings. My role in it was complex, because I was not an outside researcher who was just recording the proceedings, but I was actively contributing to the way in which the process is shaped and implemented on ground, hence performing the role of a reflexive, participatory researcher, who is documenting a process that they are an integral part of. PAR projects are messy to document and this one was no different. The layers and levels of data that was generated of the process was complex and provided fodder for academic analysis for many years to come.

The last methodological tool I used to conduct this complex action research project was to conduct historical and political analysis of secondary literature (research articles, books, newpaper articles, multi-media footage) on the history of the higher educational system in Bangladesh and the US. The literature also includes the very specific influence the US privatization policies have had on Bangladeshi higher educational models and design. This was a very important part of the entire data collection, since I needed to represent and narrate the complex history of the entire higher-educational system from the colonial period till its transition to the current postcolonial and neoliberal times, to provide insight into the connectedness of both countries' educational contexts. The complexity of this transition had to be narrated in a holistic and nuanced way, where Bangladesh's economic transition since its liberation in 1971 till the current times had to be traced and its impact on the increasingly privatized higher-educational system. This political economic analysis is an important part of this ANT-PAR analysis, since it provides the frame, which contextualizes the way in which power, context and politics affect the formation, complexity and ultimately the stability of the network.

Also, a balance had to be created in representing the voices of Bangladeshi scholars, journalists, practitioners, etc. who are writing on this topic and not having an over-representation of only non-Bangladeshi, northern voices from the US. The texts that were used for the purpose of my research were carefully sought out and selected from a variety of different institutional perspectives. This was done to provide a balanced understanding of why the higher education system looks the way it does in the US *and* Bangladesh, to trace the process in historically accurate ways and to contextualize the need for developing the participatory networks. Reading and connecting the texts to the conceptualization of BGreen was key, since as a group of community collaborators, we were conscious of designing a platform that addressed the historical challenges of both US and Bangladeshi youth and their connection to education, environment, sustainability, and social change.

Below is a snapshot of which methodological tools from above were used in the analysis chapters to address my research questions:

Chapter 3: The first analysis chapter comprises the important social and historical themes that provide the backbone and context for my research and findings. It provides the historical overview and political economic analysis of both the US and Bangladeshi higher educational systems and how politics and academic–community partnerships, models and frameworks have played out in the past before the transition of the economy into a hyper-capitalist, neo-liberal system. For the first part, I had to engage in historical and political economic analysis of reviewing and analyzing secondary texts to study and analyze the state of the larger political economic processes of higher educational institutions in the US and Bangladesh and its contested relationship to academic–community action projects like BGreen; the methodological use of secondary literature (research articles, books, newspaper articles, multi-media footage) on the history of the higher educational system in Bangladesh and the US was used to explore the colonial and postcolonial educational legacy and how it changed due to national and international funding and policy shifts. The political economy of the past and current educational system and how the discourses on the role and goal of education in both countries have shifted with the change of political economic structures is explored through these texts and of course combined with data collected while interviewing the local community partners who had knowledge on the issue at hand.

The historical and political economic analysis was combined with the qualitative data gathered from being part of the participatory planning meetings and from the interviews with BGreen's community partners to connect the historical and policy writings to actual observations and ideas of the actors/actants, closely affiliated with educational institutions in the US and Bangladesh. This chapter is important to this PAR-ANT research project, since it provides the required historical frame that communicates to readers the culture of education in US and Bangladesh and how different turning points in its history have impacted the current state of matters.

Chapter 4: In the second analysis chapter, the larger frame that drives the creation of this concept is the relational dynamics between transnational political economic systems and participatory action initiatives (on the ground and online) to create transnational participatory networks, in this specific case, the BGreen participatory network contributes to the transformation of academic–community partnerships in Bangladesh and the US. This chapter is divided into two major sections, each section focusing on the details of the Bangladeshi and the US development of BGreen. In this chapter, I engage with PAR, ANT and application of Freire's *conscientização* as the theoretical trajectory and merge it with the methodological tools of interviews, participatory research and the political economic analysis of small institutions that were the community partners for BGreen to narrate the ways in which the participatory networks on the ground contributed to the formation of BGreen. This chapter exclusively looks at the organizational networks formed and their impact of leading to other forms of networks which contributed to the development of complex, stable participatory networks comprised of organizations, people, media organizations, social networks, to name just a few components. This chapter will really bring forth the community partners' discourses on academic–community partnerships and how different aspects of the process are negotiated, when diverse people and organizations get together to design a collaborative process, one which challenges the business as usual in the differing contexts of Bangladesh and the US.

Chapter 5: The chapter narrates and analyzes the multi-media networks (social media, radio, television, print, etc) that were built and sustained while developing BGreen and analyzes the importance of developing multi-media participatory networks that help in amplifying the goals of such a community-engaged mission, which is complementary to the on-ground mobilizing and building of participatory networks. I do a political economic analysis of the relevant print, television and radio industries in both countries as they relates to the formation and amplification of the BGreen participatory network. Analysis of new media technologies such as social media and blog use is also documented and analyzed. The support of the media networks in both countries looked very different, but overall both kinds of support helped significantly to amplify and sustain the message of BGreen. The transnational multi-media participatory network contributed to the amplification of the project and in turn led to more youth and organizational engagement, hence, their role in developing a deep and complex participatory network cannot be undermined. This textual analysis of the nature of the project's coverage in the media attempts to identify the kinds of discourses that emerged as a result of this, which really helped with the proliferation of the project and aided in the development of longer-term media connections with diverse media organizations. Another point that will be explored is whether the media exposure was done in solidarity with a new model of engaged academia or whether it was done from the stand point of maintaining the status quo, which would point to the politics of the media organizations and in turn reflect the discursive identity of those entities. Also, the way in which the new media networks were formed and how the spaces were used by both BGreen's community partners and also by the youth participants will be explored. The potentials of new media and how the youth navigate this unlikely space for the realization, sustenance and application of Freire's *conscientização* to create new discourses and complex participatory networks on environmental social change is investigated using these methodological tools.

Chapter 6: The final analysis chapter narrates this environmental academic–community engaged project from the perspective of the affiliated youth. It explores global youth participants as community action agents and how their identities are negotiated when attaching themselves to academic–community movements such as BGreen as independent and key stakeholders. The chapter takes a comparative approach on how the nature of the youth involvement, initiatives and aspirations are different and similar across the two geopolitical locations in study. This chapter brings the discussion full circle, as it puts forth the voices and perspectives of the youth who are participating in this academic–community project, which was designed to provide an alternative to the way in which Bangladeshi and the US youth could navigate the educational and community organizations that they are affiliated with. This chapter is designed to represent and analyze the voices of the youth who are central to the design of the project and to explore the range of discourses that are generated as a result of this process. Through the analysis of my data collected, it brings into the forefront the need for a shift in the educational model in the US and Bangladesh, one that puts students in the center of decision-making and priorities. It provides a glimpse into the way in which the youth connected with the BGreen experience and whether they saw value in the development of an academic–community space that was designed specifically for them.

Why the environment?

My research interests are at the intersections of environment, education, organizations, youth and sustainability. Due to the surge of environmental challenges that have plagued Bangladesh over the course of its history and during the recent focus on issues of climate change, it made it easy for me to choose the environment as the unifying concept or frame through which we can address the research questions that relate to the educational sector of Bangladesh. The US has been in the forefront of environmental, sustainability and climate change debates from the global north, making it the obvious choice to research from this geopolitical location. Environment in its entirety is one of the significant actants in the building of this participatory network, since it assumes an important position in its affiliation with education in the research project. The year 2021, referred to as Vision 2021 by the Bangladeshi government, has been declared as a "development goal" as it marks the 50th year of the nation's independence and that is around the same time that a new climate change treaty will be discussed by the UN (Nagorik Committee, 2006). Being one of the most populated countries in the world, the nation's population is predicted to reach 190 million by 2025, of which 63 percent will be under the age of 30 (US Census Bureau, 2013). Currently 52 percent of Bangladeshis are under the age of 30 (Indexmundi, 2018). Hence the future of the country is indeed in the hands of the nation's youth.

Based on the new IPCC report, David Suzuki, renowned environmentalist, reports that there is increased evidence on how humans are largely responsible for global warming and how with indifference and inaction there is serious threat to humanity (Suzuki, 2013). The habits of living things have a way of affecting both the local and the global, and these very actions hold great potential in bringing about significant changes to the world's ecological systems. We are leaving environmental footprints wherever we go and our actions, choices and decisions of the way we live in one *locality* also makes its impact on the *global*. However, Suzuki also writes that there is space for optimism as well, and emphasizes the importance of awareness building and citizen action to meet the challenges.

Holding true to these ideas and working with the values of citizen participation and deliberation which was at the core of this academic–community project, I developed the idea of an interdisciplinary performative participatory action research project that involves youth in both countries, from very different geopolitical realities, in building the BGreen participatory network. The way in which the youth are mapping these links between education, environment and their collective futures in a concrete way through this project is narrated and the multi-institutional interest in maintaining this connection is also explored through the various analysis chapters. Through engaging in a collaborative academic–community project, the youth are learning the importance of inter-connectedness which usually goes against the grain of the modern approach of education that is invested in fragmenting "the world into bits and pieces called disciplines and sub-disciplines, hermetically sealed from other such disciplines" (Orr, 1994, p. 11).

Orr further writes:

> Most students graduate without any broad, integrated sense of the unity of things. The consequences of their personhood and for the planet are large. For example, we routinely produce economists who lack the most rudimentary understanding of ecology or thermodynamics. This explains why our national accounting systems do not subtract the costs of biotic impoverishment, soil erosion, poisons in our air and water, and resource depletion from gross national product . . . . As a result of incomplete education, we have fooled ourselves into thinking that we are much richer than we are. The same point could be made about other disciplines and subdisciplines that have become hermetically sealed from life itself.
>
> (1994, p. 11)

Using education as a starting point in changing the way in which such hermetically sealed systems operate and maintain themselves is an effective and deliberate starting point, since the youth can be part of changing the terms of conversation from inside-out. Hence, via academic–community action projects like BGreen that are invested in youth-engaged change, there is the potential for a true societal shift by making transparent our interdependence with the larger network of all entities—the more-than-human/non-human as well as the anthropogenic, and bringing into the forefront ethical decisions about educational futures, environmental justice and beyond.

This is a challenge, when my work is published, because there are political consequences to naming organizations and people. This is one of the limitations of a PAR project. Bergold and Thomas (2012) write,

> participatory researchers are particularly called upon to address ethical questions. The closeness to the research partners during participatory projects repeatedly requires ethically sound decisions about the norms and rules that should apply in social dealings among the participants.
>
> (p.109)

It creates a sense of discomfort in me as the principle investigator in keeping the balance between representing my information in a way that does not offend any of the actors involved, considering the way in which my interpretation and analysis of something collaborative can impact so many people's lives. For example, if there was any tension or negative experiences between/among the actors/actants, it would put people in a precarious position for it to be discussed in public through my writing. However, as per many other PAR projects, this is one of the risks of such a research design, where principle investigators often have to deal with such issues on a regular basis. The students were not expected to have any prior knowledge of the content for participating in this conference.

Freire's ideas on engaged education and specifically *conscientizacao,* was also explained in detail to also the community partners throughout the planning process, so that the core group of actors knew the relevance and importance of this concept to create discursive shifts in the way in which institutions are structured to produce knowledge. Freire's (1970a, 1970b) canonical work on changing educational and knowledge building paradigms challenges the traditional didactical relationship based on linear, top-down transfers of knowledge from a teacher to a student, which is often the route that is taken in traditional conferences, seminars or classrooms in the US and Bangladesh. Freire (1970a) used a banking analogy where the teacher is described as "depositing" knowledge that the student passively accepts. He writes,

> Instead of communicating, the teacher issues communiqués and makes deposits, which the students patiently receive, memorize, and repeat. This is the 'banking' concept of education, in which the scope of action allowed to the students extends only as far as receiving, filing, and storing the deposits. They do, it is true, have the opportunity to become collectors or cataloguers of the things they store. But in the last analysis, it is the people themselves who are filed away through the lack of creativity, transformation, and knowledge in this (at best) misguided system.
>
> (Friere, 1970a, p. 71–72).

Hence the need to break away from such a limited and problematic model of knowledge transfer was explained to the workshop leaders, although this was a difficult topic, considering the fact that I may have been perceived as questioning their ideas on teaching and/or conducting workshops. The way in which this aspect played out in the actual workshops was mixed. While some of the workshop leaders were very mindful of the concepts, and really understood my perspective and the project's goals, some resorted to straightforward conference style presentations, presenting their research or topic in a typical top-down fashion with very little interactive elements in their presentation. This inconsistency did not go unnoticed by the youth. The youth expressed their opinions quite clearly in the debrief sessions by stating in many of them how they found the workshops that were interactive to be the most useful.

One such youth expressed her opinion quite clearly that connected with the larger goals of creating a space like BGreen and of course, more importantly, the BGreen participatory network. She wrote:

> This was our chance to be part of change in the making in our country. I knew when I came in through the door in the morning, that this experience was going to be different. But what I didn't know that our participation can look so different from one workshop to the other. However, I do wish that two of the workshops lectured us less and instead followed what the others did, of engaging us in conversation and brainstorming.

The youth facilitators who were trained to moderate and engage them in the process were also very satisfied with the way in which the participants really picked up on the complex ideas that were presented to them and the way in which the quality of the youth participation evolved as the day progressed. In a post event de-brief they unanimously agreed that the youth participants felt quite empowered and got increasingly confident about their participation as the day went by and were able to discuss and articulate complex ideas amongst themselves. Each workshop and its experience encouraged them to open up and engage in the collaborative dialogues more and they understood the role of the facilitator better as well and how their presence made the mediation of power dynamics between extroverted/introverted participants an easier process.

As core community actors looking to develop a sustained BGreen participatory network that goes beyond the event itself, it was important to de-brief with the facilitators of the process. They were key actors in the facilitation of the BGreen action research projects as they were the people who had the closest contact with the youth participation and their perspectives mattered in knowing how the experience and process could be made better. In retrospect, the facilitators should have been given a separate questionnaire to fill out, rather than the informal discussion that they had with the core community partners after the event, which was recorded as meeting minutes as part of the data collection procedure.

Examples of successful transnational exercises

Amongst the medley of participatory workshops and exercises that Bgreen conducts in both Bangladesh and the US, one of the more popular ones that ensued within the line-up was the participatory technology assessment (pTA) exercise which was led by one of our main community partners, Consortium for Science and Policy Outcomes (CSPO) that is a think tank of Arizona State University (http://cspo.org) in Dhaka, Bangladesh. PTA, is defined as being a specific participatory model to garner citizen participation and engagement in developing inclusive scientific and technological discourses with a focus on connecting informed public perspectives with policy experts and was designed to provide "broader access to and participation in technological policies and practices" (Worthington, Cavalier et al., 2012) that challenge epistemic communities and the perpetuation of Science (Adler & Haas, 1992; Latour, 2004). It is one process which genuinely has infinite scope of using Freire's idea of *conscientização*, in really using citizens and experts in dialogue and a two-way exchange of perspectives that reframes complex, "expert" issues for the public to meaningfully engage and deliberate with it in their relevant and familiar dimensions.

The pTA exercise was done in four stages to deliberate about social, environmental, economic, and ethical issues about a proposed nuclear power plant with each other and with subject matter experts to develop their consensus opinion about three policy options and present it in a mock public hearing to a panel of expert stakeholders. To address the research questions, we collected demographic data on the applicants and participants, pre-survey/questionnaire of participants' activities, knowledge and expectations and a post-survey/questionnaire on project ideas and participant learning, and quality and policy relevance of deliberations. Then in the second half of the first day, the first set of deliberations followed by citizen testimonials that they presented to community experts (academics, industry experts, policy-makers) who were working on nuclear power and its future in Bangladesh. This particular pTA exercise was based on the Science, Policy and Citizenship (SPC) program led by Dr. Mahmud Farooque of Arizona State University's Consortium for Science, Policy and Outcomes (CSPO) and I. The participants were challenged to deliberate on issues at the intersection of science, society and policy based on balanced background information, peer discussions, and interaction with real world experts.

The specific goals of BGreen's pTA exercise was to:

1. get youth's views on nuclear power in Bangladesh
2. give youth a chance to express opinion and develop recommendations for decision and policymakers
3. decide for themselves what roles they want to play
4. equip themselves with tools for informed decision making
5. develop new procedures for engaging citizens on energy and environment issues (Worthington, Cavalier et al., 2012).

In the actual deliberation sessions the students were quick to adapt to the deliberation pTA technique, which follows a very specific model that engaged facilitators heavily working together with the youth participants. The students were able to follow the procedure very closely and were able to engage in direct and informed conversation with experts and stakeholders working in the technical, educational, economic and social issues and policy and advocacy aspects of energy and environmental challenges facing Bangladesh, which in most other scenarios would never have been possible for the youth of Bangladesh, with the current educational structure there.

Through facilitated discussions, dialogue, and debates, they were able to develop and present their recommendations for the future of nuclear energy in Bangladesh, and the students developed detailed recommendations on which kind of educational and policy directions Bangladesh needs to go before introducing nuclear technology to the current mix of renewable energy options. The success of the process was an example of how it was able to break down the idea of epistemic communities, where the youth were actively discussing and deliberating on an issue that they are kept away from in their educational institutions and their workplaces. After a long participatory and deliberative process that involved multi-stages, in the final deliberation session, each youth group provided their unique ideas/narratives of solutions in the presence of the people to make up these epistemic communities- experts, scientists, academics and policy-makers who were present at the event. One youth expressed in their feedback on this session,

> This was such a unique and fascinating process. It really enabled us to understand the complexity and nuances of nuclear energy and its future in Bangladesh and at the end of it, I participated in formulating informed opinions on the future of renewable powers in Bangladesh which was heard by policy- makers. I was able to understand and collaborate with my group-mates to come up with real solutions by applying our academic skills in order to address something of importance for our national future. Woudn't it be amazing if we could use this process in our schools?

This was quite a nuanced response from a youth participant, since she was able to connect the value of participatory processes across her institutional affiliations and pointed directly how perhaps, embracing participatory processes such as these could be a better way of connecting academic "training" with social change. Throughout the deliberation process the different stages of magical, naïve, and critical emergence was at play, since the youth went from not being aware of the nuclear realities of Bangladesh, to connecting it to their personal futures and then ultimately the national and regional futures of Bangladesh and what its impact would be in the Bangladeshi context. This form of a participatory process helps to "motivate, enable, and empower the public to make decisions" about topics that are selected and highlight the importance of understanding how "Science" and the public decisions around it cannot be separated from values, political context and reinforces the need to come up with new "sciences" rather than upholding "Science" (Worthington, Cavalier et al., 2012) (Latour, 2004). Iterative processes like these rely on the participation of citizens, in this case, youth to really work through the concept of *conscientização* to help them understand the deeper implications of current policy making in Bangladesh around diverse issues, in this case, nuclear technology.

It provides a mechanism to utilize the Freirean concept of *conscientização* to really grapple with the issue in a holistic, multi-faceted way that goes beyond standard frames of economic growth, progress, profit-making, which are associated with the dominant discourse on the incorporation of nuclear technology in Bangladesh. This process also brings forth the importance of these participatory processes and how the element of *conscientização* that is at work in the process has the potential to have multi-institutional impact, across all the diverse human and non-human actors/actants who were involved in the process, which may change the way in which systems of knowledge or structures themselves are held falsely "functional" (Couldry, 2009). Challenging the false "functionalism" of structures can perhaps be made possible with the incorporation of these participatory processes, which when combined with *conscientização,* could perhaps result in *organizational conscientização,* which could have much wider and fruitful multi-industry implications.

Bibliography

Adler, E. & Haas, P. (1992). Conclusion: Epistemic communities, world order, and the creation of a reflective research program. *International Organization*, 46(1): 367–390.

Agamben, G. (1993). *The coming community*. Minneapolis, MN: University of Minnesota Press.

Anzaldua, G. (1999). Borderlands/La Frontera: The new mestiza. San Francisco: Aunt Lute Books.

Bergold, J. (2007). Participatory strategies in community psychology research–a short survey. In A. Bokszczanin (ed.) *Poland welcomes community psychology: Proceedings from the 6th European Conference on Community Psychology*. Opole: Opole University Press, pp. 57–66.

Bergold, J. & Thomas, S. (2012). Participatory research methods: A methodological approach in motion. *Historical Social Research/Historische Sozialforschung*, 13(1): 191–222.

Burr, V. (1995). *An introduction to social constructionism*. London: Routledge

Busch, L. & Juska, A. (1997). Beyond political economy: Actor networks and the globalization of agriculture. *Review of International Political Economy*, 4(4): 688–708.

Butler, J. (1998). Performative acts and gender constitution: An essay in phenomenology and feminist theory. *Theatre Journal*, 40(4): 519–531.

Callon, M. (1987). Society in the making: The study of technology as a tool for sociological analysis. In W. E. Bijker, T. P. Hughes and T. Pinch (eds) *The social construction of technological systems: New directions in the sociology and history of technology*. Cambridge, MA: The MIT Press, pp. 83–103.

Callon, M. & Latour B. (1992). In A. Pickering (ed.) *Science as practice and culture*. Chicago: Chicago University Press, pp. 343–368.

Cameron, J. & Gibson, K. (2005). Alternative pathways to community and economic development: the Latrobe Valley community partnering project. *Geographical Research*, 43(3): 274–285.

Cameron, J. & Hicks, J. (2014). Performative research for a climate politics of hope: Rethinking geographic scale, "impact" scale, and markets. *Antipode*, 46(1): 53–71.

Cammarota, J. & Fine, M. (2008). *Revolutionizing education: Youth participatory action research in motion.* New York: Routledge.

Cardoso, F. H. & Faletto, E. (1979). *Dependency and development in latin america (Dependencia y desarrollo en América Latina).* Berkeley, CA: University of California Press.

Cardoso, F. H. & Font, M. A. (2001). *Charting a new course: The politics of globalization and social transformation.* Lanham, MD: Rowman & Littlefield.

Castree, N. & MacMillan, T. (2001). Dissolving dualisms: Actor-networks and the reimagination of nature. In N. Castree and B. Braun (eds) *Social nature: Theory, practice, and politics.* Malden, MA: Blackwell Publishers, pp. 208–224.

Colombo, M. (2003, May). Reflexivity and narratives in action research: A discursive approach. *Forum Qualitative Sozialforschung/Forum: Qualitative Social Research, 4*(2).

Cooks, L. (2001). From distance and uncertainty to research and pedagogy in the borderlands: Implications for the future of intercultural communication. *Communication Theory, 11*(3): 339–351.

Couldry, N. (2009). Rethinking the politics of voice: Commentary. *Continuum, 23*(4): 579–582.

Couldry, N. (2012). *Media, society, world: Social theory and digital media practice.* Cambridge: Polity Press.

Cressman, D. (2009) *A brief overview of actor-network theory: Punctualization, heterogeneous engineering & translation.* Burnaby, BC: ACT Lab/Centre for Policy Research on Science & Technology, School of Communication, Simon Fraser University.

Denzin, N. K. (2001). The reflexive interview and a performative social science. *Qualitative research, 1*(1): 23–46.

Escobar, A. (1992). Imagining a post-development era? Critical thought, development and social movements. *Social Text, 31/32, third world and post-colonial issues*: 20–56.

Escobar, A. (2008). *Territories of difference: Place, movements, life, redes.* Durham, NC: Duke University Press.

Freire, P. (1970a). *Pedagogy of the oppressed.* New York: Continuum.

Freire, P. (1970b). *Cultural action for freedom.* Cambridge, MA: Center for the Study of Development and Social Change.

Freire, P. (1973). *Education for critical consciousness* New York: Continuum.

Freire, P., Ramos, M. B., & Macedo, D. (2000). Pedagogy of the oppressed. New York: Bloomsbury.

Gibson-Graham, J. K. (2005). Surplus possibilities: postdevelopment and community economies. *Singapore Journal of Tropical Geography, 26*(1): 4–26.

Gibson-Graham, J. K. (2006). *A postcapitalist politics.* Minneapolis, MN: University of Minnesota Press.

Giroux, H. A. (2013). *Youth in revolt: Reclaiming a democratic future.* Boulder, CO: Paradigm.

Harvey, B. (2011). Negotiating openness across science, ICTs, and participatory development: lessons from the AfricaAdapt network. *Open Development: Networked Innovations in International Development*, 275.

Harvey, B. (2014). Negotiating openness across science, ICTs, and participatory development: Lessons from the AfricaAdapt network. *Open Development: Networked Innovations in International Development*, 7: 19.

Hassard, J. & Law, J. (1999). *Actor network theory and after.* Hoboken, NJ: Wiley-Blackwell.

Hemment, J. (2007). Public anthropology and the paradoxes of participation: Participatory action research and critical ethnography in provincial Russia. *Human Organization*, 66(3): 301–314.

Indexmundi (2018). Bangladesh demographics profile. Available at: https://www.indexmundi.com/bangladesh/demographics_profile.html

Jacobson, T. L. & Kolluri, S. (1999). Participatory communication as communicative action. In T. L. Jacobson & J. Servaes (eds.) *Theoretical approaches to participatory communication*, Cresskill, NJ: Hampton Press. pp. 265–280.

Jacobson, T. L. & Servaes, J. (eds) (1999). *Theoretical approaches to participatory communication*. Cresskill, NJ: Hampton Press.

Kemmis, S. & McTaggart, R. (2000). Participatory Action Research. In N. K. Denzin & Y. S. Lincoln (eds) *Handbook of Qualitative Research*. Thousand Oaks, CA: Sage Publications.

Lassen, I., Horsbøl, A., Bonnen, K. & Pedersen, A. G. J. (2011). Climate change discourses and citizen participation: A case study of the discursive construction of citizenship in two public events. *Environmental Communication – Journal of Nature and Culture*, 5(4): 411–427.

Latour, B. (1987). *Science in action: How to follow scientists and engineers through society*. Cambridge, MA: Harvard University Press.

Latour, B. (1991). In J. Law (ed.) *A sociology of monsters essays on power, technology and domination*. London: Routledge, pp. 103–132.

Latour, B. (2004). *Politics of nature*. Cambridge, MA: Harvard University Press.

Law, J. & Callon, M. (1986). *Mapping the dynamics of science and technology: Sociology of science in the real world*. London: Macmillan.

Lindlof, T. R. & Taylor, B. C. (2010). *Qualitative communication research methods*. Thousand Oaks, CA: Sage Publications.

Manzo, L. & Brightbill, N. (2007). Towards a participatory ethics. In S. Kindon, R. Pain & M. Kesby (eds). Connecting people, participation and place: Participatory action research approaches and methods. London: Routledge.

Maxwell, J.A. (2004). *Qualitative Research Design: An Interactive Approach* (2nd edition). Thousand Oaks, CA: Sage Publications.

McChesney, R. W. (2008). *The political economy of media: Enduring issues, emerging dilemmas*. New York: Monthly Review Press.

Morgan, D. L. (1997). *The focus group guidebook*. Thousand Oaks, CA: Sage publications.

Morley D., Chen K.-H. (eds) (1996). *Stuart Hall: critical dialogues in cultural studies*. London; New York: Routledge.

Mosco, V. (1996). *The political economy of communication: Rethinking and renewal*. London: Sage Publications.

Murdoch, J. (1995). Actor-networks and the evolution of economic forms: Combining description and explanation in theories of regulation, flexible specialization, and networks. *Environment and Planning A*, 27(5): 731–757.

Nagorik Committee (2006). *Bangladesh Vision 2021*. Dhaka, Bangladesh: Center for Policy Dialogue (CPD).

Nancy, J. L. (1991). *The inoperative community*. Minneapolis, MN: University of Minnesota Press.

Nordtveit, B. H. (2005). The role of civil society organizations in developing countries: A case study of public-private partnerships in Senegal. Dissertation, University of Maryland.

Oberhauser, K. & Kountoupes, D. (2012). Citizen science and youth audiences: Educational outcomes of the Monarch Larva monitoring project. *Journal of Community Engagement and* Scholarship, *1*(1): 10–20.

Orr, D. (1994). *Environmental literacy: Education as if the earth mattered.* Barrington, MA: Schumacher Center for a New Economics.

Patel, L. (2012). Contact zones, problem posing and critical consciousness. *Pedagogies: An International Journal*, *7*(4): 333–346.

Reason, P. & Bradbury, H. (2001). *Handbook of action research: participative inquiry and practice.* London: SAGE Publications.

Reid, C. & Frisby, W. (2008). Continuing the journey: Articulating dimensions of feminist participatory action research (FPAR). In P. Reason & H. Bradbury (eds) *Sage Handbook of Action Research: Participative Inquiry and Practice.* London: Sage Publications, pp. 93–105.

Servaes, J. (1989). Cultural identity and modes of communication. *Communication Yearbook*, *12*: 383–416.

Servaes, J. (2002). The European Information Society: much ado about nothing? *International Communication Gazette*, *64*(5): 433–447.

Servaes, J. (ed.) (2008). *Communication for development and social change.* New Delhi: Sage Publications.

Servaes, J. & Malikhao, P. (2008). Development communication approaches in an international perspective. In J. Servaes (ed.) *Communication for development and social change.* New Delhi: Sage Publications, pp. 158–179.

Sparks, C. (2007). *Globalization, development and the mass media.* Los Angeles: Sage Publications.

Spinuzzi, C. (2008). *Theorizing knowledge work in telecommunications.* Cambridge, UK: Cambridge University Press.

Stovall, D. (2006). Forging community in race and class: Critical race theory and the quest for social justice in education. *Race Ethnicity and Education*, *9*(3): 243–259.

Straubhaar, R. (2014). A place for organisational critical consciousness: Comparing two case studies of Freirean nonprofits. *Comparative Education*, *50*(4): 433–447.

Suzuki, D. (2013). *Getting dirty is good for your immune system.* The Georgia Straight, 5 November.

Tuck, E. (2009). Suspending damage: A letter to communities. *Harvard Educational Review*, *79*(3): 409–428.

Wadsworth, Y. (1998). What is participatory research? *Action Research International*, Paper 2.

Wallerstein, I. (1974). The rise and future demise of the world capitalist system: Concepts for comparative analysis. *Comparative Studies in Society and History*, *16*(04): 387–415.

Wasserman, S. & Faust, K. (1994). *Social network analysis: Methods and applications.* Cambridge: Cambridge University Press.

Worthington, R., Cavalier, D., Farooque, M., Gano, G., Geddes, H., Sander, S., Sittenfeld, D. & Tomblin, D. (2012) Technology assessment and public participation: From TA to pTA, *Expert and Citizen Assessment of Science and Technology (eCAST).*

3 Transnational political economic realities and their impacts on social transformation

The political economic realities that shape the development of educational systems in Bangladesh and the United States is explored and analyzed in this chapter. It is important to analyze the relationship between the structural realities and education, to understand better the acceptance and/or rejection of (transnational) academic–community projects as tools and solutions for sustained social change in both geopolitical locations. The differences and the similarities in the ways in which networks are built, based on the complex intertwining of various social, cultural and economic factors in the context of global north and south is discussed in this chapter. The unapologetic and unchecked global neoliberal agenda has directly impacted the educational systems of both countries. Following the story of global privatization, economic movements provide a valuable compass for investigating and analyzing the adoption of this profit-driven system's effects on youth and their connection to educational institutions in both nations.

I engage with the existing literature focused on US and Bangladeshi higher educational systems and their contested relationship to politics, youth and social change in this section, and make connections with Freire's political approach of *conscientização* in developing an educational project that is community engaged and geared towards social critique, inclusion, innovation and transformation. This chapter provides some insight into the cultural and social context that frames my research which deals with the potential and strength of academic–community projects, and points to the possibility of transforming and transgressing the limited, neoliberal models of education that are invested in separating community and academia in the US and Bangladesh (Brown, 1995; Karim, 2008; Nath, 2006; Muhammad, 2003).

When we delve into the historical and political economic analysis of the formalized higher education institutions in Bangladesh, it is amply clear how US-backed global educational policies and privatized, market-based funding structures have impacted the course of education in Bangladesh. Hence, the commentary on the political economic structures of education and funding is blurry and encompasses very similar realities for both nations. In order to make sense of these institutional dynamics, strategies and decisions that have shaped the educational experience of youth in both Bangladesh and the US, a political economic analysis is required because, as Mosco (1996) writes:

> This formulation has a certain practical value for students of communication because it calls attention to fundamental forces and processes at work in the marketplace . . . . But political economy takes this a step further because it asks us to concentrate on a specific set of social relations organized around *power* or the ability to control other people, processes, and things, even in the face of resistance. This would lead the political economist of communication to look at shifting forms of control along the circuit of production, distribution, and consumption.
>
> (p. 24)

The way in which power operates on the ground and at the top has the capacity to frame and limit the possibilities and potentials of a small, counter-culture project like BGreen. Therefore, this complex interplay of power, networks (non-human and human actors/actants) and politics is an important point to consider and understand in an informed, systematic way to map the context that frames BGreen. This knowledge can help researchers and community actors to understand the way in which educational policies came into being as part of a strategic, political project that has been consciously adopted, and what local innovators can do to change the situation. It will help actors/actants who are involved in developing projects like BGreen to understand the constructed, ideological and political economic realities that they are up against in every stage of their participatory network building.

Knowing the current structure in more detail will provide clues to actors/actants as to how *conscientização* could be used as a transformative concept and tool to critique and change pedagogical processes in the context of the current political economic structure in both the US and Bangladesh. Educational democracy rises to the top as being one of the key needs of the higher educational sector in both nations today to build the next generation of critical, socially aware and engaged individuals involved in sustaining true democratic values in society that are putting into practice some of the values of Freire's visions of education for social change. The construction of the higher educational system, public or private, in the US and Bangladesh largely depoliticizes the importance of addressing socially relevant causes and instead takes a mercenary approach to education which serves global capitalism and explicitly follows a neoliberal agenda, resulting in an incomplete, disengaged, uncritical and ungrounded form of education (Giroux, 2013). The parallels between the educational politics of the two nations are glaringly obvious, which has made it difficult for educational democracy to prosper as a process of social change. This is a result of a profit-seeking system that is invested in dismantling state support for social services and the commons, by following a hyper-capitalist US model of economic growth. Instead there is a push to using deregulation, liberalization and privatization as a strategy to bring about economic progress in developing countries such as Bangladesh. As scholars Rahman and Wiest (2003) say:

> The global institutions such as World Bank and the IMF, determine every aspect of Bangladesh's economy and society including its agriculture, environment, occupations, waterflow, state of industry and even the mind set of the so-called civil society in the process of integrating Bangladesh into world capitalist system.
>
> (p. 17)

The funding source of the majority of higher education system in Bangladesh is no different and, as my narrative will show, the introduction of the World Bank and IMF into the educational industry has resulted in a much more precarious educational situation in Bangladesh, coupled with the nation's unstable and corrupt political system. In the US, while political scenarios in the Bush, Obama and Trump era have radically polarized the daily operationalization of academic institutions, the general road safety and related logistics have largely remained intact. In the case of the incessantly unstable, corrupt and unreliable political system in Bangladesh, often academic and non-academic institutions remain shut down for indefinite periods of time due to threats to citizen safety causing civil society chaos on a regular basis.

The structure and curricular goals of most universities at present in both nations, amplified by both their polarizing, unstable and corrupt political systems have acutely impacted the scope and potentials of developing an educational project with *conscientização* as one of the driving forces of the process. The attention is just not on developing a fairer, just and socially relevant mode of education. The aggressive market-driven approach is designed to omit the voices and needs of youth, and reduces youths' rightful and central place in the design of the educational model to that of mere consumers of a profit-driven educational approach (Giroux, 2013). The attention is on profit maximization rather than developing a curriculum that supports creative and socially engaged ways of learning and applying knowledge. This educational model does not have their best interests in the philosophy, design and structure of the educational model as their core goals have been shifted by market-led forces that relegate youth to being mere consumers. In this chapter, the significance of BGreen as a counter-cultural academic–community engagement transnational project is interwoven into the narrative to set the stage for an alternative vision of engaged academia for youth of both nations, using education as a tool for bringing about environmental social change.

Why BGreen?

As discussed earlier, *conscientização* is one of Freire's most powerful contributions to this project, which has the potential to transform people, organizations and societies. *Conscientização* is a social, psychic phenomenon, which can be used as a transformative tool that can help entities in learning to perceive social, political and economic contradictions, and to take agency and action against the oppressive elements of reality, to develop effective *praxis* for social change (Freire, 1970a, p. 35). According to Freire, "the awakening of critical consciousness (*conscientização*) leads the way to the expression of social discontents precisely because these discontents are real components of an oppressive situation" (Freire, 1970a, p. 36).

Hence the exploration of these discontents with the support of multi-institutions and industries and the emergence of the critical consciousness of youth and other actors, stakeholders and organizations/institutions connected with them (and from participating in processes of change such as BGreen) can potentially be the turning point for the downward spiral of these educative platforms in the current state of education globally. It is important to navigate the supposed "functionalism" of political economic structures for not only a better understanding of how political economic structures maintain power through the sustenance of epistemic communities, but also to understand how participatory networked processes can be used to navigate and unsettle this false construct of functionalism that is still at work in the understanding and application of both classic and critical political economic theory (Couldry, 2009, 2012).

Education was being hailed by the Bangladeshi government as the savior for the masses after the liberation in 1971 and the only way to achieve sustainable development (Kabir, 2010). However, this project has shaped up in the current times in Bangladesh in the most unsustainable way. The term "sustainable development" was coined in 1987 by the Brundtland report, which was the result of the work by the World Commission on Environment and Development (Nordtveit, 2005, p. 21). The idea of this concept of sustainable development was one that was theorized as developing strategies and processes that "improve human well being in the short term without threatening the local and global environment in the long term" (p. 21). Nordtveit (2005) furthers Mehmet's (1999) ideas, who wrote that as a project, sustainable development emphasized a "holistic approach to development" (Mehmet, 1999, p. 133) and "harmonization of economic growth with other human needs and aspirations" (Mehmet, 1999, p. 133) and how, in the 1990s, the notion of sustainability was adopted by most international development agencies, who eventually became donors for higher educational systems in developing nations (p. 21). In the case of Bangladesh, the path that connects this idea to achieve sustainable development via education has been a very flawed one, which has resulted from the compounding of the political economic failures of national governments, international development funding agencies and mindless emulation of the US privatized educational system.

In the case of the US, the acute privatization and commercialization of education is at an all-time high, with drastically reduced budgets for the proliferation of sustainable, socially relevant education. Capital-driven globalization has been a significant game-changer for both the Bangladeshi and US higher education systems and the kind of education they are "selling" to the global youth are reducing them to being mere "consumers" of a decontextualized, homogenized, profit-driven, top-down process. Nordtveit, (2009) reflects on globalization's two-fold effect on education and writes:

> Globalization can therefore be said to have an impact both on the delivery processes of education (which are now more market based) and on the content of education (which is now more economy centered). The Freirian model of education as critical dialogue has increasingly been considered as threatening and regressive by education policy makers.
>
> (p. 10)

Hence the development of platforms like BGreen is an important political project, since it is designed to be an educational-praxis platform based on transnationally involved participatory processes, with a bridge connecting and communicating youth aspirations to academic and civil society organizations. Projects like BGreen support youth in being involved in developing participatory networks to solution-building by using the structural advantages of different industries to cooperate, communicate and collaborate together to address growing local and global sustainability concerns.

Conscientização could be a very potent tool in transforming the structure of business-as-usual in diverse institutional and industry platforms in the US and Bangladesh, which is one of the key goals of my research. It is appropriate to compare the state of higher education of Bangladesh to what Giroux (2013) reflects on about the state of higher education in the United States, due to the shared privatization of the educational project. Giroux (2013) aptly writes:

> Public and higher education, increasingly shaped by corporate and instrumental values, must be reclaimed as democratic public spheres committed to teaching young people about how to govern rather than merely how to be governed in an increasingly authoritarian society.
>
> (p. 22)

Therefore, in order to challenge this decontextualized, socially irrelevant, money-driven model, which involves multi-industries in order to make funding for education possible, it is necessary to combine the same multi-industries and institutions with youth voices and aspirations so that there can be meaningful communication about the urgent change required in the educational system that is not currently serving either youth or larger society. This allows for unsettling the dualities of power and binarism inherent in such structural constructs and allows for ideas like *conscientização* to perhaps be developed as tools in reconfiguring the way in which *organizational conscientização* could look like in diverse multi-industry settings.

I am proposing that a shift in the organizational structure of educational systems is an urgent need in the US and Bangladesh, which can be built off of youths' efforts to develop their individual and collective *conscientização*, which may result in the creation of a critical, socially engaged new generation of Bangladeshis. The US does not have a history of youth political movements, however, the youth engagement process is especially relevant to Bangladesh, since youth have historically been active agents of positive social change in the nation's history (Kabir, 2010; Quddus & Rashid, 2000) at different crucial periods of time. Why do I think educational platforms, combined with youth can be the answer to the ecological crisis? Youth citizen action has historically been successful in all aspects in Bangladesh, as recently as the Shahbagh phenomenon. As Freire (1970a) states, "people come to feel like masters of their thinking by discussing the thinking and views of the world explicitly or implicitly manifest in their own suggestions and those of their comrades" (p. 124).

Hence, replacing the learning void with a critical and engaged pedagogical process in Bangladesh (and of course the US) that foregrounds empowering and socially transformative knowledge production processes for social change is a goal for academic–community projects like BGreen that want to achieve *organizational conscientização* (Straubhaar, 2014). However, the success of BGreen as a one-time project is not enough to bring this forward either in the US or Bangladesh. As emphasized earlier, to bring about structural discursive shifts, participatory networks like BGreen need to become a regular feature in academic institutions globally, where ideally youth actor/actants can apply their critical ideas that are generated as a result of their journey through magical, naïve and critical consciousness. Ultimately, processes like these may help facilitate debates among youth, educators and administrators that extend beyond educational institutions, which will connect the emergence of critical consciousness with transformation of multi-industry political economic structures with which they are affiliated (Lewis et al., 2016).

Brief history of higher education institutions in Bangladesh

Formalized higher education in Bangladesh started through the inception of the University of Dhaka in 1921 during British rule, adding to the list of higher education institutions via the University Grants Commission (UGC) that rested in University of Kolkata (in current day India) (University Grants Commission, 2007). Much like other colonial global educational projects, the British wanted to create knowledge centers that aided in the strategic plans of the British Raj and to use the resulting educated class in Bangladesh/India/Pakistan to be educated to meet the British Raj's needs. As Kabir (2010) writes, "they wanted to create a class who would be Indian in blood and color, but English in taste. Therefore, indigenous history and customs gradually disappeared as the colonial powers enforced their colonial ideas on natives" (p. 25), using education as a means of social control.

However, soon after the end of British rule in 1953 when Bangladesh became a part of Pakistan, Rajshahi University (which is the second largest university of Bangladesh) and subsequently a few more higher education institutions were initiated (University Grants Commission, 2006; Kabir, 2010). There was a change in goals of developing higher education under the Pakistani regime from 1947 to 1971 as well, since there was more of a focus on using these knowledge centers, their students, staff and faculty as instruments of social change against a common cause—liberation from the Pakistanis (Kabir, 2010; Quddus & Rashid, 2000).

Historically, students' political involvement contributed significantly to the establishment of freedom and democracy in Bangladesh, which ultimately led to the formation of the free country, no small feat or contribution by a segment of the population who are constantly ousted from national debates around the world (Quddus & Rashid, 2000). Hence, the role of youth in Bangladesh in challenging the power and binarism that are held stable in key political economic structures (such as the government) with the support of academic institutions is not a new phenomenon in Bangladesh. While the connection of youth and politics has had mixed results in Bangladesh, it is necessary to revisit this complex phenomenon in this research, since a new politicized form of education is desired.

From national independence in 1971 until 1985, the country had more universities sanctioned by the state, following the newly born country's overall development, which was built on the policymaker's ideas, which believed in education being the great equalizer. It was envisioned that with access to education, the economically disadvantaged had means to secure economic and social advancement, however, growth did not unfold in the way in which it was envisioned by these short-sighted policies (Quddus and Rashid, 2000). Since the 1990s, the attitudes and policy implementations of the education sector (especially higher education) had largely shifted to one that was market-regulated in Bangladesh, following the need for more universities in the country, which was largely funded by the World Bank. The World Bank funding propagated a market-led model for the emerging economy, which is operated within frames of cost-effectiveness (Nordtveit, 2009). Nordtveit (2009) further writes about the role of the World Bank and its integral relationship to global private sectors:

> The World Bank aims at strengthening the private sector. It also often promotes market-based solutions for implementation of public services, generally because these private implementation methods are said to be more effective than state implementation of services. It seems that the change of social service provision from government to the private sector, whether justified by evidence of better performance or not, is linked to global policy changes, frequently known under the term *globalization*. Policies favoring market solutions to delivery of social services are increasingly employed in most countries.
>
> (p. 7)

Globalization was viewed as being the panacea for achieving economic growth and so the entire funding for the development and flourishing of the private higher educational sector in Bangladesh was secured from international financial institutions (IFI) led by the World Bank. IFI generously supported the growth of a corporatized, revenue-focused private higher educational institution and culture in Bangladesh (Kabir, 2010) as well as many other majority world nations globally. Neoliberal policies of the international financial institutions (IFIs) play a crucial role in formulating various socio-economic policies in postcolonial states such as Bangladesh, and this nation's higher education sector is no exception. Upon maturation of the plans of developing a new, privatized education system in Bangladesh, in response to the public model that was showing cracks in its administration, The World Bank allocated US$100 million for the reformation of the higher education sector (Ovimot, 2006). To be specific, Bangladesh was one of the very first countries in the world amongst 35 nations to receive the Extended Structural Adjustment Facilities of the International Monetary Fund in 1986 and 1989, which was one of the first programs of financial assistance given to "developing" countries from December 1987 through 1999 through the International Monetary Fund.

It was the first time the World Bank had provided financial assistance for the higher education sector with a very specific vision for shaping the structure of the university system in Bangladesh. This vision has led to the state of the higher education sector in Bangladesh (Faruque, 2005, cited in Ovimot, 2006). For Rahman, who was the Finance Minister of Bangladesh at the time, the investment in the educational sector was treated in the same way as any other sector of the economy (Ovimot, 2006). To add to the gross de-contextualization that framed the thinking behind the development of this new educational system further, The World Bank provided direct recommendations to the government with conditions for its financial and technical support for the development of the new educational sector in Bangladesh. The recommendations were market driven, which shifted the goals of using education as a tool for achieving *conscientização* and instead took a cost-benefit approach to this process.

With the guidance of the IFIs, the government of Bangladesh has drafted a Strategic Plan for Higher Education (SPHE) in Bangladesh: 2006–2026 (University Grants Commission, 2006; Kabir, 2010; Varghese, 2006; Quddus and Rashid, 2000) that upon examination is clear in its vision of connecting education with market-driven economic forces. UGC finalized a 20-year Strategic Plan for Higher Education (SPHE) in April 2006 which, upon investigation, shows a clearly developed education plan that is driven by market forces (Kabir, 2010). Following the discourse of neoliberalism as followed by the US educational system, the youth citizens are treated like commodities in a market that is primarily concerned with profit-making rather than knowledge production for social development and change. Also, often the new private universities are set up and controlled by their own infrastructure, with weak guidance from UGC, providing a narrow range of academic majors, focusing only on business and technology related majors (Kabir, 2010).

The analysis and review by the World Bank mission was followed by an Education Ministry request for assistance in developing a 10-year Strategic Plan for Higher Education. There is acknowledgement to the World Bank in developing the document and its content and the final version of this 20-year SPHE document that UGC formulated was made official in 2006. However, the overt extent to which the international organization contributed to its formation is never made clear at any point, except for the direct link to the educational funds that can be traced back to the World Bank, that pushed for a market-led, privatized model of education (Giroux, 2013; Kabir, 2010, 2011). Students' democratic involvement with the SPHE would help to address their perspectives on what type of higher education institution they would like to have in Bangladesh that would meet their educational and social needs. It is exactly this kind of provision that may be possible with the development of participatory cultures within educational institutions, via deliberative methods where youth and other concerned stakeholders could get together to address the future of SPHE collaboratively, where the youth citizens' needs and voices are represented in the reformulation of the document, which upholds the power of epistemic communities within such political economic setups.

Following the formulation of the 20-year SPHE document, the Bangladeshi government followed the US privatized educational model and ratified the Private University Act back in 1992, and the first private university, North South

University, was established soon after that year which has become the most renowned private university in Bangladesh to date (Quddus & Rashid, 2000; Varghese, 2006). The national count for Bangladesh's universities until 2008 was 29 public universities and 51 private universities offering different courses at undergraduate and postgraduate level, even though the number has gone up in the last seven years (University Grants Commission, 2008). As Quddus and Rashid (2000) write about the emulation of the privatized US educational model in Bangladesh, "increasingly, societies now regard higher education as more of a 'private good' with not enough immediate and positive externalities (characteristics of a 'public good') to justify public support" (p. 29). This view of education is a highly problematic one that reduces education and the emergence of *conscientização* to merely one that is dictated by monetary and profit-seeking considerations where education and young people have been "increasingly removed from the inventory of social concerns and the list of cherished public assets, and in the larger culture they have been either disparaged as a symbol of danger or simply rendered invisible" (Giroux, 2013, p. 19). Again, the Bangladeshi educational system is mirroring the political economic realities that have shaped the identity of the US educational system, driven by profit maximization.

Conscientização was developed as a powerful pedagogical and social transformative tool based on the idea of public service and wellness by Freire, which sharply contrasts with this vision of education, which does not allow for the growth of critical thinking that has transformative social potential. Hence, citizen-science approaches that really combine the diversity of social human and non-human actors/actants, in this case youth, to develop a new culture of engaging with knowledge building and the subsequent discursive shift (structural, individual, social, ideological) as a result of this, seems to be an appropriate strategy for beginning to engage with this challenge. One of the key objectives of these unchecked neoliberal policies is to design an environment for the market that can run all sectors of the economy, by introducing suitable laws and institutions to suit its needs (Olssen & Peters, 2005; Kabir, 2010).

Since the 1980s, Bangladesh has adopted neoliberal economic policies in various sectors of the economy, for instance agriculture, industry, and finance and banking (Nuruzzaman, 2004; Rahman, 2011, 2014) to achieve "growth", which in turn has directly impacted industries like education, which is now largely dictated by the neoliberal agendas that are governed and designed to serve markets rather than socially engaged knowledge building. Hence, for citizen-science driven approaches to work and to develop sustained participatory networks such as BGreen, we need the inclusion of global and local multi-institutions to bring about change. This claim will be supported, via the exploration and analysis of the contribution of multi-institutional actors/actants in developing the BGreen participatory network, in the following chapters and how the complex interplay of all these entities forms the basis of a stable, open and growing participatory network. Through such a generative and participatory process, youths' can apply the critical consciousness that emerges to their future/current workplaces which potentially can redefine the way in which structural functionalism operates within institutions, *and* diverse political economic institutions can provide the architectural support that can add to the complexity, deepening and stability of the participatory network.

The story so far

Higher-educational institutions in the US and Bangladesh at this current point in time, come with an entire baggage of issues, irrespective of whether they are public or private institutions. While public and private higher education institutions have different problems that are unique to their lineage and traditions, the end result remains the same: youths who are enrolled as students suffer the brunt of administrative and curriculum deficiencies that are driven by profit or politics. Giroux's (2013) account about the US approach to such hyper-capitalist approaches to education rings true in both nations about an anti-Freire approach. He says, that the hyper-capitalist approach to education in the US "confuses training with critical education" and encourages the "withering away of the public realm, public values, and any viable notion of the public good" (p. 131). The comparison of the US higher educational system with the Bangladeshi one is important to make since the US model has been closely duplicated by the majority of the Bangladeshi private higher educational institutions that came into being from the late 1980s onwards. The emulation of the curriculum structure of US liberal arts institutions is widespread in Bangladesh as the US model of education is resulting in profit maximization for the owners of the private schools, colleges and universities that are mushrooming everywhere in Bangladesh. Also, many of the private academic institutions in Bangladesh have some level of affiliation with US-based academic institutions and are always looking to secure partnerships with US-based institutions.

Education remains one of the key targets of the neoliberal project because of the sheer market size (Giroux, 2013). The global spending on education is more than $1 trillion (Ross & Gibson, 2007; Kabir, 2010). As Ross and Gibson (2007) make clear, neoliberal policy in itself is a monolithic political project, one which is driven by profits, hence targeting one of the key industries that has the potential to shape young people's ideologies and worldviews (Ross & Gibson, 2007; Giroux, 2013). To elaborate on the specific case of the educational system in Bangladesh, there is a long history of state politics being interwoven into its structure, which showed sparks of being a democratic process in its inception. However, over time this educational and political mixture created a corrupt, greedy and monstrous system that was developed only to serve and enhance the power and agendas of competing political parties of the times rather than providing students in universities the opportunity to manifest their academic desires into socially relevant and beneficial projects (Kabir, 2010; Quddus and Rashid, 2000).

Public universities in Bangladesh explicitly and/or secretly always maintain political affiliations with the dominant political parties. These unwieldy, politically motivated relationships place educational endeavors in a precarious and peripheral position in Bangladesh (Kabir, 2011). Kabir (2011) writes:

> It is generally recognized by all concerned that the administrative system is primarily based on elections in the public universities and has become dysfunctional due to political linkages with governments with power. Hence, the autonomy, as given in the university acts, has become nominal and the party in power effectively controls the university. Teachers and students have become linked to student's politics.
>
> (p. 25)

Therefore, the whims of the political demands of the time, that serve a select party's propaganda to build further power over the populous has been central to the educational structure, decision-making and output of these institutions, rather than focusing on using these political affiliations to address local and national social concerns. Over time, this same cycle, which leads to on-campus and off-campus violence and also *session jams* (which is the name given to a major delay of 2–3 years in degree completion due to political conflict on campuses) created a sense of mistrust amongst students and parents in attending public higher educational institutions. It created a genuine desire for educational institutions that really filled the needs of the students and parents in having a safe, non-partisan learning environment—a gap that was swiftly filled by an imported private higher education system, with its many shortcomings, following a brutal, profit-making approach.

These private universities were designed to be intentionally "apolitical spaces" that are free from political affiliations, upheavals and complications from the public university model to a point where the focus of these institutions was to train youth to become passive consumers of their socially disengaged and mercenary approach to education. This was a deliberate attempt to move away from the corrupt, short-sighted and greedy aspect of student politics, which has been the defining factor of the controversial past of public universities, only to be replaced with another aggressive global political project, namely neoliberalism. One of the key features of such a privatized higher educational system today in Bangladesh is one that tries to build a distinctly apolitical image, one that identifies as "politics-free campuses" (Kabir, 2011), again following in the legacy of US academic institutions. The development of this privatized, non-political educational project could have been the solution to the ongoing public and corrupt higher educational system, however, much like the US privatized higher educational system, its Bangladeshi counterpart succumbed to hyper-capitalist politics, driven by corporate, profit-seeking, neo-liberal greed, that designs education as a money-making business venture.

This approach to higher education has created hindrances to the development of engaged educational models and successful academic–community projects like BGreen, all over again, due to a different set of reasons than Bangladeshi public universities. A youth action research academic–community project like BGreen goes against the grain of what education has come to mean today in Bangladesh, since it is not rooted in profit and instead is rooted in educationally-driven social change. Citizen science PAR-ANT projects such as this one enable members of the public, in this case US and Bangladeshi youth, to participate in actual community engagement projects that have the potential to yield positive environmental outcomes for the wider community (Oberhauser & Kountoupes, 2012), an approach that the current educational system has silenced and omitted to building the next few generations of global youth. Also, it allows for a creative rebuilding of the ways in which structural and non-structural entities or actors/actants can interact with one another to create new kinds of participatory networks, where students and institutions can use *conscientização* as a building block to carve a new version of student politics in both the US and Bangladesh, one that is not rooted in partisan politics or profit maximization, but instead is rooted in structural and sustainable social change that will ultimately form the fabric of emerging global societies.

Social effects of education for profit

Consistent with the plight of the US economic system, market-led neoliberal values are treated as the dominant model of development and knowledge building throughout the higher education economy in Bangladesh, as discussed extensively in the previous sections. The entire funding for the development and flourishing of the private higher educational sector in Bangladesh was made possible by international financial institutions (IFIs) led by the World Bank, that generously supported the growth of a corporatized, revenue-focused private higher educational institutions and culture in Bangladesh (Kabir, 2011). Nordtveit (2009) reflects on the state of Senegalese education, which is a parallel example of a developing African nation that is working on reconfiguring its educational identity post-colonialism and also post World Bank intervention. Nordtveit (2009) writes:

> In absence of planning, and as a result of flawed implementation, global donors, and particularly the World Bank, became very influential in Senegal. Some teachers were less than enchanted with the foreign influence, and even

suggested to re-baptize the national education system as "The World Bank School System".

(p. 13)

This gap in the planning and foresight of national policy-makers mixed in with monetary greed in both Senegal and Bangladesh, is what caused the demise of the idea of developing education as a main focus of the nation and the people's sustainable development, where both nations' policy-makers too easily adopted the market-led educational ideologies of the World Bank. This combined with one of the other key features of Bangladeshi higher educational system today, which tries to build a distinctly apolitical image, one that identifies as "politics-free campuses" (Kabir, 2011) has given birth to a vacuous educational system that has no social grounding.

This approach to education has created hindrances to the development of successful academic–community engaged projects like BGreen, as this youth action research academic–community project goes against the grain of what education has come to mean today in the context of Bangladesh (and of course the US). Kabir (2011) quotes a parent of a university student that he interviewed for his article. He narrates, "Parents are scared about our main bourgeois politics and therefore parents think that if they can send their children to a private university, children will be safe from nasty politics." This on one hand targets the political affiliations, upheavals and complications from yesteryear, which has caused innumerable challenges to the educational system and progress in Bangladesh by resulting in *session jams*, which is the name given to a major delay (2–3 years) in completing the degree.

However, in an attempt to move away from the corrupt, short-sighted and greedy aspect of student politics, (since public universities in Bangladesh have always explicitly and/or in secret always maintain political affiliations with the dominant political parties), the current strategy has resulted in adding further precariousness to the approach and quality of education in Bangladesh today (Kabir, 2011). While the number of higher educational institutions has skyrocketed across the country, the educational content in most of these institutions remains questionable. Hence, the reaction to such a corrupt and state interest-based higher education system was not a carefully thought out alternative in Bangladesh— following a profit-driven, de-politicized, uncritical and socially disengaged form of higher-education (Giroux, 2005). Instead of focusing on teacher training, content diversification and rethinking the way in which education can be used as tool for social change *and* financial security, the focus on profit-building has taken center stage.

The increased corporatization of education in these two nations that focuses on excluding the academic and non-academic community from processes of active engagement, citizen science discourses are definitely on the periphery in the approach to education, curriculum planning and pedagogy (Brown, 1995; Karim, 2008; Nath, 2006; Muhammad, 2003). Muhammad (2003) advocates for this democratic shift in the global context and he writes that potentially "civil society movement could be a motive force in empowering the poor and might ensure people's participation in globalization from below vis-à-vis a pervasive top-down globalization process" (p. 11).

Even though the global youth involved in BGreen both in the US and Bangladesh were not economically the poorest in either of the nations, they embodied a demographic that has always been sidelined to the periphery as participants in "serious" decision making around "serious" matters, such as the future of higher education. In the current state of affairs in both countries, neither the current academic model nor the present youth are accustomed to combining and connecting socially driven ideas and projects with their academic/class content as the idea of education is still overwhelmingly one that is based on what Freire calls the "banking" model of education with bookish, top-down definitions of learning and relating to knowledge production. Hence this created a crippling effect to the potentials of education in both countries where one of the most important tools of emancipation is being destroyed—education (Freire, 1970a; Giroux, 2013).

Due to such a shift in the approach to education, the students are in a perpetual state of magical consciousness, or at most naïve consciousness, where most are not even aware of their contextual realities and how they connect to larger social and structural problems. Kabir (2011) specifically writes that students "have no critical insight into capitalist oppression, injustice, and the class structure of the society. The overall political culture of the society is gradually transformed into de-politicization and the term democracy is becoming a synonym for market ideology" (p. 23). This issue constantly rose its ugly head when I was developing BGreen in both nations. Even though the youth of Bangladesh were ready for changes in their education and activism, they did not know exactly what an alternative looked like, where their institutional learning could be in alignment with their desires for social change.

Thus, they were lingering somewhere between the magical and naïve consciousness stage disconnected to participatory and iterative processes that may have helped them with the emergence of their critical consciousness. This is ironic, since, at least historically in the Bangladeshi context, higher education institutions and youth had a pivotal role in making Bangladesh an independent nation by combining their personal aspirations to bring about significant structural changes that resulted in the birth of a new nation. As Kabir (2010) writes:

> Political consciousness and ideological involvement in public university teachers is not a new phenomenon in Bangladeshi society. Rather, their political

involvement benefitted the country – they had a great role from the language movement in 1952 to the restoration of democracy in the 1990s; teachers and students sacrificed their lives in the war of liberation in 1971. Therefore, how can squeezing of public university autonomy in the name of de-politicization of public universities be justified?

(p. 27)

Universities were spaces of activism and freedom, which allowed for a multitude of voices to be expressed in Bangladesh. The country's oldest public university, the University of Dhaka, was treated as the center of every democratic movement of the masses (Quddus & Rashid, 2000), which was the root of the political edge of such public institutions, a process that eventually went astray due to the corruption and misuse of these political aspirations via parties in power. The 20-year Strategic Education Plan (SPHE) formulated again falls prey to political nepotism *and* neoliberal market ideology, hence creating a bigger monster with the strengths of two powerful political projects. The committee members that designed the document were said to have been handpicked by the political parties in power without any student and community representation, which is a counter-productive process, since the needs of students are directly at stake here (Kabir, 2010, 2011).

Resistance and democratic deliberation of peripheral groups in any country is a complex task, until people are aware of the issues and see themselves as a force for social change, which is the relevance of *conscientização* as a socially liberating concept. As scholar Nuruzzaman (2004) writes:

Since 1975, the major political parties of the country have been working for the neoliberal policy agenda . . . [and] that the motivation to work for this agenda mainly lies in political interest and that without implementing the neoliberal policy agenda prescribed by IFIs the state's power cannot be sustained.

(p. 13)

BGreen is a manifestation of such an academic–community engaged rebellion, which is small in size, but one committed to bring the core issue of the failure of the educational governance globally to citizens who are unaware of the behind-the-scenes manipulations by mammoth, international and national political economic structures that are partnering up their strengths to omit citizen engagement in every sector of society.

A process of "vocationalizing" higher education is not going to contribute to the development of youth, citizens and society that is able to understand and critically engage with national and international politics, history and their development in a meaningful way (Kabir, 2012). Kabir (2012) writes, "sometimes they know of some historical events, but they are growing up without knowledge of the implications and of critical perspectives. The critical insight of students is diminished, helping establish the prevailing capitalist ideology in society" (p. 17) Hence this profit-driven training, vocationalized and "banking" approach to education will not chart a democratic future for either the US or Bangladesh. The notion of "educational democracy" (Fields & Feinberg, 2001) needs to be insisted upon in the higher education sector in order to sustain democratic values in society.

BGreen hopes to be a small disruption to such a higher educational approach that completely depoliticizes important, socially relevant causes that takes a mercenary approach to education that perpetuates an empty, incomplete, disengaged, uncritical and ungrounded form of education. The goal is to work with diverse educational institutions in global settings to perhaps develop a new educational direction as it strengthens its transnational participatory network. One of the advantages Bangladesh has over the US is its inherent disorganized bureaucratic system. The unplanned and chaotic higher education policies of Bangladesh, as developed by UGC has a very weak role to play in maintaining the educational structure. Kabir (2010) writes:

> The conclusion on quality assurance in higher education in Bangladesh is that UGC has a role in setting certain minimum qualifications for recruiting teachers in general for both public and private universities. However, it lacks the ability to exercise such control due to politicized campuses and weak structure of UGC. Individual institutions are left to assure the quality of education and research.
>
> (p. 28)

While the weak over-arching governance of the UGC is disappointing and ineffective, the broken system allows for something new to penetrate and change the way in which the policies are applied on the ground. Therefore, each and every academic institution in Bangladesh can potentially be a fertile ground for change. The breakthrough could be a harder process in the context of the US, because the neoliberal organizational systems already have a deep entrenched history and method that is supporting this long-running global hegemonic structure. However, in the case of Bangladesh, due to the weak organizational infrastructure of the individual institutions and the lack of their depth in thinking through the long-term goals of the process, projects like BGreen can attempt to bring something new and worthwhile for all actors/actants involved.

One of the most effective ways of doing that would be to engage youth in their own capacity building via participatory activities that help them emerge from the cultural vacuum of neoliberalism. Emerging from such an overwhelming and omnipresent political project such as neoliberalism needs to be followed by strategies on how *conscientização* can be developed and operationalized not only in themselves but also structurally. Hence, actors with the right ideas can take advantage of these weak policies and governance, by developing universities and institutions in a brand new way in the same spirit that BGreen has been envisioned and developed to serve youth. Academic–community processes like BGreen would allow for a place to help the youth to go through the different stages of consciousness, that they can ultimately use as a tool to achieve organizational *conscientização* in diverse institutions.

After this political and historical analysis, the following chapters add to the complexity of this participatory network called BGreen, where a unique, shifting and ever-evolving combination of human and non-human actors/actants have contributed to the development of a sustained process flowing through transnational spaces in the global north and south. The importance and inclusion of the current chapter challenges what some scholars refer to as a "strong" ANT approach that refuses pre-existing social and historical trajectories to analyze actor networks, but solely emphasizes the interactions and the outcomes as a result of it as the primary source of the analysis. The concept of a participatory network was developed to address exactly this gap, since the scope and complexity of a network cannot be understood or realized without knowing the context that frames its flow. Each of those cultural, political, social, religious, structural, spiritual, spatial (to name just a few) contextual realities add nuances to any participatory network, that is very important to understand to grapple with the foundations upon which it proliferates.

However, it is also important to be able to identify which of the actors/actants have more power in a specific context and how the unequal contribution of some actors/actants as a result, determines the complexity and flow of the participatory network. This is one of the key reasons for my adoption of the weak version of ANT that does not fetishize difference and maintains the balance between possibilities and discursive shifts that can emerge out of small processes like BGreen. However, the key is to not lose sight of the larger power structures that it is constantly touching, redefining and transforming in the process of gaining depth, complexity, hybridity and stability. BGreen participatory network explores this tension between structure and amorphous possibility and can identify the gaps that exist in the educational sector and how academic–community projects can contribute to filling the void that is negatively impacting knowledge-production and youth futures in both the US and Bangladesh.

Bibliography

Alam, M., Haque, M. S. & Siddique, S. F. (2007). *Private higher education in Bangladesh*. N. V. Varghese (ed.). Bangladesh: International Institute for Educational Planning.

Brown, M. B. (1995). *Africa's choices: after thirty years of the World Bank*. London: Penguin Books Ltd.

Couldry, N. (2009). Rethinking the politics of voice: Commentary. *Continuum*, *23*(4): 579–582.

Couldry, N. (2012). *Media, society, world: Social theory and digital media practice*. Cambridge: Polity Press.

Freire, P. (1970a). *Pedagogy of the oppressed*. New York: Continuum.

Freire, P. (1970b). *Cultural action for freedom*. Cambridge, MA: Center for the Study of Development and Social Change.

Giroux, H. A. (2005). The terror of neoliberalism: Rethinking the significance of cultural politics. *College Literature*, *32*(1): 1–19.

Giroux, H. A. (2013). *Youth in revolt: Reclaiming a democratic future*. Boulder, CO: Paradigm.

Kabir, A. H. (2010). Neoliberal policy in the higher education sector in Bangladesh: Autonomy of public universities and the role of the state. *Policy Futures in Education*, *8*(6): 619–631.

Kabir, A. H. (2011). A new discourse of 'international understanding': Nothing but 'Americanism'. *Critical Literacy: Theories and Practices*, *5*(1): 38–50.

Kabir, A. H. (2012). Neoliberal hegemony and the ideological transformation of higher education in Bangladesh. *Critical Literacy: Theories and Practices*, *6*(2).

Karim, L. (2008). Demystifying micro-credit the Grameen Bank, NGOs, and neoliberalism in Bangladesh. *Cultural Dynamics*, *20*(1): 5–29.

Lewis, L. A., Kusmaul, N., Elze, D. & Butler, L. (2016). The role of field education in a university–community partnership aimed at curriculum transformation. *Journal of Social Work Education*, *52*(2): 186–197.

Mehmet, O. (1999). *Westernizing the Third World: the Eurocentricity of economic development theories*. London: Routledge.

Mosco, V. (1996). *The political economy of communication: Rethinking and renewal*. London: SAGE Publications.

Muhammad, A. (2003). Bangladesh's integration into global capitalist system: Policy direction and the role of global institutions. In M. Rahman (ed.) *Globalisation, environmental crisis and social change in Bangladesh*. Dhaka: University Press, pp. 113–126.

Nuruzzaman, M. (2004). Neoliberal economic reforms, the rich and the poor in Bangladesh. *Journal of Contemporary Asia*, *34*(1): 33–54.

Nath, S. R. (2006). Youths' access to mass media in Bangladesh. *Adolescents and youths in Bangladesh: Some selected issues*, Research monograph series no. 31. Dhaka: Research and Evaluation Division, BRAC. pp. 147–162.

Nordtveit, B. H. (2005). The role of civil society organizations in developing countries: A case study of public-private partnerships in Senegal. PhD Thesis, University of Maryland, College Park, MD.

Nordtveit, B. H. (2009). *Constructing development: Civil society and literacy in a time of globalization.* Berlin: Springer Science & Business Media.

Oberhauser, K. and Kountoupes, D. (2012). Citizen science and youth audiences: Educational outcomes of the Monarch Larva monitoring project, *Journal of Community Engagement and Scholarship, 1*(1): 10–20.

Olssen, M. & Peters, M.A. (2005) Neoliberalism, higher education and the knowledge economy: From the free market to knowledge capitalism, *Journal of Education Policy, 20*(3): 313–345.

Ovimot (2006) *Monjuri commissioner koishol potro: uccho shikkha dongser chokkranto* [Strategic plan of the Grant Commission: A destructive initiative in the higher education sector]. Dhaka: Samajtantrik Chatro Front.

Quddus, M. & Rashid, S. (2000) The worldwide movement in private universities: Revolutionary growth in post-secondary higher education, *American Journal of Economics and Sociology, 59*(3): 487–516.

Rahman, A. (2011). A political economy of the emerging television news industry in Bangladesh. *Revista Eptic, 11*(2).

Rahman, A. (2014). The problems with reimagining public media in the context of global south. *Stream: Culture/Politics/Technology, 6*(1): 56–65.

Rahman, M. & Wiest, R. (2003). Context and trends of globalization in Bangladesh: Towards a critical research agenda. In M. Rahman (ed.) *Globalisation, environmental crisis and social change in Bangladesh.* Dhaka: University Press, pp. 3–32.

Ross, E. W. & Gibson, R. J. (eds) (2007). *Neoliberalism and education reform.* Cresskill, NJ: Hampton Press.

Straubhaar, R. (2014). A place for organisational critical consciousness: Comparing two case studies of Freirean nonprofits. *Comparative Education, 50*(4), 433–447.

University Grants Commission (UGC) (2006) *Strategic Plan for Higher Education in Bangladesh: 2006–2026.* Dhaka: UGC.

University Grants Commission (UGC) (2007) *Tetrishtom Barshik Protibedon 2006* [33th annual report 2006]. Dhaka: UGC.

University Grant Commission (UGC) (2008). *Choitristom barshik protibedon 2007* [34th Annual report 2007]. Dhaka: UGC.

4 The networked architecture of the BGreen experience

This chapter explores the relationship between academia and community engagement and how national and international community organizations and international academic institutions collaborated together to design the BGreen experience as a transnational participatory network spanning the US and Bangladesh. The process that went behind building the onground architecture of the BGreen warrants discussion in the context of the two nations' political economic realities, so that there can be an understanding of how such participatory networks can go about materializing and further gaining network stability. The political economic connections of all the organizational actors/actants who were the major global community partners for BGreen is explored and analyzed here in connection to the PAR-ANT process that ensued in order to shed light on the diverse constituents that made the participatory network of BGreen. It traces the community connections made on the ground in both countries in the creation of this unique platform by identifying the challenges and benefits of such communicative, citizen science networks and uses the methodological processes of ANT and PAR to navigate the process. The ultimate goal is to provide comprehensive perspectives on the importance of such inclusive collaborative models in the development of participatory networks that can contribute to the future of youth-led academic–community partnerships on a global scale.

The chapter interrogates academic–community partnerships from a variety of inter-disciplinary and transnational vantage points and from two geo-political locations in the global north and south—US and Bangladesh. Since the project was fluidly operating and flowing within transnational spaces, the boundaries and comparisons are often overlapping and blurry. The combined geopolitical narratives from both global north and south provide a unique counter mapping of established research on such partnerships that originate mostly from northern/western geo-political locations (Trickett & Espino, 2004; Carlisle & Cropper, 2009; Etmanski & Pant, 2007; Battistoni et al., 2009). It provides a rare glimpse of a participatory action research project that is based in divergent social, cultural, economic contexts.

The previous chapter provided an overview of the global neoliberal agenda and its deep impact on educational systems in both Bangladesh and the US. Building on that thread, this chapter will first identify the general premise of such transnational academic–community partnerships in both countries and how BGreen plays out as it flows through both US and Bangladesh as it gains participatory network stability.

More specifically, this chapter will give readers a peek into the reality of academic–community PAR collaborations on the ground from both a US and Bangladeshi context and the extent to which small cracks of change are made possible that shows the promise to challenge structural rigidity and supposed functionalism of political economic structures in society. The aim is to not only identify what makes these ANT-PAR processes unique and different, but also to identify commonalities that can be translated to similar community engaged projects in any global setting, to help change the discourses and practices around the way in which knowledge spaces are built and consumed in the global setting with the contribution of multi-institutional actors/actants. ANT's process of translation is utilized to understand the way in which the networks emerged. Emergent networks like BGreen gain stability through the process of *translation*, which in ANT is understood to go through four stages as explained earlier: *problematisation*, *interessement*, enrollment and mobilization.

The translation process is developed to help with setting a common meaning/understanding of the project at hand among the actors/actants involved in building this network and through the exploration of the on-ground participatory networks that were formed, new questions are posed that will aid in navigating these community connections that are forged to create spaces for youth to develop new subjectivities, ones that have the potential to create new environmental and educational discourses. The need for academic institutions to shift to a more inclusive, community engaged model, one that radicalizes the academy, by opening its doors to communities to impact knowledge production, application and the emergence of *conscientização* is addressed. These participatory networks will bring into the forefront the potentials of combining youth, community and academia to bring about sustained changes to the environment in a transnational, post-liberalization setting where new technologies create often a seamless, fluid transnational network while flowing through the global north and south.

Mapping the terrain

BGreen's goal at inception was to integrate dynamic US and Bangladeshi youth with diverse environmental experts, professionals and other climate-concerned global citizens in an action research platform that connects academic institutions, civil society organizations, international organizations and global youth. The key aim was to combine the strength, expertise and perspective of diverse institutions to inspire urban youth to take direct action in developing innovative plans, sustaining environmental awareness and planning for the collective futures of their communities, one that sets an example of a unique initiative that transforms the larger perceptions of academic–community divide in both countries. The way in which community is defined, used and transformed through such a process is also explored and how the industries and institutions normally separate themselves from such collaborative connections is examined. As part of the global academic system, my vision and goal was to create an opportunity for higher educational institutions in the US and Bangladesh to combine and collaborate for a larger, global cause. They did this by opening their doors to a community engaged project of this type, one which deviates from the artificial boundaries that are often created between academic institutions and the community.

This chapter will lay out the diverse nature of organizations and people that came together to build this platform for youth civic engagement in Dhaka, Bangladesh and in Western Massachusetts, US by analyzing the individual actors that contributed to the formation of a participatory network. Some of the questions that I will be addressing in this chapter are: What are the webs of connections that arise in an emerging, changing entity like BGreen to start building a transnational participatory network? How do the connections involving both human and non-human actants/actors shape and reshape BGreen's emergence through different phases? Also, do the connections result in a sustainable, new entity that goes through the process of ANT's translation that persists over time to form what is called a black box? Are there limitations to the concept of black box for a PAR-ANT project that combines both theoretical paradigms, one that can be solved by creating a BGreen participatory network instead?

Academic–community partnerships are an anomaly in the context of both Bangladesh and the US praxis of education right now. The rapidly changing social and academic landscape of education in both countries has supported the maintenance of the separation of academic institutions and non-academic actors, especially youth organizations and groups to perpetuate the isolation of and segregation of multi-institutional and independent actors/actants to amplify the un-democratization and continued depoliticization of the academic sphere (Giroux, 2005; Kabir, 2010; Khaleduzzaman, 2014;). This brings into light the urgent need of academic institutions to redefine the manner in which knowledge is produced and disseminated to potentially create inclusive spaces of politicized, socially relevant knowledge and social transformation: a site where participatory politics of engaging non-academic actors are used to construct theory which goes full circle by applying it in a setting that transcends the traditional constructs of the academy.

In the context of both nations, to understand and map the universe of academic–community engagement it is important to explore briefly the relationships of the separate actors and organizations. As we have already discussed in the previous chapter, the educational model in Bangladesh (from primary to advanced higher education) has transformed from a largely public model to a privatized model in the last couple of decades due to pressure from international organizations such as the World Bank, which has led to increased corporatization of the educational system and the total emulation of the US propagated neoliberal agenda (Brown, 1995; Karim, 2008; Nath, 2006; Muhammad, 2003; Kabir, 2010). With the increased corporatization mixed with the post-colonial system of education that focuses on excluding the non-academic community from processes of active engagement, citizen science discourses are definitely on the periphery in the approach to education, curriculum planning and pedagogy (Brown, 1995; Karim, 2008; Nath, 2006; Muhammad, 2003).

Muhammad, (2003) says, "Civil society movement could be a motive force in empowering the poor and might ensure people's participation in globalization from below vis-à-vis a pervasive top-down globalization process." Hence, neither the current university model nor the present youth are accustomed to combining socially driven ideas and projects with their academic/class content and expectations, as the idea of education is still overwhelmingly one that is based on bookish, top-down definitions of learning and relating to knowledge production in both nations. On the other hand, the civil society organizations and/or the non-profit organizations have a relatively better association with both academic institutions and youth actors, but by no means is the association an intimate one. On one hand, non-profits have always needed the expertise of academics to provide expert opinions on matters that they deal with on the ground and hence academics in such non-governmental settings in Bangladesh and the US often work in consultant/advisor capacity (Zohir, 2004).

However, it is also common to often keep their roles, responsibilities and work in both settings quite disparate to maintain distance between their two roles, rather than embracing the continuum these two roles potentially provide to bridge two industries that can certainly generate a deeper impact in society (Sandmann, 2008; Trickett & Espino, 2004). It is this continuum that speaks to the potentials of the strengths of academic–community projects, and on an individual level, points to the possibility of transforming and transgressing the limited, postcolonial models of education that are invested in separating community and academia globally (Brown, 1995; Karim, 2008; Nath, 2006; Muhammad, 2003). On the other hand, the relationship between non-profits and global youth is often a much more developed one. Non-profits are often driven by a lack of funding and have a history of using youth from local and international schools and universities to do volunteer work for them, which often turns out to be a mutually beneficial association for both parties: the students often are hungry for work opportunities that will make them competitive and experienced in the future job market and it helps organizations with a small budget to have cheap, educated and skilled labor to help them out with their various social projects. Also, with the access and proliferation of new media technologies, now global youth engagement in organizations is at an all-time high, because the youth can live anywhere in the world and still work with an organization based in a different country. In the case of Bangladesh especially, this is a very frequent phenomenon and in the case of BGreen it was very frequently the case that global youth from various countries (both global north and south) worked and collaborated together to build this transnational participatory network by using new media technologies as one of the key OPPs in the project.

In comparison, the exchange between youth and civil society organizations is designed for mutually beneficial purposes, which allows for youth voices to be included, even if in a marginal way in the context of non-profits (Flanagan & Christens, 2011; Lewis, 2004;). Due to the top-down model of education that does not have well-established mechanisms for participatory engagement of students/youth in the private or public higher-educational system in both US and Bangladesh, there is a lost opportunity for both, since such a potent combination of mixing large institutional political economic strength with ground-up youth perspectives and activism is not being given a chance to be explored. Denying such a process creates obstacles in the way in which social discourses can be generated as a result of the dialogue, deliberation and conversation between diverse actors/actants (Giroux, 2013). Reflecting on the connection between globalization, donor funding and education that is connected to following this "banking" model of education Nordtveit (2009) writes, "Globalization policies have been criticized not only for affecting the delivery and quality of education but also for affecting its substance. It is contended that economy has become economy centered, instead of child centered" (p.9).

Based on Giroux (2014) and Nordtveit's (2009) analysis, the academic space should reclaim what I consider to be the most important aspect of education as a social and sustainable developmental tool—one which aids in the production of new knowledges that is grounded in communities and lived realities rather than reproducing outdated knowledge systems that are controlled by the combination of markets working in alliance with the government to perpetuate a flawed model of education. The shift that I am proposing and actively participating in is creating space for the emergence of Freire's *conscientização*, which is a process that the World Bank finds threatening and unnecessary in their vision of education and the way it is implemented in their global decision-making (Nordtveit, 2009). Shifting the current model to one that is more inclusive towards communities and community organizations of diverse natures would be a step in the direction of the development of fresh discourses that develop the best form of theory. This form of theory emerges in connection to real communities *and* can be used to contribute to the wellbeing of those same communities.

Hence my version of the PAR-ANT approach had youth as the centerpiece in combining academic and community engagement in providing an alternative to the artificial binaries that are often constructed to separate the academy and non-academic sectors. The beginnings of a new counter-cultural academic-activist project through the webs of connections that arose out of the emerging, changing connections involving both human and non-human actants/actors to shape and reshape BGreen's emergence through its different phases is now discussed in detail. While the next chapter deals with details on the impact of digital and new media technologies (especially social media networks) as an integral actor/actant of the process, this chapter's analysis includes the important role of phone, email and Skype as key non-human vehicles of building these participatory networks alongside the human actors.

Making connections

From the project's beginnings as a transnational academic–community project, the first requirement was to find appropriate, committed academic partners in both the US and Bangladesh. I was concurrently planning action research projects in Dhaka, Bangladesh and Western Massachusetts, US, which connected diverse people in building this participatory network in various roles. In the US, UMASS Amherst was my base and home institution and I wanted a reliable and well-reputed academic partner institution in Bangladesh. I thought the most effective way to do so would be by finding an entrance into an accredited and reputed educational institution in Bangladesh. I was open to the host being either a well-known urban high school or an urban undergraduate/graduate college/university. My first choice was a higher-education institution, led by my interest in reaching older youth and academics due to their research scope and expanded networks to other industries, although I was interested in bringing in high-school youth to participate in the youth action research via the indirect route of higher educational institutions. Due to a variety of different reasons in both the US and Bangladesh, hosting an event in a university would attract a wider age group, bringing in people who are slightly younger and older than the typical undergraduate who is 19–23. However, hosting it in a high school would not be an attractive option for college and university youth, as they would feel the event is geared more towards younger youth.

It was a lofty goal to attempt to build transnational networks from the get go about a topic and process that is largely peripheral to the academic experience and design of global mainstream academia in both countries. However, as a researcher I was determined to pursue my vision. I got together an initial proposal with ideas on what my specific vision of the project was and then sent it around via email and phone to everyone I knew (professional as well as personal contacts) who had links to issues of sustainable social development and change. This list was comprised of professors, scholars, practitioners and students from my various multi-institutional national and international networks. I had emailed most people my initial proposal and a personalized message on whether they were interested in getting involved with a project of this nature or knew of an individual or an organization who is interested in collaborating on an environmental PAR project that will actively construct and generate counter narratives of global youth from under-studied, under-represented settings.

I received a range of responses from people around the world. Most people, irrespective of country and origin were very encouraging about the idea and responded with enthusiasm and curiosity and pointed out the need for developing a project like this that counter maps global youth activism and new discourse and alliance building between global north and south. This group of people wanted to know the details of the project, why I was invested in it and why I think that there is a need for this project in the context of US and Bangladesh, which I gladly provided for them. In retrospect, some curiosity about the project and I was an investigative technique employed by the people from certain organizations in Bangladesh that wanted to know what the idea really was, since the urban work culture is quite cut-throat and competitive in the upwardly mobile, urban, educated workforce in Dhaka, Bangladesh. This was not the case in the US partners of BGreen.

There were many institutions that were looking at different aspects of the environmental crisis and sustainable development from different vantage points and everyone was trying to make a difference in the larger environmental world and hence there was healthy competitiveness about my project details, none of which I hid while discussing prospects of collaboration with my potential partners in Bangladesh and the US. This point is especially important to explain since this is one of the key challenges of conducting collaborative process in the context of Bangladesh, at least in the context of urban work culture in Dhaka, Bangladesh. There is a culture of not sharing inside information about motives, event details, etc, with outsiders, since there is always a risk of someone "stealing" ideas and replicating them without proper attribution. This aspect operates with much more transparency and ease in the US context, where I certainly did not encounter such guardedness and secrecy around discussions and implementation of BGreen at any point. However, still, in the context of Bangladesh I was able to mobilize local organizations for the vision and goals of my project to develop the shared platform for the global youth of both nations, adhering to my principles of transparency and full disclosure. In the US, I encountered fear and unfamiliarity from my contacts with the transnational nature of the project and whether or not I would be able to gather all the resources and actors/actants necessary to conduct the global project. The continued success of the participatory network with increased amounts of action research in both the countries removed the fear of the US actors/actants and replaced it with inspiration, solidarity and commitment.

My transparency was received with considerable suspicion in Bangladesh initially since there is a dominant culture of secrecy in the professional world in Bangladesh, as a response to the cut-throat competition in the work setting. In fact, some people who were early collaborators, warned me about disclosing too much information about my project to others, however, I was determined about my idealistic vision and the rewards it could reap if people and organizations collaborated rather than competed with one another to work towards a shared a common goal. One of BGreen's main goals was to build on the strengths and perspectives of multi-institutional actors/actants, hence, without open communi-cation and transparency of ideas, an effective, sustained network could not be built (Arnaboldi & Spiller, 2011). *Network instability* is an issue that often plagues actor networks and I was determined to take my role at OPP seriously, since this process is a continuous one that needs to be monitored and guided, albeit with the constant participation of other actors/actants in the process.

I knew for sure that for a community-oriented project like this, having community based partnerships that were spanning many different countries and localities were key as the project was envisioned and developed with exactly that motive in mind. The project had to resonate with all the stake-holders and actors/actants alike: the youth, organizations, academics and activists had to believe in the development of combined sustained values and goals for the project to see the light of day and make it worth it. It was not that most people did not see the value in my vision, I heard excitement and genuine support in most of their voices, however, most people did not know whether as an outsider residing in the US, I was capable of making a project of this scale, one that challenged the shape that educational institutions and approaches had taken in both Bangladesh and the US. Also, some of the early advisors of the project told me specifically that the political situation in Bangladesh at that time was really challenging and they were worried about my capacity to raise the amount of funds that I needed to make this project a reality in Bangladesh in a finite period of time. Some of them advised me to just conduct the project only in the US, due to the safer political conditions.

One of the main, undesirable actors/actants that needs further explanation is the political climate in Dhaka, Bangladesh for the whole of the time I was conducting fieldwork on the action research projects. Not one project conducted in Bangladesh was untouched by the political chaos that is the norm in the daily functioning of society in the nation today. The Bangladeshi part of the project developed around extreme uncertainty and unsafety, with constant possibilities of everything being cancelled without any notice. While I was operating within the limitations of my assigned time for fieldwork in Bangladesh (as I am primarily based in the US), changing the proposed dates for most of the Bangladeshi data collection was not an option. For the debut Bangladeshi part of the action research, BGreen was scheduled for three days: January 8th, 10th and 11th of January 2014 to be specific, which was 5 days after the scheduled national elections day in Bangladesh. Historically, the nation is at its political worst in terms of safety and productivity around election time and usually transportation, mobility and road safety is a major challenge for this reason. Then again the following year in January 2015, another political crisis hit Bangladesh at the time of the action research, which caused three out of seven action research initiatives to be cancelled.

Due to these extreme circumstances, the country experienced a government-imposed standstill for the entire month of December and January in both 2014 and 2015. At that time, there were traffic restrictions for safety reasons in most areas in the city, which posed as a huge challenge throughout the planning and implementation phase. Such a precarious scenario was truly a metaphor for the old, outdated system of politics that was posing a real barrier to the development of a new and fresh democratic discourse in Bangladesh that is spearheaded by the youth. The system was crippling the people from working actively to really identifying the problem with the current situation that they are involved in. The introduction of PAR projects like these "treat young people as agents in ongoing, critical struggles" (Cammarota & Fine, 2008, p. viii) where "they begin to re-envision and denaturalize the realities of their social worlds and then undertake the forms of collective challenge based on the knowledge garnered through their critical inquiries" (Cammarota & Fine, 2008, p. 2). The political chaos and the way in which it was creating obstacles for this project to be implemented was a reminder to all the actors involved to carve out a new way of relating to one another, so that collectively we can create the building blocks of a newer process that is not bound by such power games of the controlling class. This included the acceptance of the US partners of the precariousness of the Bangladeshi partners when it came to political limitations and insecurities. The US partners had to constantly change their timelines on collaborations based on the political limitations and subsequent work freeze of the partners in Bangladesh, which often proved to be a very cumbersome process. For example, one significant BGreen action research project that was conducted in 2016–2017 in Bangladesh in collaboration with one of our US partners, Water Defense, took a year longer to conduct due to political challenges and state imposed delays.

Mobilizing and guiding the youth involved in all the BGreen projects towards using *conscientização* as a tool to enhance their modes of thinking, projects and ultimately to the way in which they express it through their current and future institutional affiliations to bring about institutional changes through the power of the people was a goal for me as a researcher. Through the development of this participatory network, I wanted to provide the youth with a sound institutional and technological support system to act as a solid foundation to build on their visions and goals. Youth movements and their connection to academic institutions are especially important in the context of Bangladesh, because the founding of the nation from Pakistani dictatorship was based on student and youth activism that took route and prominence in academic campuses around the country (Kabir, 2010; Khaleduzzaman, 2014). Through the political turmoil in all of the times mentioned above, it was increasingly unsafe for the Bangladeshi youth to travel through the city to get around anywhere, therefore the political turmoil was at its peak throughout the active planning process of every one of the action research events. Projects were very difficult to conduct, as many face-to-face meetings had to be cancelled with community partners due to such limitations and restrictions.

There was great difficulty in organizing a safe space for the meetings to happen face-to-face, and worst of all, it made everyone wonder if any of the actors could be present on the planned day of the event at all due to public safety concerns. This was a huge de-motivating factor for all the co-organizers and as the initial OPP of the process, it was my responsibility to provide the co-organizers and partners with safe meeting places, transportation support and encouragement about the bigger picture of putting effort into a process that will hopefully work out, despite the political odds. On the US end, this provided distrust and interruptions in community and alliance building. It created tremendous pressure for me as the founder and lead researcher to mediate between what often felt like disparate universes when it came to political safety and work progress. The political challenge (and the mediation and adaptability required to tackle this ongoing issue) was a key non-human actor/actant in the process, however, it was a strong example of why non-tangible forces can be so integral to adding to network instability in the ANT framework and how people can often gloss over such important factors in the process of building something like a participatory network.

However, another non-human actant was key to offset the challenges that were posed by the political instability: technological actants such as Skype, phone, google hangout and email helped us navigate through this difficult roadblock. We were undergoing the phase of *problemitisation* in ANT, when we identified this common obstacle that could plague network growth, which was the acute political instability at the time. To reach the next two steps of *interessement* and *enrollment* we all had to collectively rethink how to meet one another as a group. Through conversation we came to the conclusion that on days when we could not meet in person, our group community meetings would happen via google hangout, which allowed for video-conferencing of the multi-actors. We also created a closed Facebook group as an online discussion forum, where all the meeting minutes were recorded and added and daily updates were posted there by all the core-community actors involved in the process, as needed.

We resorted to the support of non-human actants to support the activities of the human actors, where we decided on the importance of deciding which actors could meet online consistently based on their access to the internet. This was important to identify, so that the process of mobilization in ANT could ensue, where the human actors who could not attend due to technological barriers, could be consulted via phone or other means alongside the collaborative group meeting that happened live through Google hangout. This was one of those instances where the careful negotiation of the translation process added further complexity to an emerging network. The role of technological actors/actants in this participatory process cannot be undermined. These modes of communication not only acted as nodes of information exchange, but active entities in shaping and reshaping the entire architecture of the BGreen participatory network.

These technological actants connected people from diverse fields, locations and professions through me, the principle researcher or as ANT calls it "obligatory points of passage" (OPP), who are the necessary points of information transfer in the process, whose role in being a medium of communication is entirely necessary at all points of network building. This was a major responsibility, as I had to really be diligent and persistent about the critical communication within and between isolated streams of people and had to be the sole decision-maker in the initial stages behind which actants/actors to pursue. However, as the participatory network started emerging and getting stronger, the important function of non-human actants such as communication technologies became more evident and without a doubt, these technologies became key OPPs to the growing stability of the BGreen network. Through the process of translation, BGreen was able to enlist these communication technologies to its advantage to build a participatory network.

For example, due to the ongoing unpredictability of the political situation, the morning of each action research event in Bangladesh, we sent out a group text message to all the registered youth participants to remind them that the event was indeed happening. While other factors clearly contributed to the project's success despite the political chaos, the co-organizers and organizations, the role of technology as a non-human actant cannot be undermined at all in the process of translation that ensued within this actor network that was shaped by the relational outcome between the technological and political actants and the human actors. The creative ways in which the human actants could negotiate technology that helps create an architecture of participation to better meet their goals of organizing by bypassing life-threatening political situations, is commendable and one of the key strengths using ANT as an analytic framework for this process.

In the US project implementation process, the non-human actant of using technology for communication took more of a backseat in the PAR process. Due to the safer political situation within the Western Massachusetts area in the US, face-to-face meetings and planning and implementation of the projects ensued with the numerous community partners that are located all around the Pioneer Valley. The partners that resided in other parts of the US, communicated using new media technologies as well as face-to-face communication as needed. The communication was largely limited to in person or phone and there was minimal use of social media sites or email for communication other than when absolutely necessary. Also, I reside in Western Massachusetts, USA so it made for much easier coordination and flexibility of scheduling from my part that is spread out over a much longer period of time. The limited use of technology to build the communication between community partners made the OPPs in the US process much more centered around people. However, the sheer number of people involved in building the US part of the participatory network was much fewer, hence each of the US community members assumed a much bigger role within multi-institutions. In the Bangladeshi context there were many community partners, hence dividing the action research among many more human actors.

Allies on the ground

To reflect on the initial connective processes, after the first round of introductory talks with different environmental community organizations and individuals in Bangladesh, the US and beyond, I hit a block. Very few people were willing to go forward with the actual planning and implementation of the project due to the scope of it and also got discouraged by my insistence on combining academia, non-profit and youth. The people who backed out made it clear that in the context of Bangladesh it would be very difficult for me to find a higher education institution (private or public) that would be interested in an applied and community engaged approach to knowledge formation, where they would partner up with local youth and other community organizations in any meaningful way. Most people suggested to me that I would have better luck finding interested organizations and institutions if I hosted a traditional conference, where I invited researchers and experts to come in and present their work, much like the standard top-down format of such gatherings that had no real participatory components. This advice was consistent with the shape that higher education had taken in Bangladesh and also US, hence, while it was disappointing to come across such road blocks, it did not deter me from my path to making progress.

While I was initially disappointed by their actions, I politely re-stated my idea of pursuing an engaged, deliberative format, one where the youth could be part of the process of developing solutions in both US and Bangladesh. I also emphasized the importance of different industries and institutions collaborating in this process, and how doing so may bring about a shift in the future directions of these institutions. However, because it was a community-engaged project, I did not ignore the advice I was receiving, in order to honor the process of participatory engagement of all actors/actants and instead, I took a different approach. I spoke with youth environmental community organizations alongside the academic institutions, to get advice on the kinds of grassroots environmental projects they have been involved in so far and what their experiences have been of working with local academic institutions. I wanted to verify the information and the feedback I received from the leaders in the youth community organizations, which was not any different. The same story of non-cooperation was repeated by each of them from four different youth organizations and one of the leaders said,

> While I really believe in your idea and we have been organizationally doing youth engaged environmental work ourselves, I really think you are wasting your time by pursuing universities. Why don't you just pursue this project outside of university affiliations, I don't understand why it is so important to have universities involved. You will be able to rent a commercial venue and do projects with trained civil society workers who work on the ground, instead of wasting your time on the academics who don't do a thing. The academics don't even have any relationships with their students to boast of, every student is a number or statistic to them.
>
> (Personal communication, December 21, 2013)

This quote encompasses so many of the themes that are key to this process. There was no surprise that the youth leader, based on experience felt that involving academic institutions is quite futile in the process due to their institutional disinterest in applied learning. However, the more alarming part for me was that this young man did not see the value of academia in being able to address social challenges and instead viewed academics and academic institutions as hindrances to social progress. While I am quoting only one of the many youth in the community, this perspective of academia and its divorced relationship from social realities was a popular discourse amongst all the youth that I interacted with through my research. I had to be patient through such encounters and really try to explain my perspective to them about how the model of academia did not have to be like this and instead can take a participatory shape, despite the way in which it has been running for the past two decades. Also, I really broke down my theoretical goals to them about the importance of *conscientização* and spoke in detail about the idea of academic–community partnerships as being joint vehicles for providing the youth with the opportunity and space to really critically and consciously build a new narrative.

Therefore at the nascent stage of my project, in September 2013, when I was laying the groundwork from the US via emails, phone calls and skype, I was unable to find strategic, community and/or logistical partners to actually take this project off the ground (such as providing BGreen with funding, venue, food, volunteers, administrative support, etc), all important details that are required for the project to be a success in Bangladesh. I was aware that if I was not able to acquire stable actors/actants to build this PAR project, this participatory network was going to remain a dream. However, as one of the obligatory points of passage (OPP) for the project, it was important for me to not lose faith and instead be persistent with my efforts, since I really believed in my vision. My faith in the project and the constant continuation of conversations with various people paid off when the first breakthrough happened: I was able to identify the official university that would host the action research project.

Through one of my personal contacts in the US at University of Massachusettts Amherst, I was fortunate to have connections with the Center for Sustainable Development (CSD), the sustainability research wing of University of Liberal Arts Bangladesh, which is an up and coming private university in Dhaka, Bangladesh. The goal of this university, as per their branding is "Active Learning", which played a big role in the way in which our association worked out over time in developing this project. This project started in my mind as an instinctive desire to combine academia with praxis and CSD was in agreement with such an approach. The center houses various academics and practitioners who all work in different subfields of education, environment and sustainability from a natural science as well as social science perspective. CSD was unique, since they were interested in supporting this project further due to the PAR aspect of it that broke away from the traditional conference format and included the key actants of education and environment as a central focus. They were interested in my idea of engaging the youth directly to brainstorm and solution build for the environmental challenges that the community is encountering. While this was a pleasant surprise for me, I knew that my affiliation with a US university definitely helped my case, as it gave me a social advantage, since foreign educated scholars are held in high regard, as collaborations with northern peoples/institutions is a desirable move for Bangladeshi private universities. The fact that BGreen created a transnational participatory network between two universities, UMASS Amherst and ULAB, was an attractive prospect for the Bangladeshi institution.

The Director of the Center at that time, a Spanish woman working in Bangladesh, and the Assistant Director, a French-Canadian woman working in Bangladesh, embraced the project wholeheartedly as they were waiting for a proposal of this kind to come up from their colleagues or Bangladeshi community without much success. Both expressed to me in our phone meetings and email exchanges that they were searching for a project like this, but were unsure of how to launch it in the Bangladeshi context. This is because such an active community-engaged university partnership project that focuses on citizen science is difficult to carry out and get approved bureaucratically in the university system in Bangladesh.

Historically there has been minimal support for events and strategic collaboration like these in Bangladeshi formal higher educational settings, since these projects fall under the larger theme of community engaged, youth-focused activism.

Therefore, for my project to take off, I needed innovative thinkers in academic institutions in Bangladesh alongside my growing community affiliations in Western Massachusetts who would be open to a new process of knowledge production. The two leading women in CSD gave me complete freedom to design BGreen without any interference from their end. CSD at ULAB provided me with the venue for two out of the three events and provided me with other logistical aspects such as providing me with staff, food and printing vendors for the event. As this project was based on my dissertation research, they gave me complete freedom to adapt it and choose the content in any way that the core youth partners and I wanted, as long as it was aligned with the goals of their center. CSD's goal was to "be a research center motivated by social responsibilities, moral concerns, socio-environmental challenges to provide present and future generations with relevant knowledge and expertise for a better citizenship both in Bangladesh and the global world" (http://www.ulab.edu.bd/csd/center-for-sustainable-development/).

Furthermore, their aim is to:

> Promote knowledge creation, build a model of knowledge empowerment, promote practices – and be a pioneer by implementing a green university, develop global partnerships and be recognized as a knowledge platform in Bangladesh and in South Asia.
>
> (http://www.ulab.edu.bd/csd/center-for-sustainable-development)

BGreen's goals coincided with all of the different aspects of CSD's mission, which made it a natural fit for them to host this project. They were especially interested in backing this project because the larger university, ULAB, had just announced their "Greening the University Initiative" and hosting a program like BGreen with innovative content added something substantive to their strategic plan. They welcomed the idea of partnering with the project, as the two women I was corresponding with saw it as a good branding opportunity for their center and the larger university, since doing something new, innovative and affiliated with a researcher from a foreign institution would provide them with cultural, political and economic capital.

As mentioned earlier, foreign academics in ULAB backed the project with most conviction. It was not a coincidence, since the foreign nationals were more used to the vision of developing an action research model based on community–university platform since it is more prevalent in the northern, especially Canadian context (Castleden, Morgan & Lamb, 2012). While the north/west is far from being a utopia for community–university partnerships, there is somewhat of an encouraging trend in some niche North American contexts in such affiliations that engage the non-academic communities in its design, process and implementation rather than solely relying on the dictates of "experts", an example being the World Wide Views Project (http://www.wwviews.org).

The response to my requests of collaboration were varied and sometimes completely opposite to the positive, welcoming approach of CSD, especially from resident Bangladeshis who lived and worked in Bangladesh for a variety of reasons. One of the main reasons was the unfamiliarity with the concept of PAR and citizen science, the potentials of academic–community partnerships and youth engagement, etc. Previous youth engagement programs hosted by other Bangladeshi youth groups within the country did not gain any support from the local universities, due to the lack of their academic connection/roots, which BGreen clearly had established. Current universities in Bangladesh did not want to engage themselves in any activity of political/social nature or scope, as in their prerogative, it fell into a non-academic, activist category. Therefore, the academic–community partnership that eventually was sparked, formed and sustained through BGreen was solidified as a result of finding an official academic host in Bangladesh.

This was in direct contradiction to all the other youth engaged civil society projects that were run by prominent youth environmental groups in Bangladesh which were viewed as mere activist projects, that had no academic connections, keeping the binary between academia and community organization intact. Two such prominent environmental groups in Bangladesh became our eventual partners who worked with youth engagement and environmental social change, but without any academic roots or university affiliations. Partnerships between youth groups/ organizations and universities are mostly non-existent in the Bangladeshi context. On the other hand, while educational institutions and community organizations in the US worked together more commonly in the US, the issue was with building sustained networks of academic–community engagements, rather than building superficial, unidirectional relationships with community organizations. In the case of BGreen in the US, we were able to build sustained partnerships with US local organizations like Arise for Social Justice, Amherst Media and Water Defense.

So BGreen's initiation and development was an interesting and unique one in the context of both nations due to the way in which diverse industries like academia, civil society organizations and global youth were brought together to work collaboratively to form a larger network of actors. Developing an official academic partnership was truly key to the project, since, as I was a doctoral researcher at that time, the project is an applied *and* academic one and the goal was to connect academic audiences with activists and practitioners on ground.

The second global strategic partner for BGreen was Journeys for Climate Justice (JCJ), a registered non-profit and environmental community organization based in Australia. I was connected to them via the Director of CSD, since this Australian

NGO had ongoing environmental projects in Bangladesh in the last few years and CSD had direct experience working with a few of JCJ's activists who had done different community engaged environmental projects in Bangladesh. To provide some background on the organization, JCJ is a small Australian non-profit based in Melbourne that is tackling climate change issues in the Asia Pacific region in partnership with other active organizations and/or individuals who are committed to "deliver groundbreaking environmental projects that promote sustainable lifestyles and strive for climate justice" (www.journeysforclimatejustice.org.au). Their vision is to address the "inequitable impacts of climate change, which fall on communities that have contributed the least to the problem and have the least resources to cope with them" (http://www.journeysforclimatejustice.org.au).

Organizationally, they stood out to me due to their unswerving commitment to under-represented communities in the Asia Pacific in the context of climate change and environmental tragedies. Their team was attracted to my project, due to my interest in serving the community and also because they were interested in partnering up with project leaders like me, who are interested in building long-term connections with Bangladesh and US in the environmental context. JCJ usually has representative members dispersed in various parts of the Asia Pacific engaged in different environmental projects that specifically "raise awareness of climate change issues and promote measures to mitigate emissions, empower and support vulnerable communities to adapt to the impacts of climate change, raise funds by providing meaningful alternatives to carbon offsets" (http://www.journeysforclimatejustice.org.au).

The relationship that was created between JCJ and BGreen was one that was based on trust and made possible by social media and emails, an aspect of community network building that was crucial to the success of this global undertaking. The scope of such an undertaking relied upon relational connections between human and technological actors/actants in this process to steadily build a trans-national participatory network. Because they were located outside of both the US and Bangladesh and my idea was stemming from the United States, there was a great deal of long-distance communication between us to justify the reason why I decided to focus on youth communities in Bangladesh and the US. After detailed exchanges about my goals and motives, they were completely on board with partnering up with this project.

There were definite overlaps in our larger version, which is what pushed the process forward and also the organization had also done previous climate-change related youth action, education and engagement work in Bangladesh. One of the main ideological similarities between the organization and myself, which helped in sealing the deal in getting their support to make BGreen possible, was the fact that there were fundamental similarities between our visions of social change. We both believed in the bottom-up, youth-led and participatory approach to development and social change in the context of environment. I was bringing the academic–community engagement angle to their transnational social justice angle, which interested them. In one of our early email exchanges, JCJ's co-director reflected back on a parallel environmental project in Sri-Lanka, which is led by a Sri-Lankan native. He said in an email,

> The organizer in Sri-Lanka has been very keen for youth to work initially from their own resources and their various projects, including a recent permaculture one, has been an amazing success, all of which JCJ has supported in some capacity or the other.
>
> (Personal communication, November 15, 2013)

He was providing me with an example of a success story and was hoping that BGreen's approach towards building an academic-activist platform would be a success in Bangladesh also.

The third international community organizational connection was an academic research network and organization called Consortium for Science and Policy Outcomes (CSPO), which is a research wing of the Arizona State University based in Washington, DC. According to their website, CSPO is "an intellectual network aimed at enhancing the contribution of science and technology to society's pursuit of equality, justice, freedom, and overall quality of life" (http://cspo.org). CSPO's DC office works to connect academic knowledge with decision makers, in order to bring to the forefront "complexity of science, technology and society by *communicating* knowledge and methods, *educating* students and decision makers, *forming* strategic partnerships, *participating* in science policy initiatives, and *building* a community of intellectuals and practitioners" (http://cspo.org).

CSPO has pioneered in utilizing a deliberation model to engage with citizen science in their work that is attributed to the Danish Board of Technology, which is a part of a global network of partners including public councils, think tanks, parliamentary technology assessment institutions, non-governmental civil society organizations and universities globally that are committed to bringing citizen science into the forefront as an important tool for discussion, participation, knowledge sharing and social change. The deliberative process has been used extensively by CSPO for a variety of different projects that required citizen participation in scientific processes and I wanted to design an extensive deliberative session for the youth on a pertinent environmental and educational topic for them.

This was a dream collaboration for me, since this US based organization itself provided a unique model for the current Bangladeshi private higher-educational system which is devoid of research centers such as CSPO, a research and policy oriented project of Arizona State University. I wanted BGreen to not only be an independent project, but through my action research I wanted to bring academic–

community success stories such as CSPO's to the Bangladeshi youth and build transnational scholarship, research and social change opportunities to overcome divides between nations and communities. The model of academic engaged social change that is created and used by CSPO in their deliberations work would be one way in which global youth could adapt to change their own educational systems from inside out. I wanted to introduce CSPO's deliberative model of citizen engagement to the youth in Bangladesh, to see and understand its reception and applicability in the Bangladeshi context. The initial connection was built a few years prior to the actual BGreen event, when I was introduced to the network of people who were working hard to bring deliberations to the US, through getting connected to the World Wide Views Deliberations project which was to be held in Boston, MA in collaboration with some faculty and student partners in University of Massachusetts, Amherst. A year after the event, I sent out a general email to the still active list-serve, asking if there was any interest in participating in any way in my youth action research that was happening in Dhaka, Bangladesh.

It turned out that the Associate Director of CSPO had been interested in conducting a youth engagement citizen science study in Bangladesh for some time now. My offer was convenient for him, since I had a concrete plan and had made inroads into the world of education and sustainability in both the US and Bangladesh from an academic and community engaged perspective, both of which he was interested in. His aspirations of doing citizen science driven, youth engaged work was an amazing coincidence and he had not gone forward in the past because, being an American unfamiliar with Bangladeshi culture, he did not know how to get past the gate-keeping barriers of a new place. Since I had already formed an institutional affiliation with a private university in Bangladesh, CSPO felt more encouraged by this association and they wanted to go forward with a youth-focused deliberative exercise in urban Bangladesh on a topic that we agreed on.

The next two partners of BGreen were two youth led, organized environmental groups called Bangladesh Youth Environmental Initiative (BYEI) and Bangladesh Youth Movement for Climate (BYMC), both based in Bangladesh. I had contacted both groups through mutual connections earlier in the year to develop an understanding of environmental themed youth organizations in Bangladesh and the kind of work they are engaged in on the ground, especially in the urban scene. Both organizations were pioneered by two young men who were university students with an interest in environmental social change and sustained activism in Bangladesh. This passion led to the founding of their respective environmental youth organizations to inspire and organize youth in Bangladesh for community participation and action. To provide some details on BYEI, its main goals as an organization is to equip the next generation of Bangladeshis with leadership skills, knowledge and ideas to address the environmental challenges and build sustainable futures. BYMC, on the other hand, is a youth group that is geared towards using the youth of Bangladesh to bring about lasting changes in the civil society discourse around climate change, sustainability and development. Their website narrates that BYMC was initiated to mobilize the Bangladeshi youth and build national youth alliances to take actions on climate change.

Hence from the perspective of youth driven activism, both BYEI and BYMC had similar goals to one another and also to BGreen. However, from an academic vantage point both the projects were different from my vision, because they were interested in the activism aspect of youth engagement only, while through my youth engaged participatory action angle, I was interested in bringing about a larger multi-industry shift—one where I combine academia with activism, redefining the way in which youth are involved in community–university partnerships. There was a direct focus of BGreen to use the youth's ideas to help impact the way in which knowledge is produced in academic institutions and how it is applied to the local community by involving them in integral ways in the process (Flanagan & Christens, 2011; Giroux, 2014).

Both the organizations' expertise was in working with the youth of Bangladesh and despite all the big organization connections/partnerships that BGreen had made already, it was essential that I partnered up with both of these prominent youth organizations in Bangladesh, because they specialize in directly mobilizing the youth in the country to engage in environmental movements. Their expertise in working closely with urban youth groups in Bangladesh would be key for the kind of workshops and activities that I had envisioned to do with the youth in the BGreen participatory action research project. Both the founders of BYEI and BYMC were supportive and reliable, by promising me support from their organizations, based on the collaborative goals of the project. Closer to the event, four out of the eight main co-organizers of the event were BYEI staff all of whom helped me tirelessly to make this event/project possible and the two of the remaining four were BYMC staff. These co-organizers were the human backbone behind making the movement happen and each of the organization's staff contributed to different pieces of making different aspects of the action research projects a success.

The next organizational partner was the Edward Kennedy Center (EMK) in Dhaka, Bangladesh which is a public service center that was created in 2012 through a partnership between the Liberation War Museum in Bangladesh and the American Center of U.S. Embassy Dhaka, which is a platform committed to open dialogue, informed action, individual and artistic expression, and personal and professional development. EMK Center provided BGreen with another transnational, global opportunity by opening their state-of-the-art venue to conduct action research in Dhaka. Procuring sponsorship from EMK Center in Dhaka, Bangladesh is looked at in a very positive light in Bangladesh as well as in the United States, since this implies that BGreen gets indirect support from American Embassy in Bangladesh, which funds the center and is very powerful in Bangladesh as well as in the US. For complex cultural reasons, whenever the US Embassy or affiliated projects like the EMK project back new community projects, it helps with the popularity of a new venture. In the case of the US partners, it provided them with familiarity and legitimacy in a very unstable and unreliable political climate, as they could identify with an international venue like that and allowed them with a degree of confidence about the safety of the youth participants.

Later, I will discuss the way in which the actor networks that were built through collaborating with EMK really paid off for sustaining the transnational participatory network of BGreen, helping to build a modified black box. After providing the highlights of the core organizational partners of BGreen, I will talk about the way in which all of the human actors affiliated with these institutions worked together to contribute to the large scale success of The BGreen Project that provided a promise to the development of a new form of politicized, environmental youth academic-activism in Bangladesh.

The next US-based partner was Amherst Media, which is a public access media house based in Amherst, MA. Over the years as a longtime resident of Western Massachusetts, I have always participated in community media events of Amherst Media. Amherst Media's website states that it is "a dynamic, community driven, non-profit, public access information, communication & technology center", one that is committed to merging local public access television with global and local initiatives. The organization has been a steady partner of BGreen by producing the media action research projects such as the BGreen Media Literacy Project, which is a youth focused, academic–community engaged multi-format television show that brings together academics and activists from around the world in showcasing their action projects on the ground that are geared towards social justice, community participatory mobilizing and sustained social change. Apart from the television show being screened regularly in the local television channels in Western Massachusetts, it is streamed globally through the Amherst Media website as well as transnational social media networks such as Facebook with an audience in the US, Bangladesh and many other countries. Amherst Media has collaborated with BGreen in many different formats of media action research projects with youth from many different communities, institutions and social change forums.

The second to last major US based community partner of BGreen is Arise for Social Justice, which is a member-led community non-profit based in Western Massachusetts focusing on "defending and advancing the rights of poor people and . . . having worked on issues such as housing, homelessness, criminal justice, environmental justice, and public health." (https://www.arisespringfield.org/, 2018). The organization was founded 30 years ago by women on welfare. Arise has partnered up with BGreen in multiple community engaged action research projects focusing on local environmental social sustainability and youth engaged environmental justice.

The last major community partner of BGreen based out of the US is Water Defense, a non-profit organization dedicated to "use technology and public engagement to keep [our] waterways and drinking water sources free from contamination and industrial degradation." There has been ongoing action research and community engagement partnerships with Water Defense in projects that connect Bangladeshi communities with the collaborative expertise of BGreen and Water Defense on a variety of water related environmental issues. BGreen has conducted some of its most ambitious community engaged work in collaboration with Water Defense in highly guarded natural habitats in Bangladesh, like the Sundarbans, which is the largest mangrove forest in the world.

Towards an architecture of unity

In their lifetimes, most youth in both US and Bangladesh only knew one approach to education, which followed a socially disengaged trajectory. They had trouble envisioning a different reality without some guidance, where social projects and community engaged work could be combined with the insular model of education that is being practiced in most global private academic institutions today. Expressing these similar ideas, one youth partner said:

> I am not sure entirely what we will do in the workshops, will it be like a classroom, the same way they (teachers and professors) teach us about their areas of research? I am confused because, in a lot of the workshops that I participate in outside of my university work, they are led exclusively by NGO workers and teachers/professors are usually not even involved in any of the process. Usually my university and all the other ones I know treat work like this as frivolous and then emphasis is placed on really learning from books.
>
> (Personal communication, December 19, 2013)

Hence, without even realizing, the youth themselves were becoming victims of a larger structure, one that was designed to isolate the two, perpetuating their state of being in magical and naïve consciousness. Hence, their inability to visualize a different reality and how they could engage in bringing that reality forth, was contributing to the maintenance of a false sense of functionalism in political economic structures that reinforce the ideas and maintenance of epistemic communities within and between institutions. The structural systems that they were born into were limiting their vision on how it could perhaps be possible to construct a different educational system that was focused on critical knowledge building based on grounded, contextual realities that are inclusive of a diversity of approaches, an alternative that was desired through the building of the BGreen participatory network.

Hence, the mandatory stakeholder meetings that were the backbone of BGreen as a PAR-ANT project were a transformative space for the youth, since the interactions and conversations in these spaces really acted as a space for the youth partners to have a changed state of mind about their role in gaining critical and political consciousness that can address structural limitations. BGreen as a transnational participatory network was able to craft an international team that was comprised of university academics, NGO workers and student activists, all with a common goal of designing the contents of a unique action research platform, which brought people from different global institutions together. These actors were separated by unwieldy, outdated political economic structures that needed redefining to make the most out of the structural strengths of the institutions that they were affiliated with.

The voices of all the actors were key in figuring out the content, since their feedback and ideas were critical to making a shared process work for a larger community. As a result, the participatory network that formed, was constructed and reconstructed with sometimes complementary and conflicting ideas, all of which the multi-actors/actants negotiated and reached a consensus with my guidance as the initial OPP. As it will be narrated over the course of the other chapters, the number of OPPs for the project increased due to the multi-directional growth and increased complexity of the BGreen network, which was consistent with a weak version of ANT. This points to the presence of (and the importance of having) multiple OPPs to add to the strength of diversity in the network-building process, but also recognizing the power of OPPs to shape the flow, direction and the ultimate survival of a network. The process of enrolling these actors to build the inclusive architecture of the academic–community partnerships, became stronger and more complex as we went through the different stages of the translation process to gain stability.

Alongside the conversations and meetings between community partners that aided in the process of developing the agreed content of all the action research processes, the content was also determined by reading relevant research on the current urban environmental hot topics in both the US and Bangladeshi communities that BGreen was serving at any point in time. The content selection and finalization was also a hard process, since we had to match our interests and needs with able workshop leaders, so that the youth had the best workshop leaders to guide them in this participatory process in any of the topics selected in any given point. One of the ongoing challenges of working with youth groups in both the US and Bangladesh seeking change and educational reform is the fact that many a times they were unclear on what the change could/would look like. One of the key youth actors in BGreen who mainly handles all the promotional print designs for BGreen in Bangladesh had expressed on more than one occasion:

I believe in this vision, but I am afraid that all of our efforts will be squashed by some political party on the day of or worse still the university that is hosting is will back out on the day of the event and prioritize some other useless conference, which brings in speakers to help them build their image.

(Personal communication, December 14, 2013)

This comment really emphasized the daily insecurities of the youth of Bangladesh and what they have constructed as being a normal part of their existence in relation to their educational and political futures. Far from having any faith in these institutions, which really should be one of the few safe spaces for the youth to grapple with important issues that are key to their educational and personal futures that focus on critical development along with career development. Giroux reflects on precisely this challenge that educational institutions in the US are faced with in neoliberal times which is bringing about tremendous shifts in their missions. He says,

Universities are some of the few places left where a struggle for the commons, for public life, if not democracy itself, can be made visible through the medium of collective voices and social movements energized by the need for a politics and way of life counter to authoritarian capitalism.

(Giroux, 2013)

Consistent with this perspective, the context of Bangladesh and the US in this north–south alliance-building, politics, corruption and neoliberalism form a dangerous mix, which results in the youth's mistrust of the educational system and what it can really offer them. This dangerous mix has been given slightly different twists in the two geopolitical locations. In the minds of Bangladeshi youth, there were two forms of higher education in Bangladesh, the public system with its bureaucratic, session-jammed, corrupt, politically motivated form of education that is run by the whims of national political groups or the private education system that focused on a depoliticized, socially disengaged and mercenary approach that was run without any socially relevant agenda. The youth in the US seem to share the second vision of their Bangladeshi counterparts of being jaded about the overwhelming neoliberal agenda of privatized education in the US and often seem to be at a loss of finding a strong enough counter model of community engaged education. Kabir (2012) echoes both the nations' youth's concerns that the process of vocationalising in higher education in both Bangladesh (and the US), one that is narrowly constructed towards merely getting a "good" job is unlikely to develop democratic, critically engaged societies. He says, "a democratic society requires true and critical knowledge for its social institutions to flourish" (Kabir, 2012, p. 16). He echoes the same concerns as Giroux and writes that the present generation is growing up without knowing national and international politics, history and their development and the important lessons that such an exposure provides for the future of any civilization (Kabir, 2012; Giroux, 2005).

For this reason, the disillusioned youth were taking their desires for social change outside of academia itself, organizing independently for issues they cared about, without the support of any institutions, academic or non-academic. The youth community partners in the US had a relatively easier task with mobility and safety due to the basic human safety that is provided in the context of the US. Hence, there was a lot more independent work that has been and can be carried out by BGreen US youth partners due to the basic safety and protection available in the US for the youth, a luxury that is not present in any form for the average Bangladeshi youth. Also, there has been ongoing partnerships through BGreen between US youth partners and Bangladeshi youth partners in joining forces on collaborative PAR work such as content creation website, brochures, writing journalistic articles, blog writing, video production, exchange community engagement work, to name some of the ongoing successful collaborations. Gaining strength to build a solid participatory action network often resulted in the formation of sustainable projects, ones that took its own shape and path with the spontaneous addition of transnational actors and actants.

Network stability is an important part of the ANT process, which ultimately results over time in taking the shape of a black box, which is the point in the network when it gains stability, when using the strong version of ANT. In most cases, the disillusionment of the students/youth about their education and not really making the connection between their academic knowledge and its applicability in performing long-term social change is a major hindrance to the process. Hence supportive environments like these bring out the potentials of the youth that are latent and suppressed by the system and provide a space for new subjectivities and innovative approaches to develop new participatory networks such as BGreen that address the key concerns of this PAR-ANT project.

This emphasis of ANT on the constructivist approach, one that consciously was created to steer away from essentialist, fixed explanations of systems is important to understand the flow and development of the BGreen experience, which was rapidly adding complexity to its growing participatory actor network. The fluidity of this networked process brings forth the need to be open to change and reconstitution within a process that is not fixed, static or bound, instead it is one that flows through complex political, technological, cultural, economic, social, religious spaces to carve a unique, un-fixed, unpredictable network. Through such participatory networked processes, the goal remains to combine critical PAR framework with a weak version of ANT, where a potentially well-designed participatory network is explored in all its complexity and not simply reduced to "an actor alone nor to a network . . . . An actor-network is simultaneously an actor whose activity is networking heterogeneous elements and a network that is able to redefine and transform what it is made of" (Callon, 1987, p. 93).

Hence, through this unorthodox route of participatory network building, BGreen stands to create a radical shift in the way in which higher education operates in the US and Bangladesh and how these institutions can be used to aid in the process of shifting youth consciousness about their lived, social realities. The process of translation in ANT was key to the collaborative approach. The process was new for everyone involved: it was the merging of many different individuals, organizations and industries, however, despite some occasional disagreements over the way in which some aspect of the process would run, it was a process of self-discovery, one which was based on moving the attention away from "deterministic models that trace organizational phenomena back to powerful individuals, social structures, hegemonic discourses or technological effects. Rather, ANT prefers to seek out complex patterns of causality rooted in connections between actors" (Whittle & Spicer, 2008, p. 47).

The complex convergence of actors, human and non-human organizational, political, technological, and ideological, was key to the shaping and reshaping of the theoretical vision of BGreen that I had before starting the process. The amalgamation of the complexity of all the actors/actants in building this transnational participatory network is an important one. The translation process, was long and cumbersome and really brought forth some challenging issues that had to be solved collaboratively and with the counsel of a large group of people, where the "processes of translation and purification constantly remake the entire actor-network" (Castree & Macmillan, 2013, p. 216). The process of translation of each network is unique, where some actors/actants rise to the top as having the most salient contributions to keeping the participatory network flowing. Within the discussion of this chapter alone, it is important to note that the non-human actors/actants of technology and political instability, really were key to the development of this actor network, since all the human actors who were the core community partners, really adapted and changed their approaches to communication and organizing due to it.

Bibliography

Alam, M., Haque, M. S. & Siddique, S. F. (2007). *Private higher education in Bangladesh*. N. V. Varghese (ed.). Bangladesh: International Institute for Educational Planning.

Arnaboldi, M. & Spiller, N. (2011). Actor-network theory and stakeholder collaboration: The case of Cultural Districts. *Tourism Management*, *32*(3): 641–654.

Battistoni, R. M., Longo, N. V. & Jayanandhan, S. R. (2009). Acting locally in a flat world: Global citizenship and the democratic practice of service-learning. *Journal of Higher Education Outreach and Engagement*, *13*(2): 89–108.

Brown, M. B. (1995). *Africa's choices: after thirty years of the World Bank*. London: Penguin Books Ltd.

Callon, M. (1987). Society in the making: The study of technology as a tool for sociological analysis. In W. E. Bijker, T. P. Hughes and T. Pinch (eds) *The social construction of technological systems: New directions in the sociology and history of technology*, pp. 83–103. Cambridge, MA: MIT Press.

Cammarota, J. & Fine, M. (2008). *Revolutionizing education: Youth participatory action research in motion*. New York: Routledge.

Carlisle, S. & Cropper, S. (2009). Investing in lay researchers for community-based health action research: Implications for research, policy and practice. *Critical Public Health*, *19*(1): 59–70.

Castleden, H., Morgan, S. S. & Lamb, C. (2012). "I spent the first year drinking tea": Exploring Canadian university researchers' perspectives on community-based participatory research involving Indigenous peoples". *The Canadian Geographer*, *56*(2): 160–179.

Castree, N. & Macmillan, T. (2001). Dissolving dualisms: actor-networks and the reimagination of nature. In N. Castree & B. Braun (eds), *Social nature: Theory, practice, and politics*, pp. 208–224. Malden, MA: Blackwell Publishers.

Etmanski, C. & Pant, M. (2007). Teaching participatory research through reflexivity and relationship reflections on an international collaborative curriculum project between the Society for Participatory Research in Asia (PRIA) and the University of Victoria (UVic). *Action Research*, *5*(3): 275–292.

Flanagan, C. A. & Christens, B. D. (2011). Youth civic development: Historical context and emerging issues. *New Directions for Child and Adolescent Development*, *2011*(134): 1–9.

Giroux, H. A. (2005). The terror of neoliberalism: Rethinking the significance of cultural politics. *College Literature, 32*(1): 1–19.

Giroux, H. A. (2013). *Youth in revolt: Reclaiming a democratic future*. Boulder, CO: Paradigm.

Kabir, A. H. (2010). Neoliberal policy in the higher education sector in Bangladesh: Autonomy of public universities and the role of the state. *Policy Futures in Education*, *8*(6): 619–631.

Kabir, A. H. (2012). Neoliberal hegemony and the ideological transformation of higher education in Bangladesh. *Critical Literacy: Theories and Practices*, *6*(2): 2–15.

Karim, L. (2008). Demystifying micro-credit the Grameen Bank, NGOs, and neoliberalism in Bangladesh. *Cultural Dynamics*, *20*(1): 5–29.

Khaleduzzaman, M. (2014). Students unrest in higher education level in Bangladesh a study on Dhaka and Rajshahi University. *IOSR Journal of Research & Method in Education*, *4*(2): 6–16.

Lewis, D. (2004). On the difficulty of studying 'civil society': Reflections on NGOs, state and democracy in Bangladesh. *Contributions to Indian Sociology*, *38*(3): 299–322.

Muhammad, A. (2003). Bangladesh's Integration into Global Capitalist System: Policy Direction and the Role of Global Institutions. In M. Rahman (ed.) *Globalisation, environmental crisis and social change in Bangladesh*. Dhaka: University Press, pp. 113–126.

Nath, S. R. (2006). Youths' access to mass media in Bangladesh. *Adolescents and youths in Bangladesh: some selected issues*, Research monograph series no. 31. Dhaka: Research and Evaluation Division, BRAC. pp. 147–162.

Nordtveit, B. H. (2009). *Constructing development: Civil society and literacy in a time of globalization*. Berlin: Springer Science & Business Media.

Trickett, E. J. & Espino, S. L. R. (2004). Collaboration and social inquiry: Multiple meanings of a construct and its role in creating useful and valid knowledge. *American Journal of Community Psychology*, *34*(1–2): 1–69.

Whittle, A. & Spicer, A. (2008). Is actor network theory critique? *Organization studies*, *29*(4), 611–629.

Zohir, S. (2004). NGO sector in Bangladesh: An overview. *Economic and Political Weekly*, 39(36): 4–10.

http://www.journeysforclimatejustice.org.au
http://cspo.org

5 Multi-media amplification of the BGreen Project

While the previous chapter explores the networks and connections made with the human and organizational actors/actants on the ground, this chapter narrates and analyzes the multi-media networks (new media, television, radio and print) that were built while developing the participatory action research project in the US and Bangladesh. I provide a glimpse into the actors/actants involved in the process of developing these varied media networks and the extent to which these multi-media networks helped in amplifying the goals of such an academic–community engaged environmental mission such as BGreen. The chapter is broken down into Parts 1 and 2 to provide a full spectrum of what kind of media collaborations are possible in the US and Bangladesh to develop an emergent participatory network like BGreen.

I narrate the historical background of Bangladesh, which sheds light into why the media network-building in Bangladesh was so starkly different from the US media collaborations for BGreen. This analysis is consistent with the "weak" ANT approach of this project that interrogates the connection between historical power, institutions and networked processes. The analysis also targets the unique media needs of transnational projects like these that need to flourish in order to bring about network stability. Ultimately, the question that is posed is what stream of multi-media goes the farthest and deepest to sustain movements such as BGreen that are non-commercial and constantly evolving, and why perhaps some media streams may be better than others to contribute significantly to the development of such a participatory network.

In Part 1, I provide a brief overview of the development of popular media (radio, television, print and online portals) in Bangladesh, which brings forth the way in which environmental journalistic coverage functions within the different media industries in Bangladesh, which BGreen largely benefitted from. The role of youth in Bangladeshi journalism is also central to this analysis, since youth aged between 17–25 make up most of the journalists and/or reporters (any format) in urban Bangladesh, which was a key reason for BGreen's media success in Bangladesh on a very large scale. The lack of involvement of youth in mainstream US multi-media production was the set-back faced in the US for BGreen. BGreen was instead seen to thrive in non-commercial, public access media houses in the US that had significant youth involvement.

In Part 2, the new media networks (social media, website, blogs, etc.) of BGreen are investigated and analyzed which were very significant actants in the amplification and sustenance of BGreen's participatory network stability. The nature of the media exposure (mainstream and alternative) and amplification for a non-commercial academic–community engaged project like BGreen is important to explore and provides insights into how commercially driven enterprises, such as the different media industries in Bangladesh, hold the power to significantly contribute to the organizing efforts of less-institutionally powerful groups, such as youth, civil society and community organizations. The role of youth in bringing fresh multi-media perspectives to a global audience is highlighted, which has the potential to contribute to the formation of new discourses on engaged academia to bring about environmental social justice.

Multi-media support in Bangladesh and the US

The process of translation in ANT again played a key role in really sorting out the way in which these media networks were built and how the actors/actants were involved in the four-step process to support the growth, flow and complexity of the emerging transnational participatory network. I conduct a review and analysis of select print, television and radio features of BGreen that were created by the media to build the "brand" in the eyes of Bangladeshi and US media consumers and as a result I bring forth the media discourses around an initiative like this, informed by the youth journalists/reporters that covered the event. Also, I conduct a review and analysis of the public access media support that BGreen has received to tap into a very different crowd in the US as a complement to the very widespread coverage of the participatory network by all kinds of national multi-media in Bangladesh. By supporting projects like BGreen, transnational media organizations are actively supporting and contributing to the emergence of Freire's *conscientização* and providing support for networked social change.

Part 1: Brief overview of environmental journalism and reportage practices in Bangladesh

As touched upon earlier, media journalism and reportage, like higher educational institutions, have held a significant and complex place in the history of Bangladesh from colonial times (Das, 2012). Most of the media outlets (print, television, radio or online portals) were privatized, with a neoliberal, market driven ideology.

Reflecting on the colonial roots of media and broadcasting in Bangladesh, Rahman (2014) writes that it was first introduced to Africa and India by the colonial powers, primarily "to further their own imperialist interests and policies" as well as "to deliver urgent propaganda" of the British Empire" (p.57). He continues:

> Indeed, the practice of using media for the interest of the ruling party was not intrinsic to postcolonial regimes and their political systems, but was rather an imperial/colonial legacy that the autocratic governments in the newly independent nation-states began to rejuvenate for the same purposes valued by the former colonial ruler originally: to serve the ruling power. Although the colonial state resisted the seductions of the market and extended the use of radio to include educational and community building aims, some postcolonial states could not resist the influence of marketization forces for in the long run.
>
> (p. 57)

Consistent with the way in which educational structures have been redefined through the process of economic liberalization, the media systems in many parts of the world, like postcolonial Africa and Asia, have been replaced by market-led models that determine their content and structure (Rahman, 2014; Alhassan, 2005). There is a general absence of "subaltern counter-publics" (Rahman, 2014) in the broadcast media in Bangladesh (similar to the US) and, influenced by the dominant Indian mainstream, commercialized and privatized media, there is more focus on developing entertainment over socially relevant themes. Grassroots processes are mostly structurally wiped out of the media narrative and exposure (Rahman, 2014). Despite such a reality, the heavy multi-media coverage of BGreen is a curious case to investigate, to see what aspects of Bangladeshi environmental journalism, despite its current market-driven ideology, creates an interest among journalists to feature this academic-activist work.

The enthusiasm with which BGreen was embraced by the media was inconsistent with the general apathy of media outlets towards small, community engaged projects of a non-commercial nature as explained by scholarly research done so far on Bangladeshi media. It is important to reflect on the ways in which power and privilege connect here for me as one of the key OPPs, where my educational, class and social status in the larger context of Bangladesh provided me with access to institutions and individuals who are mostly out of reach for the average Bangladeshi. However, as mentioned earlier, I did not intentionally seek my family's help, even though I would have, if I had not made any progress on my own. The complexity of my class position acts as a reminder about the limitations of a strong version of ANT, which ignores the power dynamics and unevenness within actors/actants.

However, in a weak version of ANT, this limitation is accounted for, where we can acknowledge the ways in which power operates through different actors within it, in this case, by my social privilege. This allows for a more nuanced, accurate understanding of the course, complexity and stability of participatory networks that are shaped and reconstituted quite significantly as a result.

Over the course of my interactions with media house staff in Bangladesh, it became clearer why this project got the attention of the media houses, as discussed in the next sections. Following northern/western tropes in journalism, Bangladeshi journalism has been in one way no exception, since it has always walked the tightrope between "neutral" and "participant" roles (Hanitzsch, 2005). However, quite unique to Bangladesh, newspapers have been consistently connected and politically proactive to any significant social and political movement in Bangladesh, such as the liberation war from the British as well as Pakistanis in 1947 and 1971 along with the more recent overthrowing of military dictatorship in 1990 (Das, 2012). Bangladesh has a long and complicated history of battling political injustice, including violence against the freedom of the press (Ahmed, 2009; Rahman, 2014). In the 44 years of the nation's freedom, the country has spent 15 years under military rule and, although democracy was restored in 1990, the political scene remains volatile and unpredictable (Rahman, 2014).

This same challenge had presented itself to BGreen at the time of planning and implementing the PAR event, which really threatened the process of developing media support as explored in the narration. The way in which journalism and reportage, and specifically print journalism has come to be viewed in Bangladesh is that they usually pursue a more socially engaged role in putting their perspectives forward, even if a corrupt economic system backs them in order to influence their views on an issue (Das, 2012; Elahi, 2013). This phenomenon occurs even within the limited parameters within which such narratives have space to be covered in mainstream media. In his research, Elahi (2013) writes that the links of corruption to journalism and their political leanings sway both ways in Bangladesh. He writes:

> Many Bangladeshi journalists are opportunists who at different times in the country's history collaborated with the dictators for favors. Many of them have supported the military rulers, and helped them justify and continue their rule in order to obtain various benefits from them.
>
> (p. 17)

This is an important point that helps to illuminate the nuances that make-up the journalistic culture in Bangladesh, but it is also important to know the unstable and often dangerous history of journalists that may result in them taking the corrupt, easier path. Many journalists in the past in Bangladesh who have been strongly committed to social change during the politically challenging and transformative points in Bangladeshi history have also been under constant fire from the threatened regimes, which have many times resulted in police/military torture and death (Rahman, 2011, 2014).

Therefore, the exploration of journalistic independence on most issues in Bangladesh comes with a price, quite a steep one, especially if the cause they are endorsing is challenging the economic and political order of the neoliberal times. Further research on journalism and reportage practices in Bangladesh show that television journalism in the country is often under the most surveillance by political parties, to control the discourses that are formed by the journalists (Rahman, 2012), even though newspaper and radio coverage also display these same problems of censorship and safety, even to this day. Some scholars characterize this as being a huge barrier to social progress, since it is in direct conflict with developing conditions for a Habermasian public sphere for social good (Rahman, 2007a; 2012).

Even though social coverage is within the periphery of media realities in Bangladesh today due to meeting neoliberal, profit-seeking goals, environmental journalism has always been able to maintain a specialized and prominent presence in Bangladesh with an advocacy approach (Rahman, 2012; Krøvel et al., 2012; Das, 2012). In order to take an advocacy approach, journalists and reporters also need to be well versed in areas of the environment that they are writing about. The lack of expertise amongst the young journalists often creates intense debates about the validity of this advocacy approach to communicating about the environment and other social issues (Das, 2012; Rahman, 2012). Also, it is interesting to note that environmental social justice is still in the periphery of what is considered to be hot political topics, such as government corruption or religious instability. Even though the environment and education are such important topics in the context of Bangladeshi and US society, it still does not fall within the "dangerous" topics that journalists refrain from engaging with that could threaten their lives.

Hence, the apparently "benign" topic of environment and education (key non-human actants of this participatory network), could have been good selling points for the media houses, since they did not touch upon the overtly sensitive topics that the media houses are afraid of covering. I was asked by the other community organizers to refrain from providing too much detail on the content of the workshops to the journalists/reporters prior to the event, since some of the topics could send off red flags to them and their willingness to feature us. Two of those topics were 1. The connection between the environment and nuclear power plants in Bangladesh; and 2. The environmental impacts of genetically modified food items in Bangladesh. On the other hand, I was asked to emphasize the transnational nature of the project that united two nations' youth on the combined topic of social change. The cautionary approach of Bangladeshi media community partners in engaging with social change via unconventional routes speaks to the unpredictability of political violence around certain national topics, such as the current government's strategic plans on investing in foreign nuclear technology rather than focusing on educational institutions ad programs that lead to capacity building amongst the youth of Bangladesh to learn more about nuclear technology and its usefulness in the Bangladeshi context. On the other hand, even though BGreen received much less media coverage in the US, the actual topics of action research were much less scrutinized in the production and representation process.

Forming multi-media networks: Goals and strategies

Due to this comparatively well-developed journalistic focus of multi-media (print, television, radio and online portals) on the environment in Bangladesh, BGreen received tremendous support from the media industry in Bangladesh, far beyond the support it received in the US. Before I narrate the way in which these multi-media participatory networks were built for BGreen, I had no understanding as an outsider that a youth-engaged, academic–community action project like BGreen would even need to be built. I did not know that a non-commercial project like BGreen would even have the luxury to tap into the media industry in any significant way to add complexity to the goal of building a transnational participatory network for BGreen. In the partner meetings that were conducted on a regular basis to make BGreen a reality, the global youth actors first expressed the need to build these connections and hence proceeded with the process of translating this need that they collectively expressed as being vital to building the stability of this participatory network. The significance of this aspect of network building was clear to me, since meaningful and in-depth media support and coverage makes emerging participatory networks complex and adds to the stability of their course. However, the way in which this media amplification process contributed to the larger success of making it into a modified black box, or a stable participatory network was unanticipated and inconceivable for me prior to the events that followed.

BGreen's official youth community partners on the ground in Bangladesh, Bangladesh Youth Environmental Initiative (BYEI) and Bangladesh Youth Movement for Climate Change (BYMC) really explained the relationship between youth movements and media organizations in Bangladesh and the importance of building alliances with them for sustained network building. The youth were really demonstrating the signs of an emergence of critical consciousness, which they were connecting to larger political economic structures to manifest into what could be the beginnings of youth-led *organizational conscientização*. The youth leaders from BYMC and BYEI provided me with a brief overview of the way in which media industries operated right now in Bangladesh in connection to a transnational youth-community projects like ours. According to both the groups' previous experiences in running youth-engaged projects on the ground, the media support created legitimacy to a wide range of audiences about the initiative and gained the project widespread support and acceptance.

While this was good news for BGreen, it was nonetheless quite a surprising proposition for me, since my frame of reference is the US media, having lived there for the past 14 years. In the US, mainstream national media organizations would rarely, if ever, feature small, socially driven work like this in any meaningful way, a case in point being the citizen-science deliberations project called the World Wide Views (WWV) that happened in the US (Geddes & Choi, 2015). This experience was consistent with BGreen's multi-media amplification from the US. Amherst Media, which is a Western Massachusetts media house, is a community partner of BGreen that hosts television shows on BGreen (called The BGreen Media Literacy Project) that feature the global participatory action research projects affiliated with BGreen. Amherst Media and BGreen have had a successful and ongoing collaboration on co-producing television shows that are streamed on local public access television in the US, international media networks, social media and their website. Also, BGreen has received public-access radio support in the US, in the form of interviews with me, as the lead action researcher of the transnational participatory action research project.

To revert back to the Bangladeshi multi-media example, I was curious about what kind of media the youth community partners were talking about and the questions that emerged in my mind immediately were: Are these mainstream media outlets—television, newspaper, radio, online news portals? What is the nature of their coverage of the event—does it take the shape of a mere short event coverage or do they get in-depth features? Why are these media organizations interested in featuring projects like these that have no sensational elements? Also, what does it mean for the larger cultural sphere in Bangladesh for mainstream media to be supporting and publicizing projects like these?

The most surprising element for me about this entire process was that it was indeed both the mainstream media along with alternative media that ended up providing coverage for projects that were similar to BGreen in all different media outlets. While print media and independent online news portals provided the most support for youth-engaged, social ventures such as BGreen, radio and television also provided support and meaningful coverage, the nature of which I will explore shortly. The youth partners of BGreen showed me ample examples of their past media collaborations and both the youth organizations insisted on developing these relationships and building these connections in the early stages of my on-ground planning as a group in Bangladesh. One of the youth leaders from BYMC said:

> This is the single most important part of doing any meaningful, urban focused youth work. From our experience of organizing in the past few years, we have understood that getting meaningful validation from national media really impacts the way in which the targeted youth perceives our efforts. It gives the youth and their parents who are constantly looking for career-building opportunities an incentive to participate in a worthwhile event.
>
> (Personal communication, December 16, 2013).

In some ways, I understood the power of media in shaping people's perceptions in a positive way that can be used for publicity for an under-represented topic. However, what the youth leader said also pointed towards one of my biggest issues with the educational system today in both the US and Bangladesh, where everything is viewed as a vocational, career-building opportunity that will help in the survival of the fittest, rather than engaging in socially transformative activities that are based on ideals and goals that transcend personal gain. Geddes and Choi (2005) refer to the importance of meaningful, sustained coverage rather than features that show no depth or consistency in the media world. They write about the media amplification processes of a participatory citizen-science project called World Wide Views (WWV) in the US:

> The WWViews project design assumes that by attracting media attention organizers can reach the public at large and indirectly influence the policy process because policy makers are more likely to take notice. Although it is never explicitly mentioned, these assumptions refer to agenda-setting theory. Agenda-setting theory argues that the mass media have an 'agenda-setting' capacity that serves to highlight what is important and to frame the salience of environmental issues. The media influence what we think about, rather than how we think about a particular issue.
>
> (p. 198)

Geddes and Choi (2015) add that for media features to be worthwhile and impactful, the "quantity, prominence and frequency of coverage" (p.198) are more important than superficial, one off features. Hence, following the recom-mendations of the scholars, the aim for our media outreach was to find media amplification of BGreen in a qualitatively rich and deep way, which is the most important way in which multi-media actors/actants can contribute to the complex transnational participatory networks that can sustain over time and gain network stability. The WWV in the US received minimal mainstream media coverage, which was completely the opposite case from what happened in Bangladesh, however, it is important to understand Geddes and Choi's (2015) ideas on how deeper media content is required, especially if the goal is to influence the policy agenda, within the framework of agenda-setting theory.

The university that was hosting BGreen in Bangladesh at inception, the University of Liberal Arts Bangladesh (ULAB) and the specific research unit within the institution that was partnering up with BGreen, the Center for Sustainable Development (CSD), all had representatives in these planning meetings and they also shared similar experiences of working closely with the media in disseminating information about their events on campus. They also had a media intern in CSD, which I thought was quite holistic in its visions, since the center was trying to do inter-disciplinary academic-environmental work. While it is clear that privatization controls the education sector in Bangladesh, media houses are also mostly privatized in Bangladesh, especially in the last 20 years, which has created "unequal participation by producing chiefly market-oriented and urban-centric discourse . . . a non-radical nature of political news analysis that depoliticises the political awareness of the public" (Rahman, 2012, p.47).

Our experience working with the multi-media houses in Bangladesh in order to publicize BGreen was a very enriching and fruitful experience, one that was made possible by the youth journalists with their bold visions in publicizing a project of value for the larger Bangladeshi community. It is also important to mention that the project found this much media traction due to its transnational nature, that brought together US youth with Bangladeshi youth, creating an intercultural and international network of social change. Also, the incredible multi-media coverage of BGreen in Bangladesh helped build the foundations of exposure and legitimacy of this transnational project to the local access television and radio networks in the US.

The Bangladeshi mainstream media system was taking an entirely different approach from its commercial visions when it came to BGreen and this was being made possible by the hard work and determination of BGreen's youth-led media team *and* the youth writers/journalists/reporters in making a solid case to their editors about the need to represent a project like BGreen. This was an entirely different way in which mainstream media was using its power, one that was very supportive for small, idealistic projects like BGreen that needed as much validation from diverse multi-institutional and community actors as possible to make a wider impact. One of the many functions of mass media, at its best, is its ability to use its power to disseminate information to its varied audiences, and our collective hope for BGreen was to use the audience reach of these organizations to help this participatory network gain network stability across a larger cross-section of Bangladeshi and global populations.

Development of the BGreen media team in US and in Bangladesh

In the context of Bangladesh, the community partners who had experience in taking this route to building participatory media networks suggested that for the steady progress of building media support and coverage in light of the political situation, we needed to form a sub-committee within the BGreen community partners committee, that specifically handled the media aspect of the project. This kickstarted the translation process, where we problematized the goal at hand: To build complexity via media actors/actants in our emerging participatory network. We formed a sub-committee of community partners led by youth actors who had worked with media houses extensively. I did not conceptualize the extent to which this sub-committee, BGreen's youth-led media team in the US and Bangladesh, would contribute to the building of such participatory networks.

However, after the action research event, the media team's contribution in developing and deepening the goals of BGreen as an innovative social project cannot be praised enough. In the US context, the sheer number of community partners was much lower, necessitating taking up more media work per community partner. The safer political situation created a stability that allowed for youth community partners to work more creatively to create productions alongside me that entailed travel and more longer term planning. For example, one of the US community youth partners wrote and managed the blog posts of BGreen. She would do written as well as video blogs on various relevant environmentally themed topics to promote the ongoing work of the BGreen project in the US and in Bangladesh.

This general approach to doing a collaborative, community engaged project was deeply problematic for me, especially since small counter-cultural projects like BGreen, BYMC and BYEI need the support and collaboration of larger community networks to flourish. This closed approach went against the goals of building participatory networks that were complex, open and trusting of the participatory process, a process that builds on the merging of PAR with a weak version of ANT that relies on communication and collaboration between actors/actants that are human and non-human in an organic way.

BGreen media team strategy

The global media team had a clear strategy on how to proceed, based on previous experiences and general group vision, and this seemed to be a suitable approach for all of us as long as they shared with the entire group what their exact plans looked like. This was their organized plan from the start, which was logically and effectively presented by them in one of the community partners' meetings:

1. Identify contacts in all media industries—print, television, radio, online news portals. Build on previously established contacts and also identify new contacts for growth. Notify them about the project details and how their support will be valuable to our project and the justification of our project for their audience/readers. Be the contact people for the entire BGreen project pre, during and post the event.

2. Write up a pre-event press release (in Bengali and English) to be sent out to the media organizations prior to the event to create pre-event hype and publicity in the form of features, interviews, etc. Send it to the media organizations two weeks prior to the event to provide basic details on the event and then re-send the press release the day before the event as a reminder for them to attend. Write-up a post-event press release, which would be circulated the day after the event for extended features and interviews that happen in media organizations after the successful completion of any event/project.

3. Be in constant contact with the media houses to maintain appointments for anyone they want to interview related to the project, which everyone decided should be me, the founder and any other person/organization who is relevant to the nature of their feature. This part was very important, since we needed to create a responsible and approachable image for ourselves to the media, since so much of community partnership building is about maintaining good relationships with one another.

4. Try to shape the nature of the features in the media houses: Convince them of the need to have longer features that explain the larger goals of the project and how this kind of feature is necessary to really bring to the forefront the true goals of the project, rather than short features that are often featured under the events section of the newspaper and sidelined in the television/radio outlets.

While BYMC came up with a plan to tackle the media aspect of the event, we knew of the major challenge, a powerful non-human actor/actant that was lurking in the shadows of the whole process of developing this collaborative project—the ongoing political challenges in Bangladesh surrounding the elections that have been explained already. The elections posed major challenges in developing new media relationships for BGreen. The media organizations were wary of committing to any new projects, because so many plans were being destroyed by the unpredictable and ongoing political turmoil. Hence, the media team had to work extra hard to convince them about the value of the project and display a sense of confidence that we truly did not feel about the outcome of the event, due to the uncertainties surrounding it. Media houses were hesitant to not only send their reporters for safety reasons, but they were also concerned about how much media space they could give us, while there was a much more compelling issue to write about: The national election and the havoc it was wreaking over the daily lives of Bangladeshi citizens. This again points to the deep threat of political instability as a non-human actant that constantly shaped and reshaped the flow of this participatory network and threatened its emergence and stability.

Hence, it took a herculean effort on the media team's part, with many extra conversations than would probably be required (with last minute calls on days of the event in Bangladesh to notify them that we are actually having the event) to get many of the mainstream and alternative media houses to attend our events that eventually resulted in many meaningful features on our collaborative work. Following the translation process, reaching the last step of mobilization was deeply challenging (even though it was methodically conducted by the media team) in light of the political chaos. The mobilization process was dependent on the careful negotiations that ensued between the BGreen media team and the media actors/actants, to make both parties' interests align. This was done to ensure that we could have them commit and enroll in the process of building this participatory network, where the media actors see the value of supporting and covering an event like this, in the midst of political turmoil. Hence, this enrollment stage of the translation process was quite effective for BGreen, as the narrative below will point out, where the BGreen media team was successful in really capturing (and maintaining) the attention of four key journalists/reporters who were very important to the process of media amplification for BGreen.

Understanding the media terrain

BGreen as a movement was trying to re-define the way in which youth, academia and other industries such as media houses interact with one another. The amount of media exposure that BGreen generated in Bangladesh was unprecedented; even the BYMC team members who had done similar work for their own organization's events felt that their efforts had maximum returns for BGreen, considering the major political hurdles that stood in the way of our media success. All the partners collectively were truly unprepared for the kind of attention that we all received. Also, it is important to mention that most of the writers and hosts (video and radio jockeys) were Bangladeshi youth between the age of 17 and 25, all attending various urban secondary or higher education institution. Only two out of the 30 journalists from print, television, radio and online portals I encountered through featuring BGreen were over the age of 30. Most of the journalists were young university students or recent graduates from different higher-educational institutions in Bangladesh, who worked as journalists in one of the many English or Bengali language media houses (print, television, radio and online portals).

A unique aspect of print journalism in Bangladesh needs to be discussed in this chapter to give an insight into the state of matters here, which really helped with the process of building participatory networks through media. An interesting feature of mainstream and alternative newspapers in Bangladesh, both English and Bengali, is that they all have a special youth newspaper and/or magazine, that comes along with the main newsprint, once a week. This is unique because, in the US this is not a recognized phenomenon at all and one of the main reasons for that is youth in the US do not consume print media anymore. In the US, not only youth, but a decreasing number of people of any age are getting their news from any form of print media. However, in Bangladesh, all the major and minor newspapers have at least a weekly newspaper supplement and/or magazine (sometimes two per week) that deal with youth relevant issues, that has its own editorial board with a fully functioning, professional writing team. Therefore, this allows for a great deal of youth work in Bangladesh that is of substance or interest to be publicized by the youth supplement teams.

Also, Dhaka city has an explosion of youth events happening at all times due to the heavy involvement of the urban youth in the public sphere in the past few years, thus, sometimes you are put on a waiting list, not your choosing, if there is a more attractive youth event that is happening at the same time. Also, having prior contacts, which in BGreen's case was through BYMC, helped matters a great deal more. Luckily, due to BYMC's extensive connections in the print media world in Bangladesh as well as our unique and innovative program design that brought into focus some of the key issues that Bangladeshi youth were struggling with, we struck a chord with the various print newspapers and we were able to create a solid media network with extensive articles that featured us as their main stories.

These youth journalist actors/actants really contributed in a significant way to how other key actors/actants such as the media institutions and technologies built the identity of BGreen. With the addition of new complex entities in our larger, emerging BGreen participatory network, the journalists/reporters and the BGreen media team certainly took a defined leadership position. I could step away from being the OPP as a result, so they could assume autonomy. They were in direct communication with the media houses and they had the independence in making decisions around matters such as media partnerships, coverage type and details, since as an entire group we had entrusted the responsibility of building media complexity to these youth partners. This allowed for the youth to exercise quite a position within the network, as they were translating the needs of the actor network by enlisting multi-mediated systems to work in our favor. Therefore, the youth's critical consciousness was being manifested in the form of organizing and mobilizing media industries to work in BGreen's favor to publicize a socially transformative academic–community project that was led by them.

Also, the media systems (non-human actants) themselves assumed the role of being OPPs, since they became required mediums through which actors/actants from outside of the participatory network consumed the narratives about BGreen. Therefore, the different forms of media outlets, being OPPs, really contributed to bringing about a structurally discursive shift in the way in which this participatory network was amplifying and navigating through different political economic structures. This is the peculiarity of ANT networks that makes the process unique, which allows for grappling with the true potentialities of difference in a larger, political economic system with power structures.

Both the groups of human actors (the media team and the journalists) were overwhelmingly comprised of youth (in both the US and Bangladesh), hence, the way in which the power dynamics are challenged by them being OPPs in the development of a larger participatory network, really goes to show the complexity and potentiality of this networked approach in creating a new way of dealing with political economic structures. While the association of networks and its relationship to political economic structures may be paradoxical, hybrid, complex processes and spaces require re-theorization that creatively merges processes that will only benefit from one another. In this particular case, the youth journalists were key to complicating the way in which power and binarism reside between and within large institutional bodies and individuals. Their manifestation of critical consciousness and active enrollment into the BGreen participatory network, not only added to the stability and complexity of this academic–community project, but it challenged the supposed impervious and "functional" (Couldry, 2009, 2012) state of political economic structures such as privatized media houses.

Media moment: Isolated moment of fame or towards the path of developing meaningful participatory networks?

The young journalists' involvement in the process of developing ongoing relationships with me and the other core actors is explored in the following sections, one which was crucial to contributing to the way in which power is assumed to work in a dispersed manner in ANT (Callon, 1987; Castree and MacMillan, 2001). Since the media industry is now largely being occupied by youth under 30, which is especially true in the case of print media (both in Bengali and English), the youth felt personally connected to the content and cause. The interest factor and the connection with the writers is immediate for a project like this which is targeted towards that demographic in a central way, where their engagement and contribution will chart the future for the outcome and success of the project. Both the planning of and building the architecture of media awareness, and the youth engagement in writing the content, provided an opportunity for youth to use their elevated consciousness for sustained social change. From the perspective of youth journalists, their active engagement in the process contributed to the growth of this network, which was quite a rewarding process for them as well. One of the journalists that covered BGreen was an undergraduate in one the prominent private universities in Bangladesh. He expressed to us after featuring us in multiple news articles:

> It is such an honor to be part of the BGreen family. As an engineering major, I always believed in the power of the pen, alongside pursuing what my parents wanted me to pursue academically. That is why, to balance my parent's expectations and my own desires, I wanted to be a journalist on the side and write about up and coming youth issues. There could not be a better cause to support, because, now I don't feel that I am an outsider in BGreen, I am one of the people who are part of it and are using my connections elsewhere to publicize it.
>
> (20 July 2014).

This young journalist was not only committed to writing about the project, but he led subsequent media action research workshops for BGreen in 2015 in Dhaka on multiple topics of media, education, environment and social change. His most popular workshop was on the topic of how youth journalists can work with youth community organizers to build a better system within media industries to amplify their grassroots projects. This is an apt action research workshop that BGreen endorsed readily, since it really talks about the ways in which *organizational conscientização* could perhaps be triggered by youth workers in non-educational institutions like privatized media houses. Also, by writing, these youths are participating in meaningful change, hence using the power of the pen to take charge of their own and collective youth futures. They were applying *conscientização* as a concept to actively change the media discourse around youth participation towards educational and environmental social change.

Straubhaar writes about *conscientização*, saying, "Critical consciousness is not a plateau one reaches and stays upon, but rather a state that requires continual work to maintain. This work process that brings about and maintains critical consciousness is what Freire calls *praxis*." (p. 436). Hence the way in which human and non-human actants merged in this process to add depth and complexity to the evolving network created a discursive turning point for BGreen as a participatory network. Examples such as the one above illuminate what I mean when I say that there has been a discursive turning point, however small, through processes such as these where a youth journalist is connecting his socially engaged ideas with BGreen's and trying to create a new form of architecture of participation in the mainstream media industry in Bangladesh. His active participation in the process was an incredible act of commitment and shift in discourse itself, since he used his institutional privilege to attract attention to an emerging, youth involved mission.

Telling the BGreen story

Not only was the BGreen event publicized in different kinds of media in Bangladesh, but all the partners involved with the project received due attention with extensive footage on our collective goals and individual roles in the process. Print, radio, television and online portals featured us in both English and Bengali and both the private and public media channels endorsed our event, sometimes multiple times within the week of the event. More important to our goals and the goals of PAR, BGreen had control over what was published as well, since the longer, more in-depth features were published only after consulting with us in a very detailed way. We were fortunate that the writers wanted to present a meaningful narrative of our project. Often the journalists would send us the articles (print or online) before publishing them, so that we could recheck the way in which it was being represented, and we could fix any errors in their understanding of the process and the event. This was a major luxury, the power to shape the way in which we are being written about in the national sphere and subsequently the kind of new discourses that are being created as a result of it. This process of co-writing with journalists was an interesting one from an organizational perspective, since in many ways it was a subversive approach towards writing about an issue, in its defiance of media organizational boundaries. What made the media writing even more interesting is that most of the articles written were done in collaboration with BGreen team members in the US and Bangladesh, often with communication mediated by new media technologies.

The narratives that were written and finally published were influenced by the transnational core team and myself in a very direct and specific way that bypassed their media organizational policies and rules. Shaping the narratives created a unique opportunity for the OPPs and the core community partners to really join hands with the youth journalists and reporters to aid in the realization of the process of what Straubhaar (2014) calls *organizational conscientização*. By the notion of *organisational critical consciousness*, Straubhaar (2014) means "the continual process of reflection and action which educational organisations undergo as they seek to define and achieve their mission" (p. 12). Using Staubhaar's concept to interrogate and analyze such creative solutions that were brought about by the young journalists to create the content for the features that defied organizational boundaries is a useful construct, since it allows us to conceptualize and understand the way in which youth shifts in consciousness can start showing the beginnings of organizational social change. If each of the media organizations that these reporters/journalists were working for was interpreted from the perspective of ANT-PAR analysis, then what was happening was that each unique "closed" media black box (TV, radio, print, online portal company, etc.) was lending itself to the formation of a deeper participatory network called BGreen, which is an open, hybrid, complex and messy process that is constituted of diverse human and non-human actors and actants. This challenges the notion of the closed black box that strong ANT advocates for, which is defined by a common-sense, automatic and closed approach to its functioning. Instead it points towards an open, messy, complex, deepening, yet evolving participatory network, one that needs constant work and monitoring to keep afloat and gain network stability.

Our coverage was extensive in both English and Bengali language newspapers in sections as diverse as cultural events, city events, youth events, national events, etc. We made it on the covers of two major weekly magazines that are supplementary to two of the widest circulated English language newspapers in the country, with images from our event making up the front page. Even though we were expecting to be featured extensively in only youth sections, we were written about in meaningful ways in much larger cross-sections of the media. One of the most interesting aspects of the features was the way in which the longer articles were written, to make them as close to BGreen's vision as possible. When I say meaningful coverage, I am referring to the writing about BGreen that went beyond doing a short event round-up (with merely logistics and a short summary).

Instead I am referring to lengthier coverage with photographs and longer narratives about key points such as (but not limited to) the goals of the project, what it meant for the educational and environmental future in Bangladesh, what the youth felt about such a process, the outcomes, future plans, inspirations, etc. A large number of the articles took a meaningful, deep approach to representing the event and its goals, by incorporating interviews and photographs of the participants and the workshop leaders, as well as supplementing it with my perspective as the principle researcher of project. Over the course of four years of working on transnational participatory action projects via BGreen (since the time of my fieldwork in late 2013–early 2014), four Bangladeshi journalists have been instrumental in providing us with frequent coverage, even beyond the time of the event. They have followed my research and the growth of this action project and all four of these journalists are in constant contact with me and the remaining community partners, even one and a half years after the first big event in January 2014. Also in the US, Amherst Media has provided BGreen with continuous support in developing television shows that cater for the emerging projects of BGreen, and allowing for the project to deepen with its continuous support of working with new, untested ideas. Three out of the four journalists in Bangladesh wrote for major English language newspapers in Bangladesh and one of them founded and wrote for Bangladesh's first environmental themed online news portal.

There was a pattern in the features of these four journalists, since they had a commitment to the project beyond just providing a straightforward summary, they were performing the roles of OPPs in adding complexity to the project and they were in direct and constant communication with the BGreen media team in order to draft the media message for them. All of them combined event summary and description with a narration on my professional background and what the concrete goals were for the future of this project. For example, one of the articles by a young male journalist, who has developed an ongoing relationship with BGreen in the last two years, wrote about the value of projects like BGreen and merged it with details of me as the founder of the project, while also featuring the future plans of BGreen. On top of a standard event line-up, he also really explored my background (albeit with some inaccuracy) and then really focused his narrative on future plans of BGreen in sustaining the participatory network. He wrote:

> The most exciting project of BGreen is perhaps a multi-format television show that is in the pipeline. In collaboration with Amherst Media, Communication for Sustainable Social Change and the BGreen Project, the BGreen Media Project will be developed as a multi-format television show, which will go on air from November this year. This will help the youth, activists and scholars around the globe to come together in their attempt to work for the environment. Every episode will focus on specific environmental challenges that the world faces at the moment. Fadia said, "My vision is to connect the youth all around the world and engage them in bettering our environment. The TV show will help to this do this."
>
> (http://newagebd.net/50797/involving-youth-in-environmental-
> issues/#sthash.QoAiAzB8.cvnFM4Q6.dpuf")

The other content by our longer-term journalistic partners was quite similar in its approach to representing the event in more complex and deeper ways. This was evident in the way in which the writer really tried to move away from the event itself, and focus on the larger, strategic and organizational goals of BGreen as an academic–community project. This captured the key aim of the project, which was meaningfully elaborated in the feature. He wrote:

> I am not suggesting a magical solution that will bring an end to the world's problems. Claiming the power to understand and decipher information, take responsibility and act on them in good faith is a damn good start. On one hand, there needs to be systemic, institutional and scientific changes made and on the other hand there is a real need for accessible information to be circulated to the masses to encourage change and action: Education and media literacy can be used as an effective tool for the demystification of a phenomenon that

is often presented to people in a cryptic, ambiguous and overwhelming manner. A lot more needs to be done. There needs to be effective risk communication strategies and networks developed across media, political and educational industries, to sustain such efforts of generating an informed public, which will culminate into informed policies that target the issues at its core.

(http://news.priyo.com/2014/01/18/understand-
embrace-and-then-do-it-fadia-hasan-97809.html)

On top of extensive written features, we also landed covers of magazines and news supplements in Bangladesh, with the main story in the magazine being featured around BGreen and its goals for social change. This was significant for us, as this one particular newspaper has the country's third largest readership.

These four journalists who have done repeat coverage of us over the past four years have now become crucial actors/actants for the success and proliferation of BGreen. Whenever BGreen is working on a project that requires media support, just contacting any/all four of them personally is all I need to do to have them write on any of the recent PAR events. In the initial stages, about four years ago, these same journalists (and also others) had sent the BGreen media team a request to formulate the questions, so that we could help the audience better understand our true goals. This gave us immense control over the content and we were able to emphasize the core ideas of this action research project and use the power of the pen to really represent our narrative to the entire nation, which is no minor thing, for a counter-cultural project. Working with the core BGreen team from the start in such an intimate way, enabled them to really understand and internalize the goals of BGreen and what it is that we are all trying to do with the educational system of for global youth in both the US and Bangladesh. Also working with young, friendly and inquisitive journalists was an advantage, since they were open to new ideas and approaches, without the jaded attitude of some of the older people that we encountered throughout our collaborative work, who were suspicious of our approach of involving youth in solution building and generally had a dismissive attitude towards any project that presented a new way of doing something.

In the case of television in Bangladesh, the viewership has steadily declined, especially among urban youth, because Bangladesh has largely become a "mobile first" nation, but even then, with the expansion of the private media industry, there are many available television channels that have some viewership from youth. While there are many shows that are designed to attract the youth, amongst the plethora of television channels that are mushrooming in Bangladesh, the show that gets most recognition amongst urban youth in Bangladesh in dealing with relevant, popular content of interest to them is called *Young Night*. This is an hour-long talk show produced and aired live via one of the oldest and most prestigious private

Figure 5.1 BGreen media amplification.

channels, called Channel I in Bangladesh. Through our BYMC networks, BGreen was able to secure an entire episode prior to the event, which was aired on national television and widely served as a key tool in disseminating in-depth information about the action research project, its goals and my visions as a founder and researcher.

The show's set-up required two guests and I was accompanied by one of the two members of BYMC, who was performing the role of BGreen's media manager in the context of the community partnership. It was an in-depth interview that presented a deep, long perspective on the project, which really launched BGreen in the best possible light to people who were watching the show, an audience of mainly Bangladeshi youth. After the show was aired, we received immediate messages from many Bangladeshi youth who expressed their desire in wanting to be part of the action research project at the current time and in the future. Three other mainstream television networks (one English language and two Bengali language) featured us in their national news features, and framed us as an academic–community engagement conference that was designed to target environmental and climate change challenges in Bangladesh, with some brief interviews with me as the founder and an event summary with video footage of our goals.

For BGreen's television coverage, two out of three features were conducted with a great deal of positive enthusiasm and interest in understanding the goals of the project and our follow-up ideas, but the third news feature was conducted with a different, more skeptical approach. The news reporter who interviewed me had an antagonistic attitude about the entire process without knowing the details, and his skepticism was apparent in his condescending questions that surrounded the feature. He was an older, middle-aged journalist from a prominent television channel who was sent to cover the main event, which seemed, from his attitude, was against his liking. He framed his questions in a suspicious tone about my intentions about the project, which I dealt with as patiently as I possibly could. After asking some standard questions about the aims and visions of the project, his final statement leading to his last question was:

> We see many "conferences" come and go, where experts sit in air-conditioned rooms, do big talk about social change and then leave after the conversation is over, never to be found again. What makes this project any different? Also, what is the point of such a process that never leads to anything?
>
> (Personal communication, Jan 12 2014)

I did not appreciate his antagonistic attitude about our project, but his comment also summarized some realities about so-called community engaged projects that were done without paying true attention to local realities and including local stakeholders, which often pose barriers for the ultimate sustenance of these projects. Also, his suspicion had to do with the fact that I was an outsider coming in to conduct a project and then presumably leave after my work was done. He expressed concern about the numbers of foreigners that come and go and never develop a true connection with the local, on the ground community, hence bypassing the deeper social challenges in Bangladesh. He was worried about the uneven power relations between the US and Bangladesh and that ultimately the US youth and organizational structures would benefit more from this process than the Bangladeshi counterparts of this transnational participatory network. My answer to him was a short one, since I knew it would be quoted in national news, and I was put on the spot to address this major issue that would get televised around the country. I said:

> While I understand your concern for the long-term usefulness of the project, this was envisioned as being an alternative and answer to spaces where youth come in to sit and listen to "experts" speak and present information in a one-way process and instead it was developed in a participatory manner, where the youth will be the main actors who will work alongside experts and mentors to share and generate knowledge and solutions. The goal is to use the collaborative new discourses generated to create action projects that take these ideas forward to start with small projects of change in the youth's communities.
>
> (Personal communication, Jan 12 2014).

While the journalist looked slightly appeased, he still seemed skeptical, and I ended my interaction with him, by inviting him to attend the workshops if he had time to really witness the participation process in action. However, I seriously paid attention to his concern and grappled with that issue while developing BGreen on the ground, since I really wanted to make sure that this project was designed with the active input of the community that it was planning on serving. I was always sensitive to the fact that due to my many years of living in the US, my identity was a matter of confusion for most people around me in Bangladesh, where they did not quite decide on whether to consider me as an insider or outsider, and in most cases treated me as an outsider in Bangladeshi society.

In the case of radio, we received support from both the national public radio (which is broadcast in Bengali and English) and one of the mainstream, privately owned and popular radio stations with youth in Bangladesh. In the US we received the support of student-run radio shows in university campuses to feature BGreen's work. In Bangladesh, we received long, in-depth interview features in both the national radios with half hour slots exclusively dedicated to BGreen, with questions on the project's detailed goals and visions. These interviews focused on my academic and work background as well, as the radio jockeys wanted to know what my personal goals were for the youth community in Bangladesh and how they could use their educational training to contribute to something useful for the environmental future of the nation. While the English language program was targeted towards the urban, English speaking population of the country, I was especially interested in the Bengali feature, since the national public radio is one of the few most effective ways in which I could reach a demographic that was out of my research design—rural Bangladesh.

The national radio was the medium with the widest reach in rural Bangladesh and my hope was to connect to them, since the eventual goal would be to bring projects like these to even underserved communities in both countries: To youth across the nation, creating a bridge between the urban and rural. One of these interviews happened on the first day of the actual event and one of them happened after the completion of one of the major action research processes, focusing on the wrap-up of the project goals and what lay ahead for BGreen in the future. The third interview happened on site for one of the action research events, in the form of a small call-in segment of a popular weekly show that is focused on important youth events in the country. It was short and effective, since it got directly to the youth demographic in urban Bangladesh, the target of our action research at that time. The radio jockey enthusiastically asked me questions about the event and its goals, which was broadcasted live as part of a larger show on weekly youth happenings. In many ways, the radio interviews covered a really large scope in terms of reaching diverse demographics, with the mixture of languages and public versus private broadcasting about the event, since radio is widely consumed across the country, again with the advent of mobile phone technology.

The fourth kind of media coverage we received was from online news portals that have swiftly made inroads into the mainstream of news readership in Bangladesh. While all the major newspapers, in Bengali and English, have websites to publish their news as well, there is a different stream of widely followed independent, online-only news and cultural portals that have been gaining wide popularity and acceptance amongst Bangladeshis living within the country and abroad to develop credible journalism using new media technologies. These online portals are mushrooming in large numbers, with varied quality and focus, but some have gained recognition already as being reliable online news and cultural hubs. Most of the online news portals that featured us were written in the English language and were amongst the reputable ones with a wide cultural and social focus and only one of the portals was specifically dedicated to carrying environmental news. These online portals wrote a few different articles about BGreen and they also did an hour-long video interview feature of me which they aired a couple of weeks after the event was over. The online portal's coverage was similar to the way in which we were featured in print, with the only exception of one portal, which has the environment as their specialization. This specific portal, which was started by a group of young university graduates, provided the most continuous and in-depth coverage of BGreen until now. They believe in the values of BGreen as a project and regularly feature our workshops and events in their portal, which they heavily promote via their social media networks.

In terms of logistics and technological sophistication, the online portals were the easiest to work with overall, since they have a great deal of ease in maintaining online archives of our features, while some of the major newspapers that featured us do not have updated online records of our articles, which makes it very difficult to access data a year after the event. Also, the online portals (as they are more specialized) provided more in-depth, specialized features and frequent coverage, since online portals are a recent addition to the media universe in Bangladesh as well as in the US. The online portals also made the global media access for the Bangladeshi as well as the US partners much easier, as the internet served as a convenient connect for both countries' participants for BGreen. Online portals are also well synched with social media networks, and the cross-pollinations of these two key new media actants is helping to build a strong transnational readership online, and in turn redefining the way in which social media networks are being utilized by users beyond their personal life.

Overall, in the case of media amplification of BGreen, both large and small media, public and private, English and Bengali, provided equal amounts of support in Bangladesh. The media support was clearly not the same in the US, providing more evidence about the peripheral nature of such projects in the US mainstream media imaginations. The current transnational media team at BGreen is in constant touch with our two trusted online portals on any event that we participate in and they dutifully do in-depth coverage of all our action research. Hence, these deeper and more sustained relationships are significant to the process of building network stability of the participatory network for BGreen. The shorter features in some of the big newspapers that BGreen received with decontextualized event summaries played a role in the short-term memory of readers in getting the attention of a wider group of people to build immediate publicity around the event. However, the sustained participatory network that BGreen had envisioned is being lived through the deeper commitment of the many journalists/reporters who were committed to doing long, meaningful, multi-perspective features, on not only the action research event itself, but the process and the building of a new kind of participatory network post the initial action research event in January 2014. Through their commitment to BGreen, they are engaging in the collective emergence of critical consciousness in this complex, hybrid, networked political economic space.

One of the four key journalists that eventually has become a personal friend of mine, had said to me in one of our early interviews,

> I am not sure how you will be able to maintain this momentum with your action projects since you divide your time between multiple countries. However, I attended your events, all three days and I realized that what you are trying to do with BGreen is really affecting the way in which the youth participants were understanding their active roles in society. From speaking to the participants it seems as if, maybe you don't need to be here yourself

> if your local partners really understand and can grapple with the idea of
> re-igniting consciousness amongst them again.
>
> (Personal communication, Jan14 2014)

This observation touched upon many of the tensions inherent to ANT-PAR projects, where network instability and dissolution is a serious concern. Indeed, this journalist was referring to one of my biggest concerns that I have to grapple with every day since the success and unprecedented growth of the project. I reflected on my role as one of the OPPs and in conversations with the local partners on the ground in both the US and Bangladesh, asked them what they thought about my continued involvement in the process and whether it was necessary to continue the project forward. The local partners in both countries insisted on my active participation and even leadership, and making the difficult decisions, since they admitted to relying on me to initiate ideas as well help them refine theirs. This brings into the conversation, one of the key limitations of a truly participatory process, where all the actors/actants are faced with this participatory paradox.

My leadership deviates from a process that is participatory in all stages and complicates the way in which power operates in the strong version of ANT. Hence, even though there have been other OPPs that have emerged (human and non-human), my place as the founder, or as the "lead" OPP, seems to have stayed stable through the longer term networked process, where BGreen is surely and steadily gaining network stability. All publicity about BGreen has an emphasis on my achievements as the founder and often includes a photograph of me along with images from the actual events. This points to the way in which the weak version of ANT is really necessary to understand the complexity of such participatory networks where power manifests in a predictable way within the formation of such actor networks. It points to how some actors/actants exercise a much greater level of control and power within the sustenance of the network (in this case me), which strong versions of ANT does not explore, one of the key weaknesses of such an analysis.

Reflections: participatory media networks for social change

We have maintained communication with the media houses as an entire group by interacting with them over social media sites to advance our professional and personal equations. It is important to reiterate the average age of the Bangladeshi journalists (as well as the media producers of BGreen in non-mainstream media networks in the US) irrespective of their medium of choice and its connection to the process of emerging *conscientização* in the youth. All the reporters/journalists/producers that featured us in all the different forms of media barring just two people were under the age of 25. They brought a very different kind optimism, interest, curiosity and perspective to the framing of the entire project, where the young people were really committed to developing a new narrative on the importance of youth voices in the changing of outdated social systems that were not serving anyone's interests other than those of the proverbial 1 percent of society. Their willingness and lack of jadedness in trying new alternatives to bringing about environmental social change was helpful to us, however, it also provided BGreen with the huge responsibility of being honest and ethical in its claims towards being an alternative academic–community engagement project.

Hence, their inexperience worked in our favor, since they were very open to suggestions, but it gave a strong moral responsibility for us to adhere to it in dealing with such benevolent, supportive partners, since we had to be very mindful when it came to exercising influence over enthusiastic, young journalists who were willing to strongly support a growing cause like BGreen. The popular discourses that emerged from the youth's representation of BGreen, were very positive, hopeful reviews of the innovative structure of the event and larger processes. Often, the features include details on the unique and socially relevant content and also a romanticized narrative of my visions of social change as a young woman in a male dominated field. Youth voices are the ones that are running the show in all the media houses, hence if these same youth could be trained in "a code of ethics, followed by ethics education, it may encourage journalists to openly discuss ethical issues in the newsrooms, at least for the sake of improving their own credibility and survival" (Elahi, 2013, p. 202).

This is where Freire's three stages of consciousness (magical, naïve and critical) could be applied in very specific, productive ways in training youth in understanding the value of the process and how it can be used in their journalistic work to not only change the way in which new discourses are informed and developed as a result of them. Also at its best, their thinking and writing from such a deeply transformative space could be catalysts for inspiring change in not only the organizations that they are working out of, but also in the readers and viewers of their multi-media content. In the journalistic scene in Bangladesh, it seemed that despite the privatization of media outlets, the presence of youth has given the process of journalism a very unique twist, where corporate needs are being reconstituted by the visions of the youth journalists/reporters to some extent.

Hence, providing training and institutional support to these emerging youth voices is quite necessary, which can help these youth actors navigate the complexities of working and maneuvering political economic realities and perhaps using their consciousness as a catalyst for the crafting of new social realities. This would help young journalists create a moral universe from which they could operate, which could potentially help them overcome the issues of corruption and political coerciveness that have historically affected and limited Bangladeshi journalism and perhaps in result in building journalist/reporter safety participatory networks that can challenge the violence that is often inflicted upon them (Das, 2012; Rahman, 2007a). The topics that the youth reporters are picking to be represented and written about are ones that they feel most connected to and feel would potentially have good results and opportunities for the larger community. Therefore fresh subjectivities are being expressed through the media and new discourses are created as a result.

Part 2: New media technologies

The intricate relationship that was shared by the youth who were reporting on BGreen via their different media systems is example of how BGreen as an emerging participatory network enrolled and translated the media to join with its cause to add to the deepening of its blooming participatory network. As with all participatory networked processes, if they can proliferate, it opens up the possibilities of touching upon established, closed political economic structures like the media houses in the US and Bangladesh. Hence this process of adding media complexity to BGreen really brings together many diverse industries to work collaboratively to create something bigger than each unit individually. In this section, I explore how this multi-media network building was complemented and in many ways surpassed by the architecture of participation that was created by the active work using new media technologies by BGreen youth partners. As a result of the prior mentioned media amplification in Bangladesh and the US, the project came to be widely circulated in transnational social media networks of the media houses and found a massive following online, within Bangladesh, US and beyond.

The extent to which new media networks, specifically social media (mainly Facebook and Twitter) contributed to the growth and sustenance of the global BGreen network. I examine the way in which social media networks such as Facebook and Twitter were a canvas for the youth in realizing the youth's *conscientizacao* that holds the potential to transform the concept and practice of *epistemic communities* (Haas, 2001) in and within diverse organizations, institutions and industries. Through the lens of BGreen, I trace the role of new media in amplifying the BGreen participatory network and the potentials of new media as a subversive space for the youth in forming such transnational participatory networks and the subsequent ways in which new discursive spaces that involved the youth were created as a result. The formation of such online (and offline/on-ground) networks challenge the power dynamics that are inherent to youth-led international development projects in the global south because BGreen started (with collaboration) from the bottom-up and has the potential of penetrating and impacting often the insular institutional structures of different industries that hold the power to bring about social change. However, as I have demonstrated in earlier chapters, the case for BGreen was a curious one, since we also received structural support, hence new media networks were incorporated to enhance the complexity of this emerging participatory network.

The surprising integration of print and digital media with social media such as Twitter and Facebook helped build credibility for project partners in the US and Bangladesh and beyond, who were supporting our project from afar and were proud to have been represented in a prominent manner by the national press. It provided validation for everyone involved in the process and allowed for meaningful representation of all partners and goals, which helped justify and sustain BGreen's transnational partnerships. The youth's participation in constructing the coverage of BGreen demonstrates how it could potentially build a different future for the youth of Bangladesh and the US, by merging different transnational industries to work collaboratively with one another, forming wide-reaching participatory networks. This again points to the importance of analyzing non-human actants and their relational dynamics with human actors within the ANT paradigm, but this particular case of cross-media pollination, points to the importance of looking at the ways in which different forms of non-human actants (in this case different forms of media) interact with one another to build stronger actor networks. The combined use of social media and other traditional forms of media was one of the key contributions that added to the emergent stability of the BGreen participatory network.

This is a very hopeful future for global youth, from my perspective, as a participatory action researcher who is involved in a social movement with the goals of transforming society in a meaningful way bringing together disparate industries (ones mostly driven by profit) that are not expected to work for the service of one another from very different global, geopolitical locations. This aspect of participatory network building is actively contributing to the creation of new discourses, where youth voices are really being expressed, which is creating the building blocks of the emergence of *conscientização* in the youth *and* organizations that are relying on youth voices to create national texts. Hence, in the case of the journalism industry in Bangladesh, the youth have the power to shift organizational identities in the realization of Freire's ideas of *conscientização,* which can be "achieved with neither verbalism nor activism, but rather with praxis, that is, with *reflection* and *action* directed at the structures to be transformed" (Freire, 1970a, p. 125).

This approach of using mainstream media for the publicity of non-commercial, small community engaged projects is a very promising and counter-cultural approach and provides a big opportunity for social change and gaining visibility, in a way that is quite inconceivable in the US. BGreen's strong and stable long-term collaborations with the public access television and media houses in the US has enabled the project to have prolonged new media presence as each episode that is produced with the US media team is circulated via new media networks continuously for long periods of time, amplifying and proliferating the message and intent of the transnational action research network. This section navigates the different kinds of human and non-human actant/actor processes that added to the complexity of BGreen's participatory network. In this chapter, another key actor/actant, new media technologies is explored and how this thread contributed to deepening, stabilizing and amplifying the participatory network, that was required to complement and supplement the on-ground mobilizing and organizing as well as the multi-media networks for the realization of BGreen.

The important part to understand about the process of achieving this participatory network is its heavy dependence on relational dynamics and interactive processes between these diverse actors/actants (organizations, people, media houses, political instability, etc) since, it is this essential interaction that causes the deepening of the network, that ultimately helps in gaining network stability, which can form what an ANT calls a black box. The proliferation of these multimedia streams of communication and the subsequent stability the network gained as a result allowed for the multi-directional growth of this citizen-science project and in turn led to more transnational youth and organizational engagement that surpassed my initial expectations of building networks via participatory action research.

Harvey (2014) interrogates the capacity to building an architecture of participation via in social media networks, and investigates the role of such "mediating" technologies, which are not passive or neutral, but rather allow the youth engaged to be engaged as/in "simultaneous products and producers of the environments and contexts in which they are put to use" (Harvey, 2014, p. 21). I also look at the compounding of using new media technologies such as Facebook and Twitter and the various forms of multi-media coverage (that were converted to online articles, videos, radio coverage, etc) in building this framework of architecture of participation, which led to the deepening of the BGreen participatory network. I discuss as well the ways our social media pages became an important, non-human OPP for the BGreen network.

This is an important idea that will be explored in this section, since, despite the isolated instance of BGreen being able to successfully enlist the media into the emerging BGreen participatory network to a satisfactory extent (as explained in the previous chapter) the conventions of mass media coverage still framed the final way in which BGreen was crafted to the public. Harvey's (2014) idea of architecture of participation found real shape via the social media networks that the global youth were affiliated with in BGreen, since they were able to exercise a level of freedom in expression that was not bound by the same kind of political economic limitations of media organizations. The chapter brings into the forefront this highly engaged online sphere, which is an interactive, supportive and productive space for the youth in the creation of new environmental subjectivities and subsequently complicated the concept of "epistemic communities" (Haas, 2001) as understood in classic, international development and social change discourses. I will be exploring what happens when youth aspirations and activism go online and what kind of opportunities are developed for academic–university partnerships because of this phenomenon and how academic–community partnerships can benefit from such a fertile and well-utilized platform of the Bangladeshi youth.

The extent to which new-media provides a space for realizing Freire's ideas on *conscientização* for the under-served and under-represented youth is explored in this paper. New media, in this case, specifically social media, becomes a channel through which the global south youth can voice their environmental concerns and supplement their organizing action plans to create new, creative, participatory networks of solution building that holds the potential to perhaps transform the power relations within and between organizational structures. The manner in which the youth consciously and unconsciously are navigating this unlikely space for the realization, sustenance and application of Freire's concept of *conscientização* is narrated and analyzed to make way for perhaps a more inclusive, localized definition of *epistemic communities*—one that contributes to the proliferation of the participatory networks that were formed and sustained through BGreen.

A central point of inquiry is to investigate the impact of this e-activism, one that the global youth in both the US and Bangladesh are engaging in via participatory social media networks to voice their opinions and realize their *conscientização* on environmental social justice. While the cooperation between multi-industries is key to solving the educational challenge in Bangladesh today, the emergence of *conscientização* using new media networks without any specific, localized organizational affiliations that bypasses institutional structures of universities and civil society organizations, can provide fecund ground for supplementing efforts to achieve *organizational conscientização*, that can create a participatory network that can sustain a community of idea exchange, action using the power of the internet as a space for transformative action and new discourse building.

In the context of Bangladesh, this research is one of the first studies that are being done to study the intersection of social network sites and youth in Bangladesh. One study by research duo, Jahan and Ahmed (2012), explores the way in which social networks possess great opportunities and challenges for transforming education in countries like Bangladesh, but no research so far has looked at the intricate connection between e-activism, social networks and youth in Bangladesh. This is an important process that needs to be documented, explored and analyzed because of the sheer impact of such online participatory networks in transforming the ways in which epistemic communities operate within organizations that are designed to limit youth participation and instead aid in the realization of *conscientização* for radical social change. Cooks (2001) points to the importance of doing research on new media and its connection to community building in the context of the US. She writes:

> Some scholars have discounted the possibilities of true "communities" existing on the Internet (e.g. Beniger, 1987; Peck, 1987) while others have praised the possibilities for new nationalisms, empowerment and social change. The former set of critics presupposes the physical constraints of space and place as necessities for the true formation of community, while the latter assume the collapse of these constraints, and thus the pure possibilities for equality in the formation of community.
>
> (p. 476)

Connecting the research on new media, and in this case, social media, to the larger social, cultural and political processes in both the US and Bangladesh was an important aim for the development of the BGreen transnational participatory network. As the narrative below will show, through the proliferation of the new media networks, complexity is added to the process of building an innovative, counter-cultural project, which has been using this non-human actant of social media as a space for transnational community-building.

Brief overview of internet use in Bangladesh

Online activism, or e-activism, seems to be the future for global youth, as they are deftly using the nebulous space of the internet in creative and effective ways to express, organize and mobilize on social issues that they believe in. In the case of US, access to the internet has been very widespread for a much longer period of time than in Bangladesh, with much more developed technological infrastructure and access. Internet use via computers is still rare in Bangladesh, due to the technological divide that is persistent in developing countries such as Bangladesh (Kepes, 2016). However, government and local non-profit initiatives have undertaken the responsibility to address educational and economic inequality in Bangladesh by increasing the accessibility of the internet for the under-served and economically disadvantaged regions in Bangladesh alongside the solidification of internet use amongst the population that are already internet users (Kepes, 2016).

The surge of cell-phone technology and affordability has changed the way in which Bangladeshi people, rural and urban, relate to technology and the outside world (Kepes, 2016). Even though Bangladesh is a low-technology, high income-inequality country in South-Asia, cell-phone technology (along with phone internet) has overtaken every other form of telecommunication and media net-work in the current time (Hussain & Ullah, 2013). Along with this increase in cell phone internet use among the class of people (usually urban) who can afford it, the significance of Facebook and Twitter to the urban youth internet users in Bangladesh to navigate their personal *and* professional endeavors cannot be over-emphasized (Jahan & Ahmed, 2012; Pachi et al., 2010; Hussain & Ullah, 2013; Barrett & Pachi, 2012;). The affordability factor of cell-phone technology is a huge contributor to this trend of using the internet aggressively to network personally and professionally, especially for young school/college/university going people who have a tight budget and are always on the move and interested in staying engaged and connected to the world around them.

The youth's viewership of traditional television is on heavy decline, while there has been a very big radio revival in the country due to various factors that are beyond the scope of discussion here (http://www.omrglobus.com/BangladeshTV MediaReportQ12015.pdf). Hence, cellphones and the internet subscriptions that come with them are the most used media tool for urban people who are constantly on the move to stay connected to the world, especially via the use of social media networks such as Facebook and Twitter. The use of social networks by Bangladeshi youth is an understudied, important recent trend that needs to be narrated and analyzed, especially since, in the case of BGreen, their conscious participation and use of these online/new media networks is contributing to meaningful environmental social change. On the other hand, extensive research has been conducted on the habits of US youth and the internet, all of which points to a much lower connection between social media use and social activism (Giroux, 2013).

Even though the youth involved in my research were certainly not the most economically disadvantaged or vulnerable in the context of Bangladesh and instead were lower to upper class urban youth enrolled in higher educational institutions, it is important to know a brief background of strategic, top-down ICT interventions that have been planned for the country, in order to truly understand and explore the scope of new media and internet in the Bangladeshi sphere of BGreen. According to Social Bakers (https://www.socialbakers.com/, 2015), Bangladesh ranked in the 51st position in May 2015, which accounts for more than one-fourth of all the internet users in the country and shows promise of further sharp increases in the near future. This is due to the aggressive push of the Bangladeshi government for constructing, developing and embracing Digital Bangladesh which emphasizes "technology and knowledge-centric growth" that facilitates "forums for free-flow of ideas and concepts enriching current thoughts on Information and Com-munication Technologies (ICT) for development" (http://www.digitalworld.org.bd/digital-bangladesh-and-ict).

The Digital Bangladesh movement is a landmark ICT-based initiative of the Awami League administration, the oldest political party in Bangladesh, which took office in 2009. Digital Bangladesh has been "heralded as a mindset change within Government to embrace ICTs as a powerful enabler for the nation's socio-economic transformation" (Kepes, 2016). The Digital Bangladesh Initiative is planning to use ICT-based interventions to bring radical improvements to education and governmental services, particularly to the most economically disadvantaged and vulnerable groups (Kepes, 2016). Due to a persistently low internet penetration rate countrywide—only 3.7 percent of Bangladeshis were internet users in 2010—there are many obstacles to using this new medium in a mass scale, especially to rural Bangladesh where broadband service is often unavailable (Kepes, 2016).

However, with 46 mobile phones for every 100 people in Bangladesh, mobile telephony has far greater reach in comparison to the internet. However, the merging of internet and cell-phone technology in Bangladesh is what is revolutionizing the internet user's frequency in using new media streams in urban Bangladesh (Kepes, 2016). In Bangladesh, cell phones are already being used as educational devices. For example, the BBC has teamed up with local telecom providers to offer low-cost English language audio lessons via cell phones (Bunz, 2010; Kepes, 2016). Therefore, given the wide reach and potential of cell phones with internet in rural and urban Bangladesh, cell phones are already acting as an important vehicle for bringing about social change in Bangladesh.

Internet, social movement and the amplification of BGreen

Based on Bangladesh's rich history of youth movements, as recent as the Shahbagh Movement in February 2013 (http://ireport.cnn.com/docs/DOC-926210), the hope was to start a new educational-environmental movement in the country, one that had a very specific academic–community affiliation. The Shahbag Movement in Bangladesh can be summarized as organized mass-protests of Bangladeshi youth against the Islamic extremism that is on the rise in the country, which heavily used social media to form national and international networks (Ganim and Kamaruzzaman, 2014). The parallel between the Shahbag Movement in Bangladesh and BGreen is an important and relevant one, since,

> In the early days of the Shahbag movement, Bangladeshis were both dumbstruck and fascinated by the young bloggers who had sat down at Projonmo Chottor. The uniqueness of their action lay in its spontaneity; never before had a small group of individuals, in a matter of days, attracted hundreds of thousands of young people to a single place to engage in protest. Shahbag also surprised the public with its web-based approach; the protests were largely organized, orchestrated, and "exported" around the world using the Internet rather than more traditional methods of assembly.
>
> (Alaldulal, 2014b)

The Shahbagh movement thus could be called a participatory network, one that followed its own path of combining elements of ANT and PAR to gain a level of network stability, which over time, based on the intersection of many factors, either gains network stability or dissolves or merges with other participatory networks. The Shahbagh movement fizzled out and the actor network could really not sustain itself over a long period of time, hence never quite becoming what ANT refers to as a black box. The crowd that had gathered physically and virtually on the ground and online dispersed themselves over time. However, I have a different interpretation of the way in which the Shahbagh actor-network was dissolved. From applying the idea of a participatory network, which combines elements of PAR and ANT into forming the definition, Shahbagh as a network diverged and merged into other movements and networks that the actors/actants found suitable to their values.

While it never reached the ANT's black box, which is a closed, stable, black, contained network, it instead morphed into something that had more openness to it, where it meandered and merged into other social movements. This process is much like that of a complex, flexible process like a participatory network, that relies on being open and forming new alliances and hence shaping and reshaping its identity as it flows through diverse spaces. Understanding the evolution of the Shahbagh movement is important, as it provides some parallels (and also some important contradictions) to the way in which the BGreen network evolved as its flowed through both Bangladesh and the US. Also, the realities of the Shahbagh movement provides an apt background to the political, cultural and social contexts that the youth are a part of in Bangladesh today.

On an ideological level, Shahbagh movement displayed something much more long term. It made it clear for Bangladeshi youth that another way of life is indeed possible and that their voices, needs, subjectivities and demands for a different future for them was possible. It made clear that these non-tangible, non-human actants/actors like emotions, ideas and visions, were integral to the process of shaping the Shahbagh networks. Hence, Shahbagh, in my perspective, played a very important role in triggering the youth's re-imagination of another world that can be made possible, through their participation, by finding creative ways of working through established structures. This point of analysis is very important as it brings forth the important contribution of non-human actants that are often driving forces of such actor network building.

Cooks (2001) in her research on internet communities based in the US (and generally the global north) and their connection to democracy, points to both extremes of this phenomenon. She writes, "Early theorizing on the impact of cyberspace and communication technologies on concepts such as the nation, culture and identity posited the end of the hierarchies of race, class, gender, age, physical appearance, and the re-birth of democracy through the *horizontalizing* of communities via computers" (p. 472). At the opposite end of the spectrum, she points out how some theorists remain skeptical of the true abilities of the internet to create space for community building and how "communication technologies claim to be erasing boundaries when in fact they are creating and re-inscribing the same hierarchies, between rich and poor, male and female, young and old, citizen and non-citizen and, of course, first and third world" (p. 472). Unsurprisingly, both extremes are exactly that: extremes. Both interpretations are missing the nuances of the interactions and interplay between human and non-human actors/actants in the process of community-building via new-media technologies with the important addition of the social, cultural and political realities that necessitate the ways in which new media technologies are used for a myriad of different reasons. The rest of the section will delineate, the unique political, cultural and social realities in the US and Bangladesh today that really speak to the need and success of the use social media networks and other online platforms in the building of the BGreen transnational participatory network.

Why BGreen?

The chord that BGreen hit with the global youth, in my perspective, was one that was led by needs and emotions around what was missing for the global youth in the current educational and environmental sectors in both the US and Bangladesh. For BGreen, I am referring to high school and college students from various urban schools, private and public higher education institutions from various parts of the US and Bangladesh, who sincerely continue to give their time to the sustenance of the project. Movements like Shahbagh and BGreen as I will demonstrate below are very good examples of phenomena that use new media technology as a transnational connection across communities from different geopolitical realities.

The practical need for wanting a participatory platform for social change and the desire for wanting to be an active part of a process that uses non-human actants such as new media networks to create something larger than themselves drove the youth to use these mediums for social change. Social networks gave the youth the freedom to express and organize, by creatively bypassing on-ground organizational structures that have posed as barriers for them historically in both the US and Bangladesh. However, in the case of BGreen, the organizational collaboration with the global youth created an unusual experience for them, where they were using new media technology to enhance the on-ground participatory network building, rather than using it as a substitute. As mentioned earlier, Shahbagh fizzled out, however, BGreen's transnational participatory network became stronger and complex over time. While the reach of social media networks is extensive and potentials unlimited, the difference in the course of the two participatory networks Shahbagh and BGreen can be connected to the lack of institutional support that Shahbagh was able to generate in its flow, hence never really developing the complexity of a networked political economic space. The emergence and eventual stability of the BGreen participatory network was dependent on such well constructed synthesis across transnational organizations, big and small.

The development of BGreen via social media networks was unprecedented where at this current point in time, the youth-movement's Facebook page boasts of over 18000 followers and rising (https://www.facebook.com/BGreen Bangladesh?ref=hl). The common term that has been popularized by the global youth actors is BGreeners, to refer to the growing group of youth followers online. It has become the most effective way of engaging with the global youth interspersed in many countries around the world, communicating our plans and sustaining the project's interest among the targeted demographics. In BGreen's case, the global youth actors who are engaged in maintaining the social media page is not only using new media technologies to apply and amplify their critical consciousness, but using such non-human technological actants as a tool to engage the BGreeners in going through the process of magical, naïve and critical consciousness. This is happening via the transformative educational and environmental content that the social media managers are posting to generate discussion amongst the wider followers on larger social issues that they can engage in via these online networks to strategize on how to bring about social change.

The architecture behind the BGreen social media pages

The goal for developing the Facebook and Twitter pages for BGreen was to create an organized space that engages with the multiple discourses on environment in Bangladesh as well as creating the space for sustainable community building across many different social groups. We wanted to create an architecture of participation that embraces political economic power-structures and new media technologies to cooperate for the enhancement of a youth project. Reflecting on the complexity and desirability of such a synthesis, Cooks (2001) writes, "power has never been contained or possessed simply in people, objects or spaces, but in the interactions that produced perceptions of and consequences for their value" (p. 487). She reminds us of the nuances of looking at power and its complex relationship to transnational networked political economic spaces. Based on her observation, we have to be mindful of both manifestations of power in every step of the way: 1. as being fixed and perpetuating binarism and contributing to creating asymmetry and *also* 2. as being soft, dispersed and ultimately a more fluid process that needs certain complex social configurations to maintain the façade of functionalism to support itself.

The high-school and college bound youth are largely untapped demographics in discussions, deliberations and solution building in Bangladesh, so this participatory experiment was built to potentially redefine the way in which the youth engaged in social change. Also this demographic is so intimately connected to social media that it is no surprise that this new medium largely contributed to success and proliferation of this participatory network. The mobile and internet sector in Bangladesh has privatized some newly developed government and civil society attempts to create access by the under-privileged class to technology, vis-à-vis the Digital Bangladesh Initiatives already discussed above allude to some huge shifts in Bangladesh in the coming years. Cell-phone and internet users like the youth rely on their private and independent resources to have access to these technologies. Therefore in the context of Bangladesh, with the proliferation of internet technology in urban areas, especially in the capital city, Dhaka, the urban youth population is saturated with internet and cell-phone technology and the yearning to be connected to the outside world.

The on-ground and new media goals of BGreen were to develop a consistent, collaborative platform that unifies various dispersed youth environmental efforts under one roof to work jointly devoid of competition, but creating a safe space for building increased awareness and community action among the youth in urban, privileged areas. BGreen was successful in not only being able to generate interest via Facebook and Twitter prior to the event, but it would not be incorrect to say that social media has become the most effective way to maintain the momentum of the work that BGreen has continued to do. Social media has been one of the most important actants/actors in the process of realizing and sustaining BGreen's participatory network stability.

Again, drawing parallels to the Shahbag Movement, Parker Ziegler (2014) writes,

> This technique has remained highly specific to youth protestors, who have employed a combination of viral videos, Tweets, Facebook posts, and blogs to encourage both physical and cyber activism. This new technology has also allowed youth from around the world to play a role in these movements regardless of their geographic location.
>
> (cited in Alaldulal, 2014b)

This has gone a long way in challenging the power dynamics of typically "powerless" youth on the ground/in the periphery and the all-"powerful", large decision-making institutional bodies who are often placed at the core. Online activism is gaining momentum as youth often do not find easy access into traditional organizations to participate in dialogues due to the current limiting structures of epistemic communities that govern them that limits youth, "non-expert", or sometimes even localized participation. Also, specifically in the context of Bangladesh, online activism may be the safest route forward due to the ongoing political challenges that restrict people from safely participating on the ground. For example, the acute political challenges (strikes, road blockades, politically motivated street violence) that surrounded my action research created unavoidable, dangerous barriers and uncertainties towards the safe development of citizen-science initiatives like BGreen.

As Lopez (2010) writes in the context of global networked societies,

> the emergent practices of new media users, such as open source, peer-to-peer sharing, and creative commons, all of which are vital characteristics of living and open ecological systems. As such, the Internet has the potential to facilitate communities of practice, reassert a creative and cultural commons, and to be an organizational tool for people helping each other and to make connections.
>
> (p. 102).

The peer-to-peer platforms that were being created via new media networks allowed for the youth of both countries to unite—really create small, organic yet effective transnational creative, cultural commons, that used the scope and potentials of the internet and specifically, social media in a subversive way to express and formulate their discontents with business as usual. They emphasized the formation of subversive participatory networks in a brand new way—one which used Facebook and Twitter to spread the message and do meticulous organizing to build a social movement, by traversing the on ground instability that is brought on by the constant strikes and political turmoil on the streets. One of the main themes that emerged on why the youth insisted on the heavy use of new media technologies to assist in the building of our participatory network was how these technological systems could provide the youth with a powerful tool to challenge the limiting power structures of big institutions. For example, when the youth partners were asked about what strategy they would use to change the way in which educational industries operate in both the US and Bangladesh, a large number of them said that self-organizing via new media technologies (most often via Facebook and Twitter) was the route they endorsed. There were recurring themes of distrust and antipathy of any large, structural organizations and instead faith on the potentials of their own capacities when combined with new-media technologies. One such youth actor/actant said in an action research workshop in the US:

> This is the first ever environmental event that I have participated in and the ideas that we discussed and the brainstorming that generated action plans is something that will inspire me for months to come. But after that,

responsibilities will set in and such inspiration will become a distant memory. Our institutions will fail us again with uninspired, irrelevant training that has no interest to us. So I think using Facebook to spread the message and to do follow up on what will happen after the event is the way of keeping us notified and connected for future events and work opportunities, that we can engage ourselves with as a supplement to our educational pursuits.

(May 12, 2016)

This quote illuminates some shared challenges: the student's dissatisfaction with the educational system is obvious. However, it also brings into forefront the responsibility of the sustainability of projects like BGreen that is the importance of these projects to gain network stability. This would validate that such academic–community partnerships do not have to reside in the fringes as exceptional, isolated projects, but instead provide examples of creative, success stories from the emergent citizen sector. The growth of such participatory networks could push the educational institutions to transform themselves from inside out, by focusing in on the needs of the youth and larger society and hence achieving organizational *conscientização*.

More than 4 years after the event, due to our continued use of the medium in developing BGreen, as user and researcher, I encounter hundreds of new socially oriented youth groups that are formed and administered via Facebook on a very regular basis in order to mobilize global youth on urgent social causes. BGreen was one such cause that successfully found its audience through the expanding network that was made possible through Facebook and Twitter. Despite the problematic privatized structure of these social media sites that participate in data mining and privacy violation in the form of surveillance, these platforms are still free to users and presents itself to them in a way that starkly contrasts with the political and institutional confinement that the youth have been socialized to consider as being part of a "normal" existence. This lack of obvious institutional structure is what appeals to the youth and allows the medium to be a huge success, since all you need is a paid subscription to the internet from anywhere and then you can log into the endless possibilities and potentials of these social networking platforms—which the youth are taking full advantage of (especially in Bangladesh), without having to worry about their safety and institutional injustice, to name just a few things.

A large number of prominent or aspiring youth organizations, groups and individuals use social media platforms, especially Facebook and Twitter, aggressively to publicize their causes, big or small, non-profit or for-profit, work or pleasure. Even though there is a new wave of commendable but scattered youth environmental efforts (youth-led community organizations and projects) in both the US and Bangladesh that have been popping up in the last 5 years, a much more sustained use of new media and on-ground network building amongst all the efforts is desired. BGreen hoped to be the pioneer of these movements in the context of networked environmental social change. Some names of the prominent youth-led environmental organizations/communities are Bangladesh Youth Environmental Initiative, Bangladesh Youth for Climate Change, One Degree, Bangladesh Climate Justice Project, to name just a few (http://www.byei.org, http://bymc.weebly.com, http://1di.org), all three who were strategic partners with BGreen during the multiple participatory action research events in Dhaka.

All of these groups were doing different kinds of youth-led environmental activism projects sporadically and they lacked the consistency in their use of social media networks to sustain their organizing efforts, which in turn affected their ability to maintain the momentum of their on-ground presence. One of the big lessons of developing a participatory environmental platform is the importance of having an online identity, which does not equate to just having a modern, cell phone compatible website. Through developing BGreen in the last 2 years, one of my biggest lessons as the founder and initiator is the importance of having an active and dynamic Facebook and Twitter page, a requirement that supersedes the need for even having a website. This became apparent when one of our youth partners from Australia developed the first website for BGreen. Aesthetically and functionally the website was very well done, however, the community youth partners in Bangladesh, after looking at the website, all provided me with the same feedback.

They all expressed to me that while a website is important for the future of BGreen for an international audience, for example, for fundraising, however, for the purpose of connecting with the youth, it is almost irrelevant in the context of Bangladesh. One of the youth community partners, who has eventually become the lead new media manager of BGreen now, expressed this sentiment in one of the community meetings:

> First of all, this website needs to be made phone-adaptable, because absolutely no one in Dhaka will look at this from anything but a phone. Also, we need to really place our attention on building the Facebook and Twitter page with a lot of care, because that is how we will be able to reach the youth in Bangladesh.
>
> (Personal communication, December 17, 2013)

This comment was especially relevant coming from a young Bangladeshi male who was an undergraduate student in Computer Science running a successful web-designing start-up company on the side in Dhaka, Bangladesh. The other youth partners were in complete agreement with this and insisted on the speedy yet careful development of BGreen's social media pages. However, they were also quick to point out one of the challenges with the way in which some youth groups have run it in the past that have led to network instability and did not quite reach the stability of forming a long-term participatory network. From prior use of social media for youth organizing, the community actors pointed out that it was necessary for us to develop an interactive platform which is frequently updated and used by our community members, to avoid the pitfalls of other like projects in the past.

It is also important to note that the format and flexibility of Facebook allows more freedom in how the users and followers can interact with one another and make space for more in-depth and narrative forms of writing and communication. This feature adds to the popularity of Facebook in social organizing in Bangladesh over forms such as Twitter. Facebook allows users and followers to use it in more functional and logistical ways, such as creating events, making schedules and utilizing paid advertising, which are often important factors that determine the success of organizing and community building. However, Twitter is always used in complement with the former, especially more so, on the actual day of the event, to create "buzz" around the content, sometimes even on a minute to minute basis. For example, on the days of the action event, we had onsite social media managers, who just sat there in the workshop rooms the entire time to witness the event and do live updates to publicize the process. The live updates are done via twitter and Facebook, by capturing live videos, photographs and conversations that happen in the space and uploading them for view and discussion on the BGreen Facebook and Twitter pages.

Network building strategies

All the members of the different community organizations that I consulted before starting this project in the US and Bangladesh, unanimously emphasized the importance of utilizing Facebook and Twitter as the primary brand development, marketing and promotional tool of any youth-engaged project. As discussed earlier, the social media was not just set up as a point of publicity and marketing for BGreen. It was set up with the goals of providing an evolving, complex, deep and transnational participatory network platform for the global youth who wanted to continue to make an impact in the field of education, environment and sustainability. For BGreen on the ground in both the US and Bangladesh, the entire process of recruiting volunteers, facilitators, participants, even workshop leaders for the environmental action projects were administered and recruited through Facebook and Twitter, along with conducting traditional functions of mass media approaches, such as disseminating information about the project, keeping the online community updated on the details of the project, etc.

There was a core group of ten individuals for BGreen from both the US and Bangladesh, who were the co-organizers of the many participatory action events in both the US and Bangladesh and among them there were three people who were designated to handle the social media aspect of the growing movement. The three people who worked closely with me in crafting the social media pages, were selected based on their ability to be effective bi-lingual writers with prior experience in managing social media accounts beyond personal use. The face-to-face planning time was limited among the entire team as most of the planning happened long distance. I had started organizing about this project from the US, during summer and fall 2013 and when I was in Bangladesh for my initial fieldwork, the political instability did not allow for frequent in-person meetings. Hence, the social media coordinators who were both from the US and Bangladesh, had to pull out all stops to essentially build the BGreen online brand from scratch—based on instinct as well as keen thinking on what our needs and goals were as a platform.

The BGreen social media team and I were aware of the challenges in developing an interactive and dynamic social media space, that encouraged conversations and engagement rather than just resorting to the classic one-way internet information dissemination. Also, the second challenge was the very short window of time, to develop and create a whole new brand in front of the eyes of the youth in both the US and Bangladesh who are very Facebook and Twitter savvy and are bombarded with new and upcoming social causes very frequently. Despite these very real limitations, the team went forward fearlessly in carefully crafting the image and constructing the page in order to create our own identity as a youth social movement, one that was designed to collaborate rather than compete with other youth environmental projects that are popular today.

The website for BGreen was simultaneously developed by a French-Australian web-developer, who worked with me closely via Skype in developing a web-home for it that justified the movement and the visions, which upon completion, was synced with the Facebook and Twitter pages. Also, BGreen's Facebook and Twitter handles were working collaboratively with the unprecedented journalistic coverage (TV, print and radio) that BGreen received in Bangladesh. For every feature that was done on BGreen in mainstream media, the social media team at BGreen amplified the coverage, by sharing it via the social networking sites. In the current media scene in Bangladesh, it is considered quite irresponsible if a project that has been endorsed by mainstream media is not shared widely in social media networks, a point which the writers and editors did not hesitate to tell the BGreen social media team repeatedly. Hence, this merging of separate actor processes is a crucial point for the ANT-PAR networked analysis, since it brings forth the importance of combining multi-actors/actants to really shape and reshape the becoming of a participatory network.

Through the use of social networking, a new way of building transnational participatory networks to aid the environmental social movement was made possible before, during and after the research process. BGreen's Facebook Page and to a lesser extent the Twitter page, became a space for the global youth to understand the purpose and goals of my action research and whether they were interested in joining this participatory environmental justice program that allowed for voice of their unregulated opinions on environmental social justice that bypasses the rigid institutional structures of universities and civil society organizations. While the enrolment process happened on the ground, as well as the committed actors who joined the BGreen participatory network, this same process of enrolment took a completely different scope via the use of new media technologies.

The number of global youth that started becoming active users of Facebook rose dramatically and in the context of ANT, the social network pages became OPPs, non-human actants, that were key and mandatory entities through which communication and information about this emerging network filtered through. Social media pages in combination with the youth social media managers created a collaborative architecture of participation of the BGreeners online to engage in the Freirian process shifting from magical and naïve consciousness to critical consciousness. Many youth, who had never attended a BGreen event in both the US or Bangladesh or any other social change platform previously, sent frequent messages to us to Facebook, expressing their thankfulness to us for creating a space for them to engage in social issues related to environmental and educational issues. Also, these letters often included their inquiries on how they could get engaged in future BGreen projects as active global youth citizens committed to social change.

Hence, the moral of the story was that if a new project cannot hold the attention of people on Facebook and Twitter, then the project will likely have trouble in engaging citizens on the ground in being part of projects that are designed for social change and transformation. It is important to note, that the purpose and nature of the BGreen Facebook and Twitter pages have shifted in the last 2 years quite distinctly. While the team worked hard to create an interactive space for the subscribers, at the time of inception, the page was largely under-utilized by the youth participants who were engaged in my research despite our best efforts in encouraging dialogue. For example, prior to the first action research event that happened in January 2014 in Dhaka, Bangladesh, despite our continuous attempts to make the space interactive, very minimal interaction actually happened. For example, the team of youth partners who were managing the pages had run similar social media projects before, since the use of social media is very active in all commercial/non-commercial youth-led events in Bangladesh. Hence upon discussion with all the other actors, they had clarified to one another that we were going to craft our interactions as dialogues and questions that are inclusive, rather than having only a one-way information delivery process.

However, some of those goals were inconsistent at that time, due to the needs of the larger BGreen network to really establish itself first as a new identity in the youth scene in Bangladesh. Hence, prior to the action research event, the use of the online space was more one-sided as much as we tried to avoid this, as we really needed to build our brand identity first. In its inception stages, we needed to share administrative and logistical details to the youth about the progress of our planning in the midst of all the political chaos. We needed to send constant updates to the youth that the event was indeed happening amidst all the political uncertainty and used images from our planning meetings, conversations and broad partnership goals to develop the language around BGreen. We did not have a lot to work with in developing the language around BGreen, until a week prior to the event, when we had our official banners, t-shirts, pamphlets printed and our workshop leaders confirmed. In the week building up to the event, we created an attractive preview of what the youth could look forward to, always keeping in mind that absolutely everything could still be cancelled due to road violence even on the day of the event.

As I just mentioned, we had a dearth of what we could use to promote the event in the initial stages, since it had not happened before and hence we did not have any multi-media content (photographs, videos, etc.) to attract the youth in a complex way. This is why developing media networks (TV, print, radio and online portals) simultaneously was an important need to achieve network stability, since in the beginning of the process, their amplification before the event added depth to our social media networks. Having traditional media exposure added a sense of validation for the youth who were following us on the Facebook and Twitter pages. These simultaneous and concurrent actor networks between industries and actors added the necessary depth and legitimacy to such a new, innovative academic–community project, since in the eyes of the media consumer, anything being featured in national media is of some level of relevance and importance socially, which makes national media a non-human OPP of the project.

Over time, the convergence of media and new media networks, two non-human actants, really has become the strength of the BGreen project, where they both build off each other's strengths and aid in the process of network stability and over time, achieving participatory networks. Now the ongoing episodes of BGreen as produced by Amherst Media play a big role in sustaining the discussions of BGreen among the transnational, global youth in both the US and Bangladesh, by circulating the episodes using social media networks. This goes on to show the importance of ANT in navigating this limitation of PAR, which has no mechanism to evaluate or make sense of the relational dynamics between human and non-human actors/actants. The use of the Facebook and Twitter pages changed considerably after the participatory action research and the new discourses that were formed and generated via workshops seemed to transform the way in which the social media networks were operating. It distinctly took a more engaging and conversational shape, post event, which is growing stronger even now, where the youth participants, even outside of the ones who are the youth co-organizers post regularly on our page.

This happened for a variety of different reasons. We had more content to display and talk about in videos, photos, audio recordings, experiences that we could build of on, that the youth were part of, hence creating a community online, one which included them in the flourishing of BGreen's identity via social networks. Also, with the deepening of our relationship with journalists and media houses, our press coverage has become much more frequent, which allowed for cross-network alliance building, which was made possible in an interactive platform such as Facebook and Twitter. We have found a big group of loyalists on our social media page who are engaged with our cause in different ways.

Their interactions are of three kinds: 1. they post relevant environmental/educational articles that they find important in the context of global youth, which often sparks conversations among loyal followers; 2. they respond to our frequent post on Facebook and Twitter about BGreen and our politics; 3. they pose questions that relate to BGreen events. This points to the importance of the reliance of diverse actors/actants in shaping such a participatory network, where the synergy between both working simultaneously to make the process deeper, stronger and sustained and brings forth the importance of time in developing truly participatory networks. The importance of maintaining prominence through active academic–community youth work, beyond the first action research event and our continued use of the social media site in the last two years, has resulted in the building of this trust amongst the social media users, where over time, they feel like they are part of a larger, community, one where they refer to themselves as "BGreeners" and feel at home in the platform to voice their ideas, their relevant projects and pose questions to one another.

Now, more than 4 years after the first action research event, which was the official period of my fieldwork, BGreen's current youth team and I have to work harder than ever to maintain our social media presence. Two of the youth community partners have committed themselves to handling the Facebook and Twitter pages. They are keeping the momentum going in a number of different ways: they update the photos frequently, do daily (sometimes twice daily) posts in the Facebook Page on interesting articles, videos or opportunities that are related to youth, environment and education and of course keep the BGreen event updates going as/when required. This points to the need to move away from the concept of a closed, automatic black box in ANT, that assumes that after networks gain stability, they can sustain themselves—it becomes "common sense and automatic". In the social media aspect of participatory community building in BGreen, the use of black box as a concept did not fit in, since the process never became automatic—it needed continuous work, redefinition and remolding to maintain the momentum of the online identity of BGreen.

Another important point to consider is the big impact of the cross-media pollination between social media networks and other media houses. Since the PAR-ANT project is currently one of the two biggest, most prominent youth environmental projects in Bangladesh and there is conversation among our core actors/actants about whether we should register it to become a non-profit, the social media managers are more than ever creating deeper alliances with the media houses, so that the project stays alive in the media. Any articles that are written about us in the media are cross-posted on our social media pages to add complexity to the participatory network that we are trying to build. BGreen has been able to maintain the social media presence over a continued period of time, which has allowed the project to gain acceptance and validation from the social media users, who now know how to differentiate this project from many other isolated environmental youth projects that could not sustain themselves for a variety of reasons.

One of the other innovative recent strategies of the BGreen social media managers to maintain interest among its followers, is to create short, interesting event wrap-up documentaries that include the youth's voices and perspectives in a neatly produced video, which often also features the workshop leaders. Here are two examples of such video narratives that were filmed and edited by the youth community partners of BGreen for some recent BGreen action workshops: <https://www.youtube.com/watch?v=a8yKBetJ0S8> and <https://www.youtube.com/watch?v=CA6aukEaAB>.

The youth constructing these videos, to represent the opinions, ideas and visions of the youth and making all the final decisions on what to include and what to emit from the final cut, is an active process of social engagement and creation of new discourses. This approach is consistent with what Geddes and Choi (2015) advocate for in amplifying PAR-ANT projects of this nature, where they point at the limitations of just using mass media as a way of disseminating the information about BGreen and instead advocate for the use of a more decentralized approach of social media:

> This dynamic was reproduced in the media strategy with its focus on managed circulation of information that limited the potential for extensive horizontal forms of communication among the public at large. Future experiments may want to focus on the potential offered by the public as an actor, particularly those who participated in the deliberations. In this instance social media will play a central role . . . . Alternatives to the mainstream media by way of blogs and social media offer a range of interesting and complementary possibilities for the circulation of information.
>
> (p. 207)

Hence, this focus on developing personalized yet stylized videos on the workshop experience has been a huge advantage for sustaining interest in our social media networks and using our own multi-media in collaboration with it to create community building and amplification of the project has made a huge difference in keeping the interest of the youth participants. The youth who are participating in the events often feel very proud to be featured in a video that they can share in their massive social networks and hence, the project and its ideas proliferated, by adding newer actors/actants along the way. Another innovative idea was presented to the entire group by the creative, young Bangladeshi youth partners of BGreen, in a post event meeting in the summer of 2014, where we were all brainstorming on how to keep the project alive in a meaningful participatory way. Consistent with Geddes and Choi's (2015) recommendations, the youth expressed interest in making a feature length documentary on an annual basis that encapsulates the yearly achievements of BGreen as a participatory network. They write:

> A good documentary film/video of WWViews activities and outcomes would, much like the social media, certainly overcome the 'event' syndrome of the major media and highlight the complexities and nuances of the 'process' in ways that are nevertheless accessible. Such a documentary might capture the excitement and enthusiasm most people have observed at the citizen deliberations. Another advantage is that it ensures greater control over a coherent message that can be readily distributed.
>
> (p. 207)

One of our international organizational partners happens to be a US non-profit that is founded by a leading Hollywood actor, with special interest in environment, education and social change. We negotiated with his organization about this proposed documentary project by the youth, since we need to raise significant funding for it to become an annual project that is managed by the youth. If this project materializes, this would be another potent example of combining media and Freirian educational narratives to frame the goals of the youth-led BGreen participatory network.

Potentials of social media in transforming academic–community engagements in Bangladesh

As mentioned earlier, there is inadequate existing research on the uses and scope of social networking sites in Bangladesh. This case study brings into the forefront details that may change the way people in Bangladesh and beyond understand the growth and sustenance of such academic–activist projects with the help of participatory network building via Facebook and Twitter. The concept of translation in Actor Network Theory (ANT) in which "Innovators attempt to create a forum, a central network in which all the actors agree that the network is worth building and defending" (Tatnall, 2012, p. 112).

It is a key theoretical point that supports the growth of this participatory action project on the ground and online. The process was new for everyone involved— BGreen was the merging of many different individuals, communities, organizations and industries in the context of contemporary Bangladesh. The role of new media technologies, especially, social media networks in the "production, validation and circulation of knowledge" (Harvey, 2014, p. 21) cannot be underestimated in this process. Hence, using new media technologies to develop online plat- forms that are complementary to on-ground, community-based platforms like BGreen is an essential part of participatory network building today, especially in projects that require transnational, multi-institutional participation and youth engagement.

Such diverse multi-media networks can take socially engaged efforts like BGreen that are conceptualized first as events in physical space, to a different level of citizen engagement, all the while utilizing the benefits of technological actors/actants working closely with human actors/actants. Social media with its reach in Bangladesh and over time with the maturity of the project can be the most integral tool to bring about a shift in public environmental citizen science discourses. Combining new media with the voices of the youth is resulting in creative multi- media productions and is facilitating emergent spaces for the youth to have conversations about new, relevant topics online. New media networks are actively shaping and reshaping a participatory network, which is bringing forth new discourses and new ways of making sense of citizen dissatisfaction over a common cause. Such a shift aids in the process of developing the youth's *conscientização*, which Friere (1970a) describes as being the moment when "humankind *emerge* from their *submersion* and acquire the ability to *intervene* in reality as it is unveiled" (p. 109).

In order to exercise their critical consciousness, the global youth are using the social media networks for processes beyond their personal purposes. They are using these sites for not only community engagement, activism work, but by participating in these networked spaces actively, they are redefining the way in which theoretical knowledge gets applied to real world challenges. The global youth are choosing the language that they want to use to communicate the issues at hand to one another, without the interference of expert epistemic communities that have their specific insular ways of producing and disseminating information. Quite to the contrary, social media is allowing the youth to challenge these traditional bound epistemic communities and knowledge forts and instead finding their own, creative ways of exploring, internalizing and then disseminating the knowledge.

Traditionally generative spaces have become stifling to the creation of new knowledge and discourses, as previously identified in chapters that explain the state of educational structures in higher education in the US and Bangladesh. The success of BGreen in sustained youth engagement shows a radically different potential, one where youth are uniting via these online platforms over common issues and goals to make a combined social impact by being involved in action projects that build social awareness around diverse issues related to education, environment and social change. New media promises an effective route towards forming sustained, deep and meaningful participatory networks and the route through which Freire's powerful concept of *conscientização* could be potentially achieved. In order to bypass such a limiting structural knowledge system that is prevalent in the US and Bangladesh, increasing numbers of global youth are using the online sphere in transformative ways to create a community of ideas, action and social change and expanding the scope of platforms like Facebook and Twitter to meaningfully engage with their contexts and work towards developing their *conscientização* which helps them "perceive social, political and economic contradictions, and to take action against the oppressive elements of reality" (Friere, 1970a, p. 35).

Just merely syncing the organizing work on the ground with their online social media goals is an important first step towards building participatory networks that have *conscientização* at the core of it. Our collective inspirations and ideas of reinvisioning a different way of producing and using knowledge is finding a physical form in the shape of BGreen and as much as possible, their feedback, needs and participation is informing the way in which this participatory network is being constituted and reconstituted. The global youth's actions are helping to build new discourses on what engaged citizenry can look like, with the help of technological innovations with multi-institutional support despite very limited funding. Through the participation of the youth in academic–community partnership projects such as BGreen, they are contributing actively to changing the insular, socially disengaged model of higher education in Bangladesh today and really challenging the power that resides within the epistemic communities that are trying to hold on to a model of insular, top-down education. Power is being dispersed in this process in the way in which actor networks are supposed to play out, reducing the binarism inherent to processes that separate citizens from experts, youth from epistemic communities. The state of power, institutional, epistemic and expert power, is challenged via decentralization processes like this. Castree and MacMillan (2001) write,

> To see power as a wholly human attribute which is concentrated rather than dispersed is, therefore, to be deceived. It is also to overstate the power of power. Once power is seen as a relational achievement—not a monopolizable

capacity radiating from a single center or social system—then it becomes possible to identify multiple points (neither social nor natural but both simultaneously) at which network stability can be contested.

(p. 214)

It makes us look at "big" power in a different way, which is made evident through the formation of these youth social media networks. I advocate for a weak version of ANT like Castree and Macmillan (2003) that really engages with this idea in a much more nuanced, cautious and guarded way, paying close attention to the fact that not all actor networks are equal or the same, hence moving away from the flattening of the process. They acknowledge that,

> these processes are social and natural but not in equal measure, since it is the social relations that are disproportionately directive; that agents, while social, natural, and relational vary greatly in their powers to influence others; that power while dispersed, can be directed by some (namely, specific "social" actors) more than others.

(p. 222)

In the specific case of BGreen, this dispersion is happening via the clever use of social media networks by youth actors who are at a strategic disadvantage in comparison to larger, political economic structures. BGreen was able to provide them with institutional support that were powerful actors/actants in the BGreen network. However the way in which the youth actors enrolled the non-human actants of social media networks to add complexity to an already deepening process enhanced the on-ground affiliations and also allowed BGreen to overcome the other major non-human actant in the process, the political instability. Hence, the complex power dynamics between the human and non-human actants were reconstituted through an unexpected and unique mix of factors.

On a global scale, the Shahbag movement also demonstrates direct youth challenge to power in Bangladesh. This was an example of a "growing transnational fervor for generational struggle, in which today's global youth are using new technologies to oppose and overcome the outdated political systems that have long kept the peoples of their nations voiceless" (Alaldulal, 2014a). BGreen is following a similar route, but the fight is being fought for a different cause—education and the environment. By using social media as an academic–activist sustenance platform, the youth are using these networks subversively since the mainstream critique of Facebook and Twitter is one which attacks these networks for contributing to social detachment, isolation, narcissism. Instead the youth in Bangladesh are doing exactly the opposite, they are using these new media networks as a way to express and manifest their emergent consciousness which is connecting to larger political and structural social struggles that is shaping their experiences as youth who have been institutionally marginalized in multi-institutional settings. They are using these new media networks towards expressing their political and social desires about actively constructing new narratives of engaging with their social realities and transforming their lived, structural realities aimed towards social good. The actors/actants are working actively to create an "architecture of participation" among the stakeholders that is operating without the support of traditional institutions.

However, the way in which the global youth actors have designed the social media networks can only benefit these organization structures. For example, CSD ULAB, based in the university in Dhaka, Bangladesh that hosted us, in a post-event actor/actant meeting, expressed their admiration for the productive and effective ways in which our social media and mass media efforts have converged. They expressed their desire to use this strategy for their future events, even though they acknowledged that orchestrating this requires an efficient, visionary group of people. Bangladeshi scholars, Jahan and Ahmed (2012) advocate for the use of new media technologies, especially social media networks, in transforming academia in higher-educational institutions in Bangladesh today. According to them, academic institutions should incorporate social media in their classrooms in relevant ways that are useful to the advancement of a socially engaged, grounded curriculum (Jahan & Ahmed, 2012).

Jahan and Ahmed (2012) also write, "Although there is no central policy regarding social media use, some academic departments in Bangladeshi universities have adopted stringent rules against using social network sites in students' computing labs and public access computers" (p. 14). They advocate for academic institutions to make use of new media technologies, since they can be used in a myriad of useful ways, an example being the youth's participation in academic– action projects such as BGreen. The nature of the youth's use of these online spaces to articulate their ideas and visions is potentially transformative. Harvey (2014) writes in the US context,

> Through these new platforms lie the potential for groups once understood simply as *end users* or *consumers* of information to become active participants and producers, assuming multiple roles as they view, respond to, amend, and share content within and among different communities of interest or practice.
>
> (p.23)

BGreen will at its best bring about shifts in the ways in which epistemic communities are shaped, formed and defined and the potential of such communities for developing sustained participatory networks that hold the potential of changing the power dynamics of the inherent structure and potentially affecting policy. Harvey (2014) points to the fact that "openness and participation are fluid concepts, and spaces for participation are contingent on a diversity of factors, including, in this case, the types of tools or resources made available for users to participate" (p. 25) and hence, the overall architecture of participation that was created by the use of social networks, was an integral part of deepening and adding complexity to the multi-layered emergent participatory network of BGreen.

While the new media space is also controlled, in the case of BGreen, these new media technologies as an actant have "fundamentally shaped the forms of openness and participation that have emerged from within the network" (Harvey, 2014, p. 27). A noteworthy shift happened in the use of new media technologies and social media networks in developing the brand of BGreen. The new media team inadvertently assumed the role of an OPP who were in charge of designing the architecture and content of BGreen. This is especially true almost 2 years into the project where apart from doing infrequent posts on the BGreen Facebook page, I barely contribute anything to the maintenance and sustenance of it. My only contribution to this aspect of participatory network building is to respond to their requests of communication with organizations/people/networks that want to reach out to me as the Founder and keeping a very relaxed eye on the content/ discussions that are generated in it.

Hence, since global youth are the main content and knowledge creators on the social media networks, this challenged the idea of epistemic communities, as "expert" topics are being communicated by them using social media as a channel of building new discourses on education, environment, youth engagement and social change. However, Harvey (2014) cautions and "calls on knowledge intermediaries to reflect more closely on the roles they (and others) play in opening or limiting these spaces, and to whom" (p. 29) and also creates the need to be constantly aware of power dynamics in the building of such an architecture of participation. This also points to the necessity of moving beyond that of ANT's black box and instead building open, complex, hybrid participatory networks, that are informed by the depth and complexity of the multitude of human and non-human actors that interact via the BGreen social media pages or the website.

In conclusion, Facebook and Twitter was an integral part of the development and success of BGreen, an environmental action movement and BGreen was able to navigate, procure and translate social media technologies to aid in the growth and formation of an emerging transnational participatory network. The design, strategy and intelligent use of these online platforms ultimately impacted the participation, promotion and impact of BGreen in both the US, Bangladesh and beyond. Hence, through such new media participatory networks a subversive "architecture of participation" (Harvey, 2011) was created for the youth involved in the process that transcended rigid institutional hierarchy and other non-human actant barriers such as ongoing political chaos. Hence, the rebellion of the youth in using new media in innovative ways to bring about social change, may be an important factor that holds the power to change the way in which academic institutions, community organizations and youth collaborate to bring about a shift in the current educational model and to bring about sustained social change.

Bibliography

Ahmed, A. M. (2009). Media, politics and the emergence of democracy in Bangladesh. *Canadian Journal of Media Studies*, 5(1): 50–69.

Alaldulal (2014a). Placing the voices of Shahbag in modern narratives of transnational youth protest – part 1. *Alalodulal*. Available at: https://alalodulal.org/2014/02/10/the-youth-in-riot-again/

Alaldulal (2014b). Placing the voices of Shahbag in modern narratives of transnational youth protest – part 2. *Alalodulal*. Available at: https://alalodulal.org/2014/02/12/youth-in-riot-2/

Alhassan, A. (2005). Market valorization in broadcasting policy in Ghana: Abandoning the quest for media democratization. *Media, Culture & Society*, 27(2): 211–228.

Bunz, M. (2010). BBC's education service Janala has delivered 1m lessons in three months. http://www.guardian.co.uk/media/pda/2010/feb/17/bbc-bangladesh-janala-lessons. Accessed 15 Nov 2012.

Callon, M. (1987). Society in the making: The study of technology as a tool for sociological analysis. In W. E. Bijker, T. P. Hughes and T. Pinch (eds) *The social construction of technological systems: New directions in the sociology and history of technology*. Cambridge, MA: The MIT Press, pp. 83–103.

Castree, N. & MacMillan, T. (2001). Dissolving dualisms: Actor-networks and the reimagination of nature. In N. Castree and B. Braun (eds) *Social nature: Theory, practice, and politics*. Malden, MA: Blackwell Publishers, pp. 208–224.

Cooks, L. (2001). From distance and uncertainty to research and pedagogy in the borderlands: Implications for the future of intercultural communication. *Communication Theory*, 11(3): 339–351.

Couldry, N. (2009). Rethinking the politics of voice: Commentary. *Continuum*, 23(4): 579–582.

Couldry, N. (2012). *Media, society, world: Social theory and digital media practice*. Cambridge: Polity Press.

Das, J. (2012). Environmental journalism in Bangladesh: Active social agency. *Journalism Studies*, 13(2): 226–242.

Elahi, M. (2013). "They are not different from others": Ethical practices and corruption in Bangladeshi journalism. *Journal of Mass Media Ethics*, 28(3): 189–202.

Freire, P. (1970a). *Pedagogy of the oppressed*. New York: Continuum.

Ganim, M. A. M. & Kamruzzaman, M. (2014, March). E-governance using social network: A model for strong democratic environment in Bangladesh. In *Computer and Information Technology (ICCIT), 2013 16th International Conference on* (pp. 218–223).

Geddes, H. & Choi, S. Y. (2015). 10 Media strategy and networks at the margins of global biodiversity governance. In M. Rask & R. Worthington (eds) *Governing Biodiversity through Democratic Deliberation*. Abingdon: Routledge.

Giroux, H. A. (2013). Youth in revolt: *Reclaiming a democratic future*. Boulder: Paradigm.

Haas, P. (2001). Policy knowledge: Epistemic communities. In N. J. Smelser & B. Baltes (eds) *International Encyclopedia of the Social & Behavioral Sciences*. Oxford: Pergamon Press.

Hanitzsch, T. (2007). Deconstructing journalism culture: Toward a universal theory. *Communication Theory*, 17(4): 367–385.

Harvey, B. (2014). Negotiating openness across science, ICTs, and participatory development: Lessons from the AfricaAdapt network. *Open Development: Networked Innovations in International Development*, 7(1): 275.

Hussain, F. & Ullah, M. S. (2013). Mobile and internet communication: Privacy risks for youth in Bangladesh. *Media Watch*, 4(2): 134–144.

Jahan, I. & Ahmed, S. Z. (2012). Students' perceptions of academic use of social networking sites: A survey of university students in Bangladesh. *Information Development*, 28(3): 235–247.

Kepes, G. (2016). Breaching the divide: "Hole in the wall" computer kiosks for education and development in urban Bangladesh. In J. Servaes & T. Oyedemi (eds) *The praxis of social inequality in media: A global perspective*. Lanham, MD: Lexington Books.

Krøvel, R., Ytterstad, A. & Orgeret, K. S. (2012). Objectivity and advocacy in global warming journalism scientific knowledge, local experiences and concern among students in Nicaragua, Nepal and Bangladesh. *Asia Pacific Media Educator*, 22(1): 15–28.

López, A. (2010). Defusing the Cannon/Canon: An Organic Media Approach to Environmental Communication. *Environmental Communication*, 4(1): 99–108.

Pachi, D. & Barrett, M. (2012). Perceived effectiveness of conventional, non-conventional and civic forms of participation among minority and majority youth. *Human Affairs*, 22(3): 345–359.

Pachi, D., Garbin, D. & Barrett, M. (2010). Processes of political (and civic) engagement and participation in the London area: Views from British Bangladeshi and Congolese youth. In *Civic, Political and Cultural Engagement Among Migrants, Minorities and National Populations: Multidisciplinary Perspectives*, June 29th–30th 2010, Centre for Research on Nationalism, Ethnicity and Multiculturalism (CRONEM), University of Surrey, Guildford. (Unpublished).

Rahman, A. (2011). A political economy of the emerging television news industry in Bangladesh. *Revista Eptic*, 11(2).

Rahman, A. (2014). The Problems with Reimagining Public Media in the Context of Global South. *Stream: Culture/Politics/Technology*, 6(1), 56–65.

Straubhaar, R. (2014). A place for organisational critical consciousness: Comparing two case studies of Freirean nonprofits. *Comparative Education*, 50(4), 433-447.

Tatnall, A. (ed.). (2012). *Social influences on information and communication technology innovations*. IGI Global.

6 Youth reflections, growth and sustenance of BGreen participatory network

This chapter explores BGreen's global youth community organizers as community action agents and how their identities are negotiated when attaching themselves to academic–community institutions as independent and important stakeholders. This chapter brings the discussion full circle, as it brings into the forefront the voices and perspectives of the global youth who are participating in this academic–community project, which was designed to provide an alternative to the way in which both US and Bangladeshi youth could navigate the academic and community organizations that they are affiliated with. As already discussed extensively, there is a need for a shift in the educational model in both the US and Bangladesh to one that puts student needs, ideas and aspirations at the core of their goals and makes youth participation, engagement and deliberation a center piece that can benefit from the established structural and political economic strengths of local, international and transnational multi-institutions and industries. This chapter solely focuses on the voices of the global youth community organizers of BGreen from both the US and Bangladesh, many of whom shared similar concerns regarding their voices in education, community engagement and social change.

The salient themes that emerged out of the process from the perspective of the youth is narrated and analyzed in this chapter in a more direct and exclusive way. This provides a deeper insight into the voices of global youth community organizers that were present in the prior chapters who participated actively in developing the architecture of BGreen in the US, Bangladesh and beyond. Through BGreen, a re-organization of the way in which these institutions and industries are currently structured and operationalized was attempted and in most ways that I had set out to conduct in this PAR-ANT project, we were able to create a new, creative process and space for the youth to engage and articulate themselves in a transnational participatory network of change and growing stability and proliferation. The global youth created effective participatory mechanisms in both countries to engage in action research classrooms, workshops, trainings, multi-media, deliberations, etc. All of these were specifically designed in a participatory manner for them to engage in a Freirian way of generating knowledge, but they were also direct actors/actants in creating the architecture, strategy and form of BGreen as a participatory network which has Freire's *conscientização* as a defining concept.

Through this PAR-ANT process, the global youth actively co-created the strategic and structural processes, like they normally are, in order to uphold the idea of epistemic communities, hence separating "average" citizens from so-called experts. The inclusion of the youth in important decision-making around creating this architecture and content, was a process that the youth showed tremendous enthusiasm for and capability in assuming leadership roles in many aspects of the process as delineated in my accounts so far. In many of the contexts demonstrated earlier, the youth were able to move from a magical or naïve state of consciousness to critical consciousness and apply it in a myriad of different ways in building the architecture of BGreen. The evolving process continues to this day as the global youth are continuing to redefine the transnational BGreen participatory network in unexpected and fruitful ways.

The voices of the youth who were actively engaged in developing this architecture of participation have been interspersed throughout the chapters that preceded this one. Their involvement in shaping and making the brand of BGreen from the nascent stages to what it is now broke away from the traditional binarism that often defines tightly guarded expert communities that are reinforced by the so-called functionalism and determination of political economic structures. The youth were the main inspiration behind BGreen and it was designed to involve them in the reorganization of transnational institutional structures as it flowed through the US and Bangladesh.

At the time of inception of this project in the US, there was no expectation of what would follow, even though there were hopes of continuing with a project that so many people globally had come together to make possible. The emergence of a BGreen participatory network based on the ongoing participatory action research work was welcomed by all the actors (individual and institutional) in both the US and Bangladesh that had enrolled into this actor network in its inception phase. The needs and aspirations of the youth found a home in the development and growth of this transnational academic–community project, since it allowed the youth to think about the connections between their education, transnational alliance building of engaged communities and intersections in their interests in brand new ways. In all the previous body chapters, I narrated the ways in which the youth were integral to the deepening of the BGreen participatory network through various political economic and network processes and how they were key to the process of translating this ANT-PAR process that eventually was gaining shape as a participatory network. However, for the purpose of this chapter, the commentary about the youth's participation was extracted from the notes taken on the interactions and conversations generated in the action research classrooms, workshops, trainings, etc over the course of the last 4 and a half years of continuing to build the participatory network of BGreen in both the US and Bangladesh.

An analysis of these texts presents new discourses of global, mobilized, empowered youth on how to be active social change agents in using Freirian frames to connect their personal struggles to larger political and structural realities. It is important to map out youth voices, ideas and aspirations due to the possibilities that emerge when global youth from the US and Bangladesh engage in an academic–community participatory action project that has been specifically designed to address Bangladesh's current educational and environmental needs. The dialectics between market exchange, and how it is appropriated by the youth actors involved is explored here. This is fertile and shape-shifting ground, where we can grapple with the complexity of networked political economic (Busch & Juska, 1997) spaces. This requires us to go beyond the determination of the economy, market, and institutions as being fixed, bound and predetermined and instead urges us to reflect on human agency, and free will, even though there are always structural constraints that shape the flow of these subjectivities and discourses.

From the experience of working with multi-community actors/actants in this PAR project, communication, cooperation and collaboration emerge as being building blocks of such a youth-engaged participatory network. Their spoken word can be analyzed based on the discourses that inform them in order to understand the important frames upon which these discursive spaces have been built. These can be complex and often contradictory discourses, "but one discourse is usually hegemonic, and thus it tends to constitute the general conditions under which dominant members of a society 'know' their world" (Bergold & Thomas, 2012, p. 215). Swidler (1986) defines discourses as "not what anyone says, but the system of meanings that allows them to say anything at all" (p. 75). Hence, the architecture of the BGreen transnational participatory network is a systematic discursive shift, albeit a small one, that is negotiating the tight space between political economic structures and the potentialities of youth on the ground globally.

Berg (2009) reminds us that in order to assess discourses we must "inquire into not only which social groups benefit from discursive power, but also, how group and individual identities (subjectivities) are constituted in power relations" (Berg, 2009, p. 219) within a discursive framework. Subsequently, a solution-building approach that fosters civic engagement and democratic social change (Lopez, 2010) which is "lively, dynamic, interactive . . . and messy" (Lopez, 2010, p. 105) in the context of the education and environment is desirable and necessary and built from the foundation of complex (and often contradictory) discourses. Hence, through the designing of the process of citizen science engagement with the global youth along with the actual ideas generated in the event process itself, there was potential to generate and develop alternative youth discourses that have the potential to shape the future direction of multi-institutional, academic–community collaborations in Bangladesh.

Lopez (2010) writes, "I have learned that we must find new communication models that don't rely on the same modes of thought that brought us to the current crisis, in particular models that respect and encourage biodiverse voices in a fluid and participatory manner. The 'shallow' method of environmental communication, I suggest, is 'mechanistic' and mass-market oriented" (p. 100). Lopez (2010) instead advocates for what he calls a "deep" method that is designed for open and local contexts, much like the participatory action research approach taken to develop BGreen as a transnational academic–community engaged citizen science platform. Hence, new discourses are created not only through the conversations that ensued in the action research workshops, but also through their very multi-faceted *actions* of participation in the building of the transnational architecture of BGreen.

To reiterate, the process of enrollment in ANT translation was crucial to BGreen, since it allowed for a new opportunity for the global youth to get engaged, which from the ANT perspective was better than other choices available at a given moment, which was crucial to building the actor network (Latour, 1987). The way in which the youth negotiated their needs, frustrations, aspirations and desires in working with other human and non-human actants adds complexity to the building and sustenance of the transnational BGreen participatory network. Engaging in projects like BGreen, its community partners and youth participants were beginning to spread rays of hope through the cracks of a dysfunctional, neoliberal system and below are some of the salient, transformative moments that really aided in the process of developing a subversive, small but expanding participatory network called BGreen.

Youth voices and the BGreen experience

As an example, it is useful to summarize some numbers from the very first action research event that happened in Dhaka, Bangladesh in Dec 2013: about 87 participants actively participated in the action research conference from a wide range of institutions with some coming from far-flung urban, coastal cities of Bangladesh. There were more males (73 percent) than females (27 percent) and more university students (73 percent) than High School students (27 percent). An overwhelming 98 percent of the participants felt that they discussed the different topics constructively and that they were actively listening and following the content as well as being respectfully treated by the youth facilitators and community partners. About 72 percent from the sample absolutely agreed that BGreen motivated them to get personally involved in societal issues on education and environment, an important statistic that will be qualitatively explored later in the chapter.

In the case of US action research classrooms in different US higher educational institutions as well as in academic–community engaged action research workshops conducted, the responses are also very encouraging. One student in an action research classroom in a private college in Massachusetts said, "This community engaged classroom and the BGreen experience has enabled me to not only engage my theories that I learn into on ground projects, but to also create multi-media outputs in collaboration with many kinds of stakeholders to bring lasting impact for my effort by creating awareness about my project, my work, my passions". The youth participant was involved in multiple multi-media BGreen projects that were produced in the US for a global, international and local audience. Hence, the process of developing citizen science initiatives and its content like BGreen could be ideal processes for global youth to come together with other students, professionals and educators from multiple industries to sit together and deliberate on the directions that they would want to go with issues of education, environment, climate change and their personal and national futures.

Based on their long experiences of working with youth in academic–community youth participatory projects, Cammarota and Fine (2008) point out, "YPAR teaches young people that conditions of injustice are produced not natural; are designed to privilege and oppress; but are ultimately challengeable and thus changeable (p. 2)". Consistent with this scholar duo's ideas, youth driven PAR (YAR) projects like BGreen, work with Freire's ideas of *conscientização* very closely, which really is meant to deconstruct the world that we inhabit in a critical way, where we refrain from unrealistic projections, such as wanting "world peace", without knowing the reason for wanting "world peace." Cammarota and Fine's (2008) comments resonate with the need to break away from the banking method of education and knowledge building that Freire discourages. Instead, frameworks that cultivate the youth's ability to connect the personal with the political, where they are guided through the engaged process of working with expanding their consciousness through the various stages.

Following a thoughtfully developed PAR process which has *conscientização* at the center of it binding human and non-human actors/actants, we carefully engage with the minds of the educators and participants alike, learning from one another, making the commitment to ask difficult questions that may not have easy answers. In a YPAR process, or any citizen engaged participatory process, it is necessary to honor the process of building strategies that are informed by the change in each actor/actant's ability to really train themselves to tap into the critical consciousness that guides them to build new discourses and new solutions thoughtfully. Focusing on the actual action research sites over the years, the observation of the youth facilitators on how each sub-group of the youth participants became increasingly more engaged and communicated better with one another over the multiple days is reflective of the way in which slow, small and guided processes can really work. One of the consistent questions that was asked to the youth was why they wanted to participate in an action-oriented, participatory, citizen science project like BGreen.

One of the US respondents said:

> From the action research schedules of the BGreen website and its Facebook page I have gathered that this would be one of the most unique environmental moots in the country yet. The workshop leaders seem experts in their respective fields and I hope to interact and problem solve with them to deepen my knowledge in the issues to be discussed.
>
> (Personal communication, May 5, 2016)

In response to the same question, a respondent in Bangladesh said:

> First of all, I've never been to any kind of environmental knowledge based training platform before. So, the first instinct was that I could use this platform to gain knowledge about the environmental issues of Bangladesh along with learning and generating solutions using a participative manner. I can perhaps participate in figuring out how to resolve it.
>
> (Personal communication, January 12, 2014)

Both participants explained the way in which BGreen's youth-engaged focus is not commonly done in either the US or Bangladesh and how this approach intrigued them in becoming engaged in the network. The intentionally created participatory formats for both the youth and experts in BGreen, were carefully moderated and monitored by the core group of community organizers, as we did not hesitate to give polite feedback to our workshop leaders after the event, on what we thought about their interactive processes. It was evident from the level of participation of the youth in all the workshops in both the US and Bangladesh that they felt empowered to actively use their educational training to participate in the process of social change in concrete ways, examples of which will follow in the next sections as well as in the conclusion. Freire (1970a, 1970b) advocated for a system of education that emphasized the use of dialogic communication, participation, and action to promote conscious empowerment, one that is of course done from the perspective of steering away from damage-centric research.

Hence, consistent with Freire and Tuck's ideas on working with peripheral communities, participatory work like BGreen needs to be done with a great deal of ethical attention to dialogical and transactional pedagogy that can aid marginalized peoples in liberating themselves from the constraints of the limited, problematic learning process. Despite the encouraging and warm reception that participatory learning processes had on the youth participants in both the US and Bangladesh, the challenges of participation certainly presented themselves as well, especially in the early parts of most of the developing processes in both the US and Bangladesh. It played out differently in different contexts. For example, when the youth community partners were co-learning facilitating dialogue building and group solution building around common issues of concern, several issues rose to the surface.

The youth facilitators at first had to un-learn the top-down, didactic process of giving instructions even within youth groups, instead of embracing their role as guides in helping each other open up about their ideas and perspectives that helps them evolve through the stages of gaining critical consciousness. They were trained on how they can become the participants' allies in the process in facilitating this collaborative process of growth. To train youth in both nations to foster collaboration and dialogue, we did a few different role-playing, ice-breaking activities to demonstrate how their role can be crucial to the process of maintaining good communication between youth participants and the community organizers. They also experienced a hesitancy to participate in dialogue in some of the community partner meetings, where the youth partners initially felt the need to respect the older partners in engaging in discussion and decision-making. As one of the main OPPs for the project, I had to play a crucial role to consistently remind everyone in the group that their voice and their approaches mattered in the way in which this participatory network gets shaped and reshaped, informed by the plurality of the voices involved. This discomfort of expressing one's opinions and voices based on seniority was more apparent in Bangladeshi youth than in American youth, which may be true due to the cultural attitudes towards "elders" in Bangladesh.

In another example, while making media production decisions on very short timelines in both the US and Bangladesh, often the idea about the final media output emerged organically and spontaneously upon group discussions. There became a pattern of creating unique solutions to each academic–community engaged project. For some group projects of the youth, they chose to create independent videos on the spot during the action research process and followed with on-site quick live editing and had the entire group watch the video at the end of the action research workshop event to reflect on the collective process together and distribute it via each and every participant's social media networks to amplify the process as they chose. Another example was when we took group decisions in creating combined multi-media action research projects—the main product on a separate day after individual group projects were conducted in different locations— and joined together to build a common media experience in our partner US media organization location, Amherst Media in Western Massachusetts, USA.

Hence, taking control of the internal translation process of BGreen was very important to its sustenance. It was important to address the complex relationship between power and democratic/participatory processes and how it played out in the building of this network. Instead of shying away from this challenge, it was important for everyone involved (older allies and the youth) to be self-reflexive and conscious of their roles in perpetuating certain power dynamics within participatory processes. It is important to identify strategies that can deal with the realities of such asymmetrical power relations that are at play, which can undermine the goals of developing such spaces to begin with. In relation to the complexity of such uneven dynamics within collaborative processes, it was apparent that not only do organizations have to change but the youth participants often had trouble understanding this inclusive approach as well, since, in their lifetime they have not encountered a model like this in their affiliated institutions.

Most youth were used to the traditional format of interacting with those who are traditionally in "power", who are older, with more education, experience, degrees, etc, where they are accustomed to listen in to experts presenting their work or research on a certain topic and they base their hopes of learning on passively listening, rather than from engaging actively in the process of knowledge transformation that may lead to social change. One contradictory recurring theme in some of the comments made by the youth participants is that through their engagement in the BGreen transnational participatory process, they were expecting to learn from "experts" on what to do about educational and environmental challenges.

For example, one participant said, "I want to be part of this action research to learn about what my peers think about environmental issues, but most importantly learn from the experts on how to tackle these problems" and another one said, "I want to gain a great deal of knowledge from listening to the work of the experts" (January 11, 2015). While there is nothing wrong with learning from a person with experience and there are benefits to such a way of knowledge transfer, in my view, following the PAR model is better and more productive to learn and co-produce *with/alongside* the so-called experts who make up the epistemic communities, rather than following the model of learning *from* them. Freire (1970a) argues that creating changes in the way in which learning happens is important because, "critical and liberating dialogue, which presupposes action, must be carried out with the oppressed at whatever the stage of their struggle for liberation" (p. 65). To bring about a shift in relating the way in which knowledge is produced and used takes time and effort, hence we knew as a team in BGreen that it was important to exercise patience through challenging points in the process of change.

However, despite the newness of the process, in some of the responses the youth blatantly pointed out which workshops could have been conducted in more of a dialogic and collaborative manner, often pointing and comparing the less participatory ones to the others in our line-up, that really involved them in developing some new observations. From the variety of responses and the enthusiasm that I witnessed while working with and observing the youth in the different sessions, it was clear to me, how quickly they understood the process of participation and how some of them went above and beyond by taking their ideas to the next level, of realizing them on the ground. Most of them needed very little guidance from the facilitators who were trained to help small student groups maintain a democratic flow of conversation and were very proactive in taking leadership in engaging in the issues that they were being exposed to for problem-solving.

This youth's inspiration and enthusiasm needs to be reflected in larger institutions in the US and Bangladesh, especially the ones that youth are affiliated with from an early age such as educational institutions. This is because a deeper kind of involvement in the learning of new things and applying it to change their own reality is a process that needs thoughtful engagement itself from educators, students and administrators alike. There needs to be attention paid to the different ways in which educators, students and administrators can create diverse strategies on how to work with youth to guide them through the stages of consciousness. Consistent with my confidence in participatory action processes, the youth participants displayed different responses about participatory processes and their roles in it after the event. In the post-questionnaire, the question around youth engagement that was asked garnered altogether different responses from the youth. One of the youth facilitators had jokingly said in the post-event de-brief,

> I have volunteered and facilitated other youth events before, but I have never seen the youth so interested in filling out questionnaires with so much care. They all looked like they were giving their final examination while filling the questionnaires out and they were also talking with one another, discussing their experiences, while doing so.
>
> (Personal communication, January 14, 2014)

This was important for me primarily and of course also for all the community partners, since such positive feedback from the youth facilitators about the youth's interest and concentration levels after the end of a multiple day event was encouraging. Also, in one of our action research events in Bangladesh, when our community partners got together to log all the information from the questionnaires into google spreadsheets as a collaborative data transcription process, we were very excited about the mostly positive feedback of all the youth. Some salient themes that emerged through the process were:

1. The youth were inspired and impressed by the participatory process of working alongside workshop leaders and facilitators in a process that was more horizontally developed to include them in the process of generating new ways of thinking that they could connect to the development of action plans on the ground.
2. The youth made the connection between these participatory/deliberative processes to the current ways in which educational processes were designed in both the US and Bangladesh and showed interest in using this participatory and socially-engaged learning format rather than the top down approach.
3. The youth overwhelmingly expressed interest in network and alliance building across multi-actors/actants to sustain their interests in social change, especially by way of academic institutions and new media technologies.

In supporting these observations, here is a look into some ideas expressed by the youth participants. An overwhelming majority of the youth were able to connect the idea of horizontal participation to a process that empowers them and changes the way in which knowledge building processes and structures are built. One youth wrote,

> When I signed up to be a part of BGreen, I assumed the program would be like the other environmental conference where experts, lecturers and initiators would deliver and promote their areas of work. But now, my perspective has been changed completely and I found BGreen to be a platform where I not only get an opportunity to learn but also feel myself to be a part of it. Together, use can bring a change.
>
> (Personal communication, January 12, 2014)

While this perspective made clear amongst many others that the youth were the people that were the biggest transformative agents that worked alongside "experts" to construct a new form of engaged, dialogic learning that is based on critical consciousness as the common thread, which at its best has the potential to bring about social change. Also, this perspective helps break down the binarism that was separating the youth from structural realities. Hopefully engagement in processes like these remind the youth that their presence and participation makes up structures alongside other important human and non-human actor/actants and that they have the power to challenge the supposedly functional structural stability that is being actively constituted to sustain power and binarism.

The two comments really connected the process to the potentials academic–community partnerships that they themselves may initiate. One person said,

> I studied an undergrad course on 'environmental conflict' that led me to this event first of all. The event allowed me to see a clear connection between my

academics and professional orientation in a way that has not happened before, where I got to sit down with like-minded people to see how they are thinking about these issues. This collective feedback is important as I can use our collective visions to bring this experience and process back to my school to start youth-led clubs that address different social concerns in a participatory setting that works alongside teachers, professors and administrators.

(Personal communication, January 12, 2014)

This really brought meaning to the process of participation in the way that I had envisioned it, where the youth could move beyond the action research events and connect the importance of including this participatory process in their educational affiliations. Their ideas for developing transformative spaces could be taken up and used ideally to create *organizational conscientização*. In the next section I will discuss more in detail how this specific inspired vision of the youth in BGreen led to small structural shifts in different academic–student communities in both the US and Bangladesh. Another salient trope that emerged was how the youth connected the importance of building networks and alliances across multi-actors/actants and how new media technologies, especially social media, could be used as an important vehicle to unite people and to create and sustain social movements. One such youth perspective was from the US:

I do believe that BGreen will enrich my knowledge about education and environment and help me to share learning with other dynamic youth change makers. This will help me to make a new network with some experts those who have same vision like me.

(Personal communication, January 12, 2014)

Another youth from Bangladesh connected it to the importance of using non-human actants like social media to aid in the building of their youth networks and said:

I would like build connections among the diverse people present here and share their ideas and views in an organized way by using Facebook, Twitter and Tumblr. Through discussion with many of us, we all can come up the strategy and take initiative on how to use social media to our advantage to help gather more support for our social projects that are not supported by our schools.

(Personal communication, 12 January, 2014)

Hence, without even knowing the exact frames that were driving my research agenda, the global youth engaged were generating responses that addressed the importance of the creative relational dynamics between human and non-human actors and actants in the building of a participatory network.

Youth working for youth

As mentioned earlier, about 72 percent absolutely agreed that the conference motivated them to get personally involved in societal issues on environment. The question specifically asked them about what they got out of this innovative, engaged design, that actively used the youth in generating new discourses on architecture of participation and taking action that were then shared with diverse epistemic communities from different organizations.

One youth participant's response was powerful and succinct. She said,

> BGreen gave us a reason to dream. My team and I have already decided that we are going to go back to our town and use this inspiration to build a student led-environmental club in our university with affiliation with the faculty and administration so that we can target the environmental challenges that people in Bangladesh face in the coastal belt that we live in.
>
> (Personal communication, January 12, 2013)

Many of the responses involved the same ideas quite explicitly, while some of the others had these sentiments, but more implicit in their writing. We did not get a single response to this question that suggested otherwise. A large number of responses were inspirational, positive and expressed the desire for change and wanting to be part of processes like these more often. Then there were responses that had specific action plans, like the one quoted above that expressed the wish to do something more concrete that translates the knowledge generated in this space into something that can help their communities. Remarkably, one youth participant, who made the above comment, followed through with his actions by collaborating with a larger group of his university's youth (who were also participants in the event). After the BGreen action research event, they founded the academic–community group called DARAB (The Disaster Awareness and Response Association of Bangladesh). DARAB was founded by a group of youth from Department of Disaster Management of Patuakhali Science and Technology University who participated in the BGREEN conference 2014 in Dhaka, Bangladesh and were inspired by the conference content to establish a student environmental movement in their region.

The group was initiated to work at the community level by campaigning on disaster awareness and emergency response on issues of local/regional environmental sustainability. DARAB mainly focuses on working in the most disaster prone areas in the southern part of Bangladesh by using the vision of the youth and incorporating the resources of local educational institutions to develop campaigns at schools, colleges, universities and at the grass-roots level of the southern part of Bangladesh. They have since then proposed to BGreen to hold the next action research event in their university. Another example of a great action project that came together as a result of this research was initiated by ten different youth participants who had contacted me post event to brainstorm about how BGreen can support them in sustaining their interests in carrying out their action projects.

They expressed their concern about the challenges that they faced as young students with difficult schedules and inflexible academic institutions and asked whether BGreen would be interested in helping them with developing their action plans, if they volunteered their time to develop a Youth Action Mentorship Program. The group of enthusiastic students provided BGreen's core community partners a brief summary of ideas and assured us that they would all take turns in running this platform for mentorship with our guidance. What they were asking us to do for them was to really provide a continued mentorship with the workshop leaders that conducted the participatory work as they wanted to further their relationships with them. Hence based on the requests of the youth participants, who formulated their goals and needs, *The BGreen Mentorship Program* was born, which is the next phase of this action research initiative, which was designed on request by these youth participants who sought structural help in giving shape to their pipe-dreams in manifesting their critical consciousness in the form of community engaged projects. The Mentorship Program was developed after meetings with the community partners, who had committed themselves to this follow-up project that was going to carry the action research event forward. Now the BGreen Mentorship Program is going strong in creating action research projects in both the US and Bangladesh.

The proposed idea of having this Mentorship Program was based on both nations' needs to develop actual action projects on the ground that are connected to research (albeit on a very small scale), which over time has the potential to bring about new discursive shifts in the way in which the architecture of participation operates within a BGreen participatory network. This Mentorship Program has the potential to launch other independent but related participatory networks such as DARAB, that lead to the complexity of the BGreen participatory network as well as supporting the emergence of a related, but distinct one. The program is still running and expanding and we now have a committed group of young professionals in diverse fields that volunteer their time to work with the youth as mentors to develop their community action projects. Some of the projects that these youth are working on are urban rooftop gardening, permaculture education, nature education to middle schoolers, developing green media campaigns, to name a few. While this is an additional responsibility that neither I nor BGreen anticipated being part of, this is an example of how a participatory network can grow and expand, where the unexpected actors/actants can join in the process in order to add difference and complexity, which makes the action networks deeper, stronger and more complex.

Castree and Macmillan (2001) reflect on the role of actors/actants in network stability: "the processes determining the constituents, stability and reach of a particular network are deemed to be *internal* to it, at some level, to involve all the network entities . . . . [O]nly *after* each network has been carefully described that explanation can emerge" (p. 212). This is an important point to understand, especially in the case of the BGreen network, since much of the complexity of this participatory network happened post-event. The associations and relationships between the actors/actants became stronger and they shifted and reconfigured to what became a participatory network that started showing signs of stability. The community that was formed as a result of the collaborative, participatory work that went into building the architecture for the event, deepened upon the successful completion of our first action research project, where most of the youth community organizers enrolled themselves to the future sustenance of the BGreen participatory networks. One interesting point to note on this is, 5 years later, among the human actors, the youth community partners are the most reliable and steady contributors to the process of building network complexity and stability.

One other important example of a student-led post-BGreen project was one that has made its way to Western Massachusetts. Some of the youth community partners, who produced our workshop wrap-up videos that were discussed in the previous chapter, expressed a desire to develop a public access television show that would be available online, free of charge to youth around the world, that would showcase youth academic-activist projects from around the world. While I knew of my logistical challenges, that I would not be able to stay back long-term in Bangladesh, their question to me was whether I could find a place in the US that would be able to produce live television shows that could be synced with their footage and videos in Bangladesh, to create a collaborative show that could be streamed online.

They wanted to use the power of multi-media to sustain the movement and this gave birth to the BGreen Media Literacy Project, which is a multi-format television show that brings together youth, academics and activists from around the world in showcasing their environmental action projects, in partnership with the Amherst Public Access Television, that has become one of BGreen's international community partners. While the show is in its nascent stages and we have only filmed eight episodes, the goal is to connect the BGreen media team in Bangladesh with the Amherst media team, to start co-producing more, to feature the shared, collaborative work that is produced by the youth. This kind of trans-national and multi-institutional collaboration is an example of a project that has created international alliances on the issue of youth action and educational and environmental change.

So far the episodes have been a mixture of interviews with individuals from a variety of professional backgrounds who have critical discussions on relevant environmental topics and special features of projects from around the world and in the immediate locality. The youth wanted to do this to continue generating dialogue and communication and fostering partnerships among various grass-roots environmental projects and academic institutions that are often under-represented in the media and finding creative ways of using the internet to build a low-cost, international new media participatory network. Amherst Public Access Television was also very supportive of this vision, when I approached them with the idea and after doing consistent work with them in the last year, the young team there has become one of our most active community partners. The complexity of the process and how the BGreen participatory network developed by making use of the web of non-human and human actors/actants is quite remarkable. This goes on to show the strength of using ANT-PAR as a tool to analyze the inter-dynamics between actors/actants that go beyond an anthropocentric lens and provide a fuller picture of how the process progressed and deepened to generate the (evolving) outcomes as a result.

Youth inspirations and participatory networks

Building on the remarkable progress of the youth in using creative, collaborative approaches to addressing the educational limitations in both the US and Bangladesh, it is important to reiterate the important historical roots of youth, academia and social change in Bangladesh and US. Youth engagement and its relationship to social change has been a double-edged sword in Bangladesh, where many of the important social changes have been accomplished with the direct intervention and involvement of the youth. However, they have also been highly vulnerable to political control, manipulation and violence over the entire course of Bangladeshi history and hence there is an urgent need in developing participatory processes that help to protect the youth's ability to attain *conscientização*. As mentioned earlier, the acute political challenge could have impeded on the youth's planning, but they found creative ways of enlisting non-human actants to work in their favor in order to beat the political and structural obstacles. Such a precarious political scenario was truly a metaphor for an old, outdated system of politics that was testing the creativity, adaptability and resilience of Bangladeshi youth, forcing them to think outside the box to beat the odds.

Some of the youth voices indicated that there was a need and value in creating academic–community platforms that would provide them the opportunity to not only work with their peers but also experts, researchers, academics, professionals etc, to develop a more community-engaged pedagogical model that has larger goals of social change. Through the different action projects that have resulted from this event it is evident that when youth are given a kind of setting that can work with their instincts, inspirations, visions and strengths, they need adult allies, in this case, me as one of the key OPPs of the project, to help them navigate institutional structures to bring these fresh discourses into a concrete shape. It is also encouraging to note that the youth can go beyond the event itself and instead connect the experience to a larger process, in which they can use their voices and strategies to bring about structural discursive shifts in the way in which youth engage with multi-institutions to realize their visions for a better future for themselves.

The examples above point to some important discursive shifts that BGreen participated in the development and growth of the transnational participatory network. In the process of developing The BGreen Media Literacy Project based in the US, our very own internationally streamed, free, public access television show, one of the main youth producers from Bangladesh had written to me about how this television show is helping to turn her theoretical video knowledge into an actual applied skill towards something much larger. She said,

> Through BGreen, I am able to use my skills that I learn in the classroom to reach an international audience in developing socially themed videos. I aspire to go to study filmmaking in the US for my higher studies, so this is such a great experience for me to be able to work with media teams from other countries to develop something beautiful and relevant together.
>
> (Personal communication, January 24, 2015).

Participants found value in using their academic training in ways that directly connected to pertinent social issues in Bangladesh and the US that affects the larger population. However, one of the interesting things to note from an ANT perspective is that, multi-media actors/actants like new media and television are allowing youth actors/actants to become creative in ways that were inconceivable before. New media is allowing the youth to build new discourses and crafting new ways of working around political economic institutional structures, where power is operating in a dispersed way. In my perspective, educational institutions in Bangladesh should take notice that students are using a relatively small opportunity like BGreen and building on it to generate new realities for themselves, with their own visions, ideas and inspirations. They are using non-human actants like technological innovations to aid in the emergence of their *conscientização* and subsequently figuring out ways of manifesting it in the form of diverse, community engaged projects. They are able to take control of their own lives and find creative, innovative ways of manifesting their ideas that may lead towards significant shifts in the way in which youth navigate their institutional affiliations.

However, while these are all inspirational examples and quite a remarkable growth from where BGreen started, it also points to an alarming trend of neoliberal economies, where projects like BGreen are doing the work that educational institutions should be doing to serve youth citizens. Hence, underfunded projects like BGreen bear the responsibility of working around and within large institutions, while large educational, often privatized academic institutions are being funded to provide education that is of little meaning to the youth for which they are theoretically designed for. Hence, in order to really tap into the abilities, interests and passions of the students and educational institutions, both K-12 and higher educational systems, should rethink their money-making strategies and instead focus on a youth educational culture that highlights their needs for developing a critical, socially engaged form of education that connects theory with praxis.

Perhaps, academic–community student groups like DARAB and media youth literacy projects like BGreen Media Literacy Project can be examples of how youth can use their voices to change the way in which large multi-industry structures work. Perhaps, this can eventually lead youth to develop closer relationships to administrative processes in their respective academic and non-academic institutional affiliations. These projects can perhaps be a starting point of change. Giving the youth the tools to be able to decipher for themselves the depth of the situation is a key first step in this crisis, which is the goal of such an applied, community engaged, educational approach that allows them to go from magical, naïve to critical consciousness. Participatory action research projects like these may act as starting points for the youth to dabble in complex issues in a non-intimidating and informative atmosphere that expands their knowledge on such issues by bringing them face-to-face with multiple realities.

One of the recurring ideas that came out of the sessions in both countries is how the youth can contribute to "greening" their education and taking control over a decontextualized model of education was the development of earth/green clubs in their schools, universities and colleges. One participant said,

> As mentioned before, I would make a green club in my school and persuade my school to facilitate us and support us to take the first step by conducting different localized environmental projects that target our neighborhood's specific needs.
>
> (Personal communication, January 12, 2014)

While this may seem like a small change, it has the power to transform institutions from within, by creating a democratic space within institutions where the youth can use their voices in dealing with issues that connect education, environment and community. This is an especially great idea, since, it does not require any large monetary investment at all, especially in the beginning and it has the power to change the dynamics and goals of institutions by engaging innovative youth leaders with their institution's administrations in a fruitful, low-stakes way. This set-up will urge the youth to find ways of maneuvering the power and binarism that resides within political economic structures. With their experience in using non-human actants to their advantage in developing new participatory networks, they would need to interrogate the factors that contribute to the assumed functionalism of such structures, which is brought about by the continuous enactment of relational processes that happen between human and non-human actors/actants to help uphold the power hierarchies within political economic structures. Potentially through small, action oriented academic–community projects such as these, the youth will be able to get the support of the institutions' infrastructure to carry out pilot discussions and projects and build participatory networks with other Earth Clubs in different academic institutions to carry out larger, localized projects around the country and world.

Three such Earth Clubs in universities and schools were started as a result of the BGreen conference, in three different urban higher-educational institutions in Bangladesh, soon after the action research event. The groups of youth who pioneered these clubs in their respective institutions, brainstormed and organized their ideas at our workshops, which eventually led to institutions backed earth clubs. Orr's (1994) suggestion that "all education is ecological education" (p. 12) really brings home the idea that the pedagogical process is not just about the one-way transfer of information, instead it is a process where diverse worldviews are exchanged, which at its best results in new worldviews, new discourses (Lopez, 2010). Bringing the environment into our classroom, into our education and into our lives, and *also taking* education out of the classroom as part of a learning and demystifying process and applying it to bring about social change, as David Orr (1994) writes in World Watch Forum 2010, seems to be a powerful, promising leap in the right direction.

Undoing the hermetic seal: a new form of education?

Bringing about discursive changes in understanding the environment, education and its connections to the youth's futures, is one that we can take in our own hands especially if it is entered into our literacy sphere, which in the context of Bangladesh and the US can really help in the emergence of *conscientização* in the youth and institutions.

Orr (2010) writes of this possibility for partnership and alliance,

Institutions of higher education—indeed, all schools—must aim to create an ecologically literate and ecologically competent citizenry, one that knows how Earth works as a physical system and why that knowledge is vitally important to them personally and to the larger human prospect. There are many challenges to actually making this a reality, not the least of which is the very real possibility of growing despair and nihilism among young people in the face of what will likely be a time of increasingly dire news and seemingly unsolvable social and economic problems. To be effective on a significant scale, however, the creative energies of the rising generation must be joined with strong and bold institutional leadership to catalyze a future better than the one in prospect.

(p.21)

I think that the project of expanding our "mappings" (Bennett, 2009) to include the more-than-human is crucial, but I also think that this work must be accompanied by a different set of conceptual tools that facilitate such mappings. The ability to participate as engaged citizenry in solving wicked problems comes from a different kind of education, one that I, along with so many other scholars are proposing. A new approach to education that does not leave out different subjectivities from the established, outdated periphery can help in the process of breaking up the ideas of epistemic communities, which has till now only served a select group of people across the world. The maintenance of these epistemic communities thrive on the defacement and silencing of voices and communities that have to live with decisions that "other" people have made from them.

The fact that the global youth are mapping the links between education, environment and their collective futures in a concrete way, where they are learning to make the connections of how these three seemingly disparate units are actually interconnected in complex ways is a good starting point. Hence, via academic–community action projects like BGreen that are invested in youth-engaged change, there is the potential for a true societal shift by making transparent our interdependence with the larger network of all entities—the more-than-human/non-human as well as anthropogenic and bringing into the forefront ethical decisions about environmental justice and beyond.

One of the biggest problems that contribute to the gap in building transnational participatory networks among different industries, which in this case (among many other bad consequences) brings about environmental challenges and ecological imbalances is what Bennett (2009) calls "distancing". Social and geographic distance makes it easy to "not see" or be concerned with the costs that environmental degradation imposes elsewhere and the planet as a whole. In reverse, such distance creates a smoke-mirror that separates us from understanding the larger motivations behind processes like neoliberalism, political and monetary corruptness that has resulted in the terrible state of the mainly market-led higher-education in Bangladesh today which reduces the youth to a mere consumer. Hence the epistemic communities held in such high regard in institutions, fall prey to such distancing, which is only designed to serve the people who are already in a place of economic, social and spatial privilege.

Another one of Bennett's (2009) concepts, that of "vital materiality" helps reduce that distance between us and all of the material processes we are intertwined with, an approach that holds promise in creating positive, sustained change and a reality that the youth may be able to connect to through the action research conference in claiming their expanded consciousness. The concept of vital materiality also echoes the same kind of ideas of embracing the performative, complex processes of actors/actants (humans and non human) in an actor network, where we are constituted and reconstituted to a continuous process of becoming— always changing, always evolving. Gibson-Graham (2006) also highlight the importance of the process of change, heterogeneity and dynamism that defines the formation of ethical, participatory and performative communities, ones that are always in the process of becoming and value difference over dominance.

Short-sightedness and imposing top-down interventions and closeted epistemic communities that have increased such distancing in development policies regarding education, environment and youth, have only contributed to the perpetuation of economic and political monopoly that have only benefitted an exclusive group of people. Business as usual has not improved the situation, and instead has spiraled the educational system down a treacherous path where the youth's right to learn is measured by market-forces, an ongoing issue in many nations in the global north and south. Giroux (2013) reflects on the problematic state of the US higher education system today, which has heavily influenced the Bangladeshi privatized higher educational system along with many others around the world. Giroux (2013) writes,

> The conditions of young people today are considerably worse as a result of the shortsighted policies of three successive US governments . . . . Arne Duncan, Obama's appointed secretary of education, appears unusually obtuse when it comes to devising a democratic vision for education, especially in light of his all-too-apparent love for market-measures, military schools and high stakes testing schemes and his evident dislike for any mode of knowledge and classroom pedagogy that cannot be quantified.
>
> (p. 19)

Hence engaging youth in a socially just oriented mission that urges the transformation of the current, disengaged form of education is a complete departure from the decontextualized way in which higher education has globally been shaped and determined by market measures. The active youth citizen participation from bottom-up may be the key factor that can truly change the course of academia as it stands in both the countries. This was an essential component of designing a Youth PAR project, as often, students may feel hesitant to use the power of their voices, since they occupy peripheral social positions due to their age and education levels, a society where "young people have been increasingly removed from the inventory of social concerns and the list of cherished public assets, and in the larger culture they have been either disparaged as a symbol of danger or simply rendered invisible" (Giroux, 2013, p. 19).

The de-peripheralizing of the youth

Through BGreen, we created an environment where the youth participants and the youth organizers felt welcomed and empowered to think differently and innovatively about the issues at hand and come up with solutions, big and small. One key aspect of the design of the participant process was to make the playing field as open and respectful as possible, to create a genuine space where *everyone's* view is welcomed and treated equally, as much as possible, despite acknowledging the limitations of how power interferes with the way in which decision-making happens in such processes. To provide a specific quote from a participant that explain how the youth's peripheral positions were shifted by this process, one participant said,

> I gained enough knowledge to be able to weigh the pros and cons of several issues all by myself. Also, the discussion with experts have also changed my opinion for the better. This opportunity has provided a lot of leverage that I will use for future reference and in not only my studies but to also apply it to my future work.
>
> (Personal communication, January 12, 2014)

On an event level, BGreen's aim was to not only provide an actual action research platform based on dialogue, but also to create a point of connection to what the youth aspire to do on the ground inspired by the collaborative, action research project that they engaged in that was designed by their peer youth group. It aided in de-peripheralizing the space that youth occupy in developing such participatory networks and also in participating in it. It allowed them to go through the phases of Freirian consciousness and see themselves in a different light—not as passive learners but as active social agents through which political and structural change can come about. The realization and initial success of DARAB, The BGreen Mentorship Project and the BGreen Media Literacy Project, provided the youth a sense of validation about how inspired and well formulated action plans can take shape and how they can be the driving forces behind bringing about such structural and discursive shifts that can shape alternative futures for themselves and political economic structures around them.

The participation of the youth actors/actants in all the variety of different ways as expressed in the previous chapters, holds the potential of contributing to the development of a participatory network that really ultimately serves them. Hence, with increased global youth mobilization around the issues of environment and education, there is potential for big change: one that may positively impact future national (and/or regional) policy-making around the issues of environment and education in both the US and Bangladesh, where, if this participatory network proliferates further can come to the attention of policy makers that ultimately holds the potential for infiltrating the closely guarded epistemic communities. Gaining network stability for BGreen, would set a good example for how multi-industries worked and collaborated together with the youth to bring about shifts in the way in which knowledge is understood, assimilated and generated.

In *Borderlands* (1999), feminist Chicana scholar Gloria Anzaldúa expresses the complexities of speaking from the peripheral borderlands to the established core and how this conversation as difficult as it is, must be made possible to create radically different value and knowledge systems that benefit more than a small, elite group of people. Taking this unconventional participatory path can be difficult, but necessary to create such alternative epistemologies and methodologies and it will require the shifting from the comfort zone of both the researcher and the "subjects". She writes that these spaces cannot be created without "a tolerance for contradictions, a tolerance for ambiguity" (Anzaldua, 1999, p. 101) and BGreen is built on the hopes of exactly such complex and useful organized dialogue and communications between groups that are placed in the periphery sharing their ideas and aspirations with the core. Hence, the youth, who are typically placed in the periphery are being asked to re-define the core, the epistemic communities, and subsequently to bring about shifts in the hegemonic educational and environmental discourses that are more commonly put forth by governmental bodies and large international organizations.

Bibliography

Anzaldua, G. (1999). *Borderlands/La Frontera: The new mestiza*. San Francisco, CA: Aunt Lute Books.

Bennett, J. (2009). *Vibrant matter: A political ecology of things*. Durham, NC: Duke University Press.

Bergold, J., & Thomas, S. (2012). Participatory research methods: A methodological approach in motion. *Historical Social Research/Historische Sozialforschung*: 191–222.

Busch, L. & Juska, A. (1997). Beyond political economy: Actor networks and the globalization of agriculture. *Review of International Political Economy*, 4(4), 688–708.

Cammarota, J. & Fine, M. (2008). *Revolutionizing education: Youth participatory action research in motion*. New York: Routledge.

Castree, N. & MacMillan, T. (2001). Dissolving dualisms: Actor-networks and the reimagination of nature. In N. Castree and B. Braun (eds) *Social nature: Theory, practice, and politics*. Malden, MA: Blackwell Publishers, pp. 208–224.

Freire, P. (1970a). *Pedagogy of the oppressed*. New York: Continuum.

Freire, P. (1970b). *Cultural action for freedom*. Cambridge, MA: Center for the Study of Development and Social Change.

Gibson-Graham, J. K. (2006). *A postcapitalist politics*. Minneapolis, MN: University of Minnesota Press.

Giroux, H. A. (2013). *Youth in revolt: Reclaiming a democratic future*. Boulder: Paradigm.

Latour, B. (1987). *Science in action: How to follow scientists and engineers through society*. Cambridge, MA: Harvard University Press.

Latour, B. (2004). *Politics of nature*. Cambridge, MA: Harvard University Press.

López, A. (2010). Defusing the cannon/canon: An organic media approach to environmental communication. *Environmental Communication*, 4(1), 99–108.

Orr, D. (1994). *Environmental literacy: Education as if the earth mattered*. Great Barrington, MA: Schumacher Center for a New Economics.

Swidler A. 1986. Culture in action: Symbols and strategies. *American Sociological Review*, 51: 273–286.

7   Conclusion

The oldest recorded higher education institution in the world, *Nalanda Mahavihara*, which began in the early fifth century, was the pride of the Indian subcontinent that served thousands of students from around the world. Nalanda was a visionary university that was based in a province in India called Bihar, which is a region bordering Bangladesh, now known for notoriously low literacy rates. The lineage of education at Nalanda remains powerfully germaine to the pedagogical needs of today, especially since the design and ethics around education are rapidly getting eroded in Bangladesh and in the US, where educational spaces are becoming solely profit-making endeavors (Sen, 2015). Sen (2015) writes:

> The pedagogy that prevailed in the old Nalanda is strongly relevant here. The school regularly arranged debates between people—teachers, students, and visitors—who held different points of view. The method of teaching included arguments between teachers and students. Indeed, as one of Nalanda's most distinguished Chinese students, Xuan Zang (602–664 AD) noted, education in Nalanda was not primarily offered through the "bestowing" of knowledge by lecturers, but through extensive debates—between students and teachers and among the students themselves—on all the subjects that were taught.

The Indian government alongside the support of a few other governments in South-East Asia have just re-opened the Nalanda university once again, on a very small scale, many years later, which while being an inspirational move, is still in the process of finding stability with a lot of religious, sectarian and economic politics getting in the way of it being established all over again in a way that embodies and promotes the participatory tradition it was known for (Sen, 2015). While regional Asian nations have collaborated to rebuild this institution, it is hardly surprising that there is no Bangladeshi involvement in this process of attempting to bring back this form of education that is "driven by intellectual curiosity and interest rather than the pursuit of material profit" (Sen, 2015).

Instead of participating in rebuilding the educational drought in the larger South Asian context (reflected not in the number of educational institutions but in the quality of education), Bangladeshi government released their fiscal national budget in 2015 in which they have reduced the funds allocated to education and technology to 11.6 percent from 13.1 percent in the previous fiscal year (*The Daily Star*, 2015). Not only this, but they also just passed the bill that imposes 7.5 percent tax on private education, which is what the majority of Bangladeshis are "consuming" (*The Daily Star*, 2015). This decision has met with a great deal of controversy as expected from many different people across the country, which hopefully will lead to some action on their part. The emulation of the US model of treating education as a privatized commodity has been well internalized and integrated in the social fabric of Bangladesh.

The notion of "educational democracy" (Fields & Feinberg, 2014) is a necessity in the educational sector in both US and Bangladesh today, as the progression of academia is on a similar path and trajectory in both nations. There is a global need for educational democracy to build the next generation of critical, socially aware and engaged individuals involved in sustaining true democratic values in society. Cammarota and Fine (2008) emphasize in their book, *Revolutionizing Education* that research that is done "with" rather than "on" youth with a hopes of a "vibrant public sphere—for a democracy (to echo Michael Apple)" worth its name is an effective strategy of building inclusive communities that are involved in building new subjectivities, discourses that are grounded on social change (Cammarota & Fine, 2008, p. vii). The importance of digressing from "damage-centered" (Tuck, 2009) research is vital to counter-map and unsettle such pathological and debilitating discourses of communities from the "borderlands" (Anzaldua, 1999), which can potentially complicate the limited concept of "epistemic communities" (Haas, 2001). The current apolitical and socially divorced form of education in both the US and Bangladesh perpetuates the banking form of mechanical knowledge building, devoid of critical thinking, one that does not encourage the formation of new knowledges and fresh discourses.

As we explored in the previous chapters, this is a result of a profit-seeking economic system that controls the funding, structure and curricular goals of most universities in both countries, which in conjunction with the unstable and corrupt political system (in the case of Bangladesh) has acutely impacted the scope of developing an educational project with *conscientização* as the central driving force of the process. The unapologetic and unchecked neo-liberal agenda provides an important compass for investigating and analyzing the adoption of this profit-driven system's effects on youth and their connection to educational institutions in both the US and Bangladesh. Educational institutions are the first systemic structures that most youth in both the US and Bangladesh (and beyond) are closely affiliated with from a young age, so it is logical to assume that the pedagogical space holds immense power and potential to influence the way youth develop their ideas of the world around them.

Paying heed to the top-down failures of many national and international governing bodies regarding issues of environmental, educational and human security in the past, there needs to be creative effort invested in localized settings that involve the local communities to engage in the process to bring about a change in systems, however big or small. My narration and analysis of the global US and Bangladeshi youth's active engagement in developing BGreen as a transnational academic–community partnership brings into the forefront the power of the youth in transforming discourses and institutions around them in small but effective ways. The globally engaged youth through the building of this transnational participatory network demonstrated creativity and growing maturity in the way in which they maneuvered through the functionalism of multi-institutional political economic structures. The growth and stabilization of BGreen points to a rare disruption of the seemingly monolithic higher educational structures in both nations today, which does not encourage participatory engagement of youth in any way.

Therefore, the mapping of BGreen brings forth examples of counter-narratives of innovative ways in which actors and actants can merge to navigate these structural challenges to create new, discursive shifts. The determination of a top-down, closed system is a lost opportunity for both youth *and* educational institutions to work together to benefit from the complexity that exists within the myth of the fixity of structures. The potentials of combining large institutional political economic strength from different countries in conjunction with ground-up global youth perspectives and activism to work together to bring forth a new architecture of participation was demonstrated by the network stability of BGreen, which was essentially operating within a privatized economic framework. This points to the disruptions and nuances that are present within privatized, market-led structures, which are ultimately built out of evolving processes that ironically rely on the *constant*, *complex* and *conscious* reconfigurations of diverse factors that contribute to the upholding of the illusion of power.

The idea of determination as it is connected to critical political economic theory (and as developed in critical cultural studies) needs some revisiting here to understand the way in which such a transnational participatory network flows through complex spaces. For some, the idea of determination comes with preordained thoughts, ideas and outcomes, but according to Hall (1996) the economic cannot "provide the contents of particular thoughts" and cannot "fix or guarantee" how ideas will be used by particular classes (p. 44). This displaces the positivist and functionalist notions that particular outcomes are universal, predictable, natural and stable, which Hall (1996) refers to as "Marxism without guarantees." In this version of Marxism, there is human agency and free will, but there is acknowledgement and inclusion of structural constraints that limit the choices one can make within it.

In this version of Marxism, the base is determinant in its structuration of boundaries that coordinate human behavior, but in the end there are no guaranteed certainties of the outcome. This nuanced theorization of critical political economy (via critical cultural studies) works well in alliance with the weak ANT-PAR approach that I used to frame, navigate and analyze this project. This version of political economic theory creates room to move away from determination, which is an incomplete framework that needs to be reconciled with the addition of networked approaches to understand complex, unpredictable processes that are in flux and ultimately form what we know as "structures".

Embracing paradox

In the context of transnational networked political economic spaces (in the specific case of BGreen) there are two processes that are important to reflect on: the architecture of building this transnational participatory academic–community project and how ultimately this action research project was used by the youth to bring about discursive shifts in a variety of different ways. These two processes brought forth the complex interactions between global actor/actant networks and political economic structures, that ultimately re-constituted both ends of the spectrum (political economic and ground-up) by unsettling and traversing narrow, outmoded constructs of core and periphery. Other than bringing about shifts in the collective youth's thinking about education and also in the political economic structures of multi-institutions, there is another important shift that is key to the process: it is the change in the way in which science is defined, knowledge is produced, social change is achieved, which allows for the outmoded, tightly-knit knowledge and expert communities, called epistemic communities, to thrive.

Latour (2004) brings forth a different approach, one that embraces the pluriversality of this world, where we change the terms of conversation and the way of business as usual by coming out of the "cave" or the "old regime", which is defined by him as the systemic, spatial and ideological barriers that allow for the sustenance of tightly guarded, knowledge and expert communities, where Science (with a capital S) resides, which in turn supports the maintenance of the façade of functionalism in political economic structures. Instead he urges for the need to develop a "new collective" that is no longer surrounded by a single nature and other cultures, but that is capable of initiating, in civil fashion, experimentation on the progressive composition of the common world" (Latour, 2004, p. 197). Latour (2004) further writes how the discourse and praxis around Science needs to shift and he says,

> I contrast Science, defined as the politicization of the sciences by (political) epistemology in order to make public life impotent by bringing to bear on it the threat of salvation by an already unified nature, with the sciences, in the plural and lowercase; their practice is defined as one of the five essential skills of the collective in search of propositions with which it is to constitute the common world and take responsibility for maintaining the plurality of external realities.
>
> (p. 210)

Latour is advocating for a definition of science that includes the reconfiguration of systems where the voices and knowledge of non-traditional scientific communities, human and non-human, are accounted for in the development of a new discursive space that does away with the "old regime". Harvey (2014) reflects on this as well when referring to the idea of creating an architecture of participation and writes,

> Given that natural sciences have traditionally been more strongly bound to a model of inquiry that privileges distance, objectivity, and authority than the development community, there has been less emphasis on inclusion, community voice, or open-ness to other knowledge sets within climate science until quite recently.
>
> (p. 22)

Harvey points out recent controversies around the transparency of the Inter-governmental Panel on Climate Change (IPCC)'s climate modeling and prediction processes that highlight the current bias toward closed "expert" dialogue in the establishment of new conclusions and knowledges, throwing light on the limitations of epistemic communities as a controlling factor in effective community governance (Tol et al., 2010). However, there is a great deal more work to be done on the potentials for drawing on participatory, citizen-driven knowledge and combining it with epistemic community knowledge, and BGreen can be at the forefront of these efforts. This discussion of Science/sciences is directly related to the way in which these epistemic communities are created and upheld that impact the formation of top-down, undemocratic, asymmetrical political economic structures. In the case of both the nations, US and Bangladesh, educational systems are systematically designed to suppress any form of engagement and questioning of the order of things, hence closely protecting the insularity of epistemic communities that is necessary to support the illusion of closed, fixed, impervious political economic structures.

The youth are directly at the receiving end of these administrative and curricular deficiencies that are driven by the politics of profit and power. However, as the growth of the transnational BGreen participatory network demonstrates as it spans the US and Bangladesh, the global youth are doing their part to creatively navigate through diverse political economic structures to use their agency to bring about small, but important discursive shifts. Using my academic training, I collaborated with the youth to design BGreen as a citizen-science academic–community platform, where youth from both nations worked with expert actants/actors collaboratively to produce new discourses, in line with what Latour called the new "sciences". The journey of this participatory network was unpredictable and could not be charted. The actors/actants who had enrolled into the process had to re-invent the ideas of participation, especially with regard to the way in which they maneuvered through the political economic structures for the emergence of network stability. To translate participatory theory into praxis via BGreen, it is necessary to pay heed to the diversity of processes and perspectives in coming up with unique strategies to challenge Science for the development of the sciences. For example, it is necessary to not only pay attention to the way in which there can be a shift in the higher-educational institutions in both US and Bangladesh, but it is also important to reflect on how other industries that are relevant to the youth, such as media houses (mainstream and alternative), are undergoing shifts as a result of such participation and reconfiguration.

After building BGreen on the ground, there was a need to develop the theoretical concept of participatory network that encapsulated the PAR-ANT experience. This theoretical contribution was important to construct, since it allowed for the synthesis and re-conceptualization of inter-connected, on-ground and on-line factors that affected the formation of the BGreen participatory networks. Building on the ideally hermeneutic relationship between theory and praxis, the goal is to build a theoretical model that is informed by on-ground realities. At its best, the theoretical concept of participatory networks after being developed can be used to understand further networked political economic spaces and their complex relationships with power, binarism, non-human and human actors/actants and participation. While the theoretical concept was developed as a result of the on-ground work done in Bangladesh, the same concept was applied to analyze the building and proliferation of BGreen.

It is in the tracing of this complex, open, fluid, unpredictable, hybrid, chimeric and dynamic participatory network, where the heart of the project lies. Engaging with the diverse ways in which power, binarism, functionalism and determination is challenged through this networked political economic process was an important goal for the development and analysis of BGreen. The way in which global youth could navigate multi-institutions to build complexity in a project like BGreen spanning different countries, could potentially provide inspiration to others to use this concept of participatory network to unite citizens, technology and structures to work together to develop new, unexpected, socially relevant results.

However, it is important to note that according to the critiques of the hegemony of neoliberal peripheral development, even counterculture transnational networks like BGreen still perpetuate and sustain a fractured and flawed system to begin with, a proposition that I have mixed feelings about. As privatization raids over the peoples and places, it pushes civil society to develop creative processes like BGreen to remedy situations. While this reality will not deter action researchers like me to go forward in building more complex participatory networks via collaborative research, it is necessary to be mindful of the limitations and asymmetry that laces such projects. This urges action researchers like me to really interrogate the place for the future of projects like BGreen within the current cultural, economic, political sphere.

One of my personal goals in the early stages of my action research was to move BGreen away from the in-between space in which it was created: the complex, fertile, under-explored and under-theorized networked political economic space that exists between the actors on the ground and the myth of functional political economic structures. The goal for me was to find entry into transforming those very political economic institutions that BGreen came into contact with (for example the host universities, media houses, etc) and then having the BGreen network become a part of an academic institution, building on the potential complexity of educational structures as displayed by ULAB's willingness to host an academic–community project. However, 2 years after my research and with extended time spent with the core youth actors and knowing what they want as the future of BGreen, we have collectively agreed that maintaining the autonomy of this transnational participatory network is of utmost importance. The youth unanimously do not want any official institutional affiliations, national or international. Instead, they want to build strong, mutually beneficial partnerships with multi-institutions that are short and long-term from within the nebulous, hybrid and complex networked political economic spaces.

Instead of BGreen being attached to any one academic institution anywhere in the world that "houses" the action research projects each time, the youth want to maintain their independence and flow, while collaborating with multi-actors/actants that they want to merge with to add to its network stability. This view is consistent with what McAnany (2012) refer to as the growth of the citizen sector in the economy that resides between multi-institutions such as business, government and other private and public sectors. McAnany (2006) writes:

> Not only is this sector growing but it has in some cases adopted practices and technologies that have made the business sector so dominant globally in the past century. This new sector has as its goals to provide increased social

benefit through a variety of new and innovative institutions that will serve those who have been left out by the economy and the labor market.

(p. 150)

All the youth actors in both US and Bangladesh have decided that maintaining this distinct autonomy of the transnational participatory network of the citizen sector is the only way of preserving the unique, participatory approach of BGreen, which allows them to work with larger institutions, but protects them from swerving too far from the project goals based on other organizations' mandates. The youth not only feel empowered by their active engagement in the growth of this participatory network process, but over time, have demonstrated concrete examples (via their leadership and decision-making) on how they have undergone the different stages of Freirian consciousness and applied them in gaining network stability in very specific ways. For example, some of the major growth points for BGreen in 2015 have all been initiated and sustained by the youth. To provide some of the highlights:

1. The youth have designed the third BGreen website (www.bgreenproject.org) with expanded bandwith that can facilitate complex and dynamic online classrooms, which was one of the most consistent recommendations of the youth actors on how to specifically sustain this BGreen participatory network. This is a direct result of the academic–community partnership and a major opportunity for the youth, since youth from both the US and Bangladesh combined to create all the new media addresses.

2. The social media coordinators of BGreen, have been from both the US and Bangladeshi universities, often collaborating through skype, email and Facebook to create transnational streams of online content for BGreen's expanding and diversified work. One of their major successes of the expanding transnational participatory network is the persistent online networking of my Bangladeshi social media coordinator. Through her avid participation in the online sphere, she connected me to a high profile, celebrity-led non-profit organization in the US that deals with water, education and sustainability, Water Defense, which brought very exciting and diversified action research projects for BGreen in both the US and Bangladesh. After negotiating how we can contribute to each other's mission, BGreen has partnered up with the Water Defense and has conducted water and education-related projects in Bangladesh.

3. The youth have created a sustained television show in Amherst, MA called the BGreen Media Literacy Project, which is a multi-media platform that connects local projects with a global audience, generating dialogue and communication, creating connections and fostering partnerships among various grass-roots

social justice projects from around the world. BGreen is proud to be partnering with Communication for Sustainable Social Change and Amherst Media for this project. All the episodes have been filmed in the studio of our partner, Amherst Media, in Amherst, MA, USA.

These are accounts of a few of the major ongoing projects. The youth have shown tremendous growth as active social agents who can connect their shifts in states of consciousness (from magical, naïve to critical) to larger structural processes that go beyond their individual realities. Instead, they are using their elevated consciousness to build a new, inclusive architecture of participation that has the potential to affect the ways in which insular structural realities are systematically constructed to silence local stakeholders. My role in the growth of the network, while important, has shifted significantly over the youth's journey to attaining and applying *conscientização* to deepening the BGreen network. At this current point in time, as the founder of the project, I provide them with the connections they need to facilitate their plans, rather than micro-managing the route they will take to manifest their ideas on-ground and on-line.

They seek me out to provide them with mentorship and leadership around issues of fundraising, resource management, project development and implementation with them. They mostly take the lead in generating new themes or programming that they believe is important for BGreen to offer the Bangladeshi youth as a service to them, while I help them in refining their goals and connecting them to useful local, regional, national and/or international organizations that they can benefit from in the development of new BGreen programs. All of these expansions were uncharted and unpredictable and happened based on the youth's vision, where I became the person that gave structure to realizing their visions, rather than being the sole OPP that set the tone for what direction and shape this network will take. Their rising confidence in how to use structures in their favor is evident through their concrete ideas in developing innovative programs that apply their elevated social and political consciousness that they are using towards strategic social transformation.

Revisiting participatory networks

The youth's success in building participatory networks necessitates the importance of reflecting on some deeper issues of understanding some of the limitations of this concept that builds upon seemingly uncomplimentary theoretical trajectories. The two aspects of participatory networks as a concept that need further reflection are:

1. Considering the unpredictable and open nature of participatory networks, how do we negotiate the complexity and participation paradox of staying

"true to the original vision" versus taking a radically different approach to reconstitute the direction, scope, goals and contents of a participatory network like BGreen?

2. Also, at what point does an *emergent* participatory network become a *stable* participatory network?

Reflecting on both these questions, it is important to reiterate how the process of translation is key to the process of stabilization of such networks. Networks need to undergo the four stages of the translation process, in order to form depth and stability. The most important part of an *open* participatory network, is that it is in a constant process of *becoming* and *evolving*, where the actors/actants are consciously negotiating and re-negotiating their relational dynamics and keeping the process *open* for merging with other networks. Harvey (2014) warns us about being able to identify when actors/actants are using the participatory frames to advance goals that are not so noble. He writes that "participation, as it is put into practice in World Bank/IMF development programming, bears more in common with popular governance under late colonial administration than with the types of empowerment with which the term is frequently associated" (p. 29). Therefore, while being cautious is prudent, it is also necessary to keep an open mind. Keeping the process open is important, because all the entities that participatory networks encounter in its course adds unique complexity to it, which is transformative on both sides.

However, the level of transformation depends on the over-arching power and binary relations that frame such fluid processes and how the actors/actants manage to negotiate it. Instead of shutting down the differing approaches that contribute to the development of such participatory processes like BGreen, it is necessary for platforms to have a clear vision (that is flexible for change as/when needed) and to be open to experimenting. Platforms like BGreen should focus on bringing together diverse forms of participatory approaches and be guided with an ethical framework that is open to different forms of solution building that ultimately enriches, deepens and complicates its own participatory network. For small, transnational projects like BGreen to sustain itself, partnerships are key, since these are the associations that can potentially lend to the participatory network in gaining complexity and stability.

However, it is also important for projects like BGreen, for these same reasons, to maintain autonomy. This is because the true participatory capacities of small but complex processes can be challenged as a result of the ways in which uneven and asymmetrical power relations between different actors and actants operate. Such complexities in power relations, if unchecked, can significantly impact the process of network stability. This brings forth the importance of understanding what is meant by the term stability itself in the context of participatory networks.

The important point to ponder on would be to explore the factors that contribute to calling a network *emergent* versus *stable*. Engaging with this question is important, despite knowing all too well that a unifying answer cannot possibly be arrived at due to the complex and unique nature of participatory networked processes, especially transnational ones. Perhaps, with the possible wider application of the concept of participatory networks, there is potential to compare different applications of it in diverse social, cultural, economic, national settings that may help articulate a better understanding of the differences between network emergence and stability as it applies to it. This is consistent with the idea of refining and redefining theory as a result of engaging with praxis, to keep the process connected and dynamic between epistemological and ontological processes.

To provide an example of how the participatory and complexity paradox played out on the ground in the BGreen process, it is important to bring forth an experience with one of our organizational community partners, Consortium for Science and Policy Outcomes (CSPO). While the deliberations conducted by the CSPO team was an integral part of the participatory content of the action event, it certainly was not the *only* participatory activity that the youth participants engaged in the course of the event. However, their participatory technique, which is the deliberations model as conceptualized by the Danish Board of Technology, was an innovative process that the youth could be a part of and make informed decisions on the chosen theme, which made BGreen's array of participatory activities and opportunities stronger and more diverse. However, at all points in creating this collaboration, the community partners were mindful not to let CSPO's needs override the rest of the workshop plans, since they had more experience in running participatory events in their own way, with their own specific agenda. This demonstrates the importance of building an open participatory network, one that is malleable enough to merge with other networks where "instead of prioritizing one 'actor' or 'group' over another, the politics of impurity highlights their ethical connectivity and the impossibility of discrete political subjects" (Castree and MacMillan, 2001, p. 220).

Another repeated phenomenon that sheds light on the complexity and participatory paradox of such participatory networks is some of the organizational partners' over-emphasis on my leadership in the process, where they undermined the crucial, participatory contribution of the youth actors in adding stability to the network. This is ironic, since these organizational partners themselves are participatory actors within the larger network, but they over-emphasized my role as the OPP and/or founder of the project, hence ignoring the other actor/actants' roles in adding complexity and re-negotiating power asymmetry within the participatory network. There is no denying that my power within the networked process *is* significant and my continued commitment to the process and the people affiliated with it provides a sense of motivation and direction to the core community actors. However, the commitment and the leadership undertaken by some of the core youth actors cannot be sidelined—they're going a very long way in re-defining and re-configuring not only my role as a founder, but also the overall network stability of the participatory network.

This urges us to engage with the upholding of power and binarism in a nuanced way, where we are acknowledging the futility of having two extreme ideas of power, one that takes a fixed, determined approach, while the other dismisses its role in networked structural processes. Instead it is important for human actors in the participatory process to be able to identify and grapple with the multi-faceted and multi-layered manifestations of power as it flows through such networks and to know how to creatively combine human and non-human actors/actants to re-negotiate and re-constitute it. In the BGreen context, with the continued flourishing of the network, my role in it is shifting and evolving into a different place than where it started. My involvement with the project is gaining more of a symbolic significance, where people outside of the BGreen participatory network refer to me as a figurehead for this project, which results in me having a huge responsibility to uphold the image of BGreen in the public domain. I work closely with the core youth actors to decide on the different ways in which through my media engagements, I can bring forth the participatory spirit of this project to the public, always emphasizing on the collaborative work, rather than crafting an identity for BGreen that is solely led by me.

Synergistic participatory networks?

The reasons for developing participatory networks as a concept that moves away from strong ANT's version of the black box was to create a process that is open, participatory and hybrid which combines with not only human and non-human actors/actants in isolation, but also other participatory networks. Creating synergies between different participatory networks can ultimately enrich all actors/actants involved. As Bergold and Thomas (2012) write:

> The participatory research process enables co-researchers to step back cognitively from familiar routines, forms of interaction, and power relationships in order to fundamentally question and rethink established interpretations of situations and strategies. However, the convergence of the perspectives of science and practice does not come about simply by deciding to conduct participatory research. Rather, it is a very demanding process that evolves when two spheres of action—science and practice—meet, interact, and develop an understanding for each other.
>
> (p. 35)

Through the collaborative work with all our partners, we were able to do many little participatory projects in both the US and Bangladesh with globally connected youth, with full logistical and financial support. For the projects to grow, flourish and gain network stability, it required many diverse human and non-human partnerships between and within actors/actants that were surprising, unexpected yet created a process of hybridity and complexity that could not have been possible any other way. This is the strength of an actor network approach merged with PAR (albeit a weak one, as I have used in my research), where the beauty of difference is highlighted in every step of the way. Surprising collaborations occurred which resulted in a hybrid, dynamic actor/actant process that may not have been possible, if all the actors/actants concerned were not open to risk change.

For example, the way in which the multi-media networks were formed was nothing short of incredible, in my perspective, where mutual trust between the media teams in both countries with BGreen and the youth journalists/reporters resulted in the transformation and growth of not only BGreen as a transnational participatory network, but also the journalists/reporters themselves, who were able to maneuver through the complex power structures of the media houses, to work in BGreen's favor on a repeated basis. The shared trust among the human actors to really come together from diverse institutions to address the ways in which such a process can take shape, where each of them could be transparent to one another about the collective, united goals of BGreen was key to the process. Each core community partner was an integral actor in the networked process and brought with them their own network complexity (their organizational affiliation, their political, social, cultural, emotional attitudes), which generated shared trust amongst the partners and added to the stability of BGreen.

Also, the collaborative and unified way in which non-human actants such as technology were used in the process was a very important factor that contributed to the BGreen network stability. Each of the smaller participatory networks merged for a bigger goal to create something deeper, richer, bigger—one where human actors/actants played just as key of a role in keeping the process afloat as non-human actors/actants such as technology, inspiration, ethics and hope. The importance of ethics and how this participatory network flourished is evident in the way in which the organizational community partners overcame their differences in approaches to working together in many uncooperative work situations where people had difference of opinions, political challenges, etc, to name just a few barriers. Instead, they took a chance to work together, framed by a shared goal, one that they knew would be evolving and changing, like all actor networks.

In solidarity with the ANT vision, Gibson-Graham (2006) writes about the *coming* of a community, one that is always in the process of transformation, definition and re-definition, but it also brings into the picture the futility of being fixed, immutable and *essential*, which is a natural process of flowing, changing directions and being open to this process of un-fixed fluidity that can redefine participatory networks. The interplay of networked and political economic approaches was an important frame to explore, especially with the inclusion of participation and *conscientização* in the mix. Exploring the tension within these approaches and bringing forth narratives on why there needs to be a rethinking and renegotiation of this divide, allowed us to develop a framework and process that combined the strengths of both approaches. Both sides can inform each other's weaknesses, as I addressed earlier, in the development of participatory networks, by addressing difficult issues of power and binarism that often plague the realization of participation as a process.

As a reminder, through this research I have tried to address this in-between space, albeit from a ground-up, participatory perspective, where the role of larger, institutional bodies is incorporated into the way in which we relate to the construction and development of small, transnational projects such as BGreen. Ultimately, through the synthesis and merging of large and small, as PAR-ANT would have it and by analysing some of the salient outcomes of this participatory network, the goal is to show that larger, political economic actors/actants like universities, media houses, etc, do not stay untouched and unchanged through the formation of such transnational participatory networks. Complexity is at the core of every structural process. It is futile to perpetuate false dichotomies that support the pseudo determination of political economic structures and at the same time, it is also incorrect to view participatory processes as being the panacea for the ills of the functionalism of structures and systems. Instead, it is necessary to try and build participatory processes that put us in conversation with structures, with the hope of unsettling such extremities and develop a nuanced understanding of dynamic processes that reside inside the illusions of a fixed, stable and impervious structure.

The neoliberal agenda of private universities in both the US and Bangladesh that are invested in creating the most socially disengaged form of education for the youth in both countries has been narrated at length in Chapter 4. However, after the successful run of the first BGreen event in Dhaka, Bangladesh, which was hosted by the private university, ULAB, even such a rigid educational set-up started showing signs of complexity. For example, the university expressed interest in hosting BGreen again the following year, if there was any interest in all the other partners in continuing with this partnership. This was expressed to everyone in the post-event community meeting, which was attended by the Vice Chancellor (VC) of the institution. The Vice Chancellor had not shown a great deal of enthusiasm in BGreen prior to the event, and the team from ULAB who had become very friendly with all the other partners after the event was over, told us that the sheer media frenzy over the event led him to change his mind and he showed interest in meeting me. The Director of CSD (the sustainability unit) in ULAB that had hosted us told me, "No other event that ULAB has hosted has ever made so much press. I think while he was skeptical at first and thought there would be no takers for this idea, the amount of media attention that BGreen got changed his mind " (Personal communication, January 16, 2014).

While on one hand it was encouraging for us and displayed the power of multi-media networks in helping sustain our larger participatory network, the VC's eventual conversation with me also pointed to one of the dangerous tropes of popularization of a process, which may deviate people from maintaining their ethics around the project. This tension exemplifies one of the shortcomings of developing participatory networks, however, on the other hand, it points to the network stability that can be achieved, if actors/actants can work through their differences. In many ways, while BGreen is structurally much smaller and less powerful than ULAB, it still needs BGreen's expertise to guide and build such action research projects with its niche expertise. It also provides global youth to use BGreen as a platform to get involved in the process of changing higher-educational structures by the engagement of youth and new media technologies, in ways they could not do by themselves.

Another important institutional shift that occurred via the partnerships was a meeting with the Director of the US Embassy in Bangladesh in January 2015, after the BGreen action research event happened again for the second time. The introduction to the US Embassy happened through our connections with the EMK Center that was our community partner for the training session from the first year of conducting the action research. The Director of the EMK Center had introduced me to the Director of the US Embassy, since the US Embassy allocates the largest amount of funds to support community projects in Bangladesh amongst the Northern embassies. The meeting with the US Embassy Director of Cultural Affairs resulted in her encouraging us to apply for a decent-sized community project research grant that she felt we would be eligible for. She was heavily supportive of our future plans and provided us with encouragement to follow our goals in sustaining this network, which is driven by the needs of youth and using technological actors/actants as their allies. BGreen is waiting to hear from the US Embassy about the funding.

At the same time, we are also aware of the risks of being funded by a powerful actor/actant such as the US Embassy. Despite the fluidity and openness of the participatory network, BGreen is at risk of being vulnerable to the power play of the US Embassy and its organizational vision. Busch and Juska (1997) warn that small networks (in relation to the mammoth proportions of US Embassy) run the risk of being "dominated and because of their position in the network have very little power to articulate and defend their interests" (p. 702). Hence the openness of participatory networks is a double-edged sword, where while it is necessary to remain open to maintaining the dynamic, participatory element of the network, it always adds to the vulnerability of the network, because of external actors/actants that may use their/its power to coerce, re-direct or re-shape a participatory network from its purpose.

However, this is also a contradiction to the process of participation, which while being complex can also struggle with maintaining the continuous flux and in making sense of the growth and direction of such a dynamic, non-static process. These instances demonstrate that for such democratically designed youth citizen science projects to work, the shift in the people and structures needs to come about concurrently, where both aspects need to be worked on as difficult as it is to do so. This is why building a complex, diverse and sustained participatory network may be beneficial, as the different actors/actants that are part of multi-institutions may be able to work together with a common goal to bring about discursive shifts in multiple points at the same time. Citizens (in this case the youth) have to identify the problem and move forward with meaningful action to facilitate change in creative, innovative, untested ways.

Organizational actors/actants comprise individual actors and their corresponding non-human actants that can be used as tools for building a new *organizational conscientização* that can be "productively theorised and utilised at the organizational" and "not just the individual level" (Straubhaar, 2014, p. 445). Consistent with Castree and MacMillan's (2001) version of weak ANT, Straubhaar (2014) also adds that while each actor network (organizations, institutions, etc) is unique and different, there are also shared lessons on the "similar regular processes of reflection and strategic restructuring that help them [organizations] refine their mission and determine how effectively they are pursuing their organisational goals" (p. 445). This perspective and use of *conscientização* is quite apt for the organizational shifts that occurred throughout the development of the BGreen project. The emergence of this participatory network re-defined the relational dynamics between and within institutions, and perhaps as a result of it, other aspiring participatory networks can have something to learn from the narration of this complex process.

At its best, BGreen has the potential to lead to more goal-oriented environmental youth projects that address the challenges that arise out of the mediated discussions across various age, social and economic groups in a supportive platform. Taking inspiration from citizen-science and environmental social change platforms such as the David Suzuki Foundation (http://www.davidsuzuki.org), 350.org (http://350.org) and World Wide Views (WWV) (http://www.wwviews.org), BGreen was developed to be a localized answer for both US and Bangladeshi youth, by incorporating the unique needs and contexts of local and global communities of the youth's interst. The goal was to challenge the insular and outmoded model of binarism that separates citizens from participating in processes of generating *and* making sense of knowledge that ultimately can impact policy shifts based on their informed decision-making. An important point to consider is that all the movements named above share some similarities in goals, but bear important differences that make them complementary, which allows for non-competitive alliance-building across projects and nations, which is much needed to solve a global challenge of epic proportions.

Based on my short experience of being engaged in developing academic–community partnerships, one lesson rises to the top. There is a need for alliance-building among projects like WWV, 350.org, David Suzuki Foundation, BGreen, etc., since such multi-directional and multi-layered synthesis helps in building network stability of each of those participatory networks, but provides opportunities for building bigger, transnational participatory networks. Each participatory network brings its own unique and complex relational dynamics between human and non-human actors/actants. This not only adds to the deepening of each smaller participatory network, but it can bring about discursive shifts when working together to form a larger, global participatory network that builds off the strengths and complexity of each individual one.

Participatory networks, youth and education for social change

The academic spaces in both US and Bangladesh should reclaim the most important aspect of education as a social and developmental tool—one which aids in the production of new knowledges that is grounded in communities and lived realities rather than reproducing outdated knowledge systems. Shifting the current model to one that is more inclusive towards communities would be a step in the right direction of developing fresh discourses that result in the best form of theory—one that emerges out of working with complex, real communities. The precarious state of politics in the country at the time of planning the project and the barrier it posed for everyone in developing it spoke directly to the unwieldiness of an old, broken system that needs to be replaced urgently, a new system that contributes to the development of a progressive, inclusive and grounded form of engaged academic–community partnerships. However, it was the commitment of the youth around me that made the project a reality through the stark obstacles, even though adult allies provided them with the guidance necessary to make this action research project a success. As adult allies of global youth, it is our responsibility to guide them and help them in the process of developing and embracing their *conscientização* by guiding them through the iterative process of Freire's magical, naïve and ultimately critical consciousness.

Reflecting on the ways in which both the US and Bangladeshi youth took leadership in engaging with BGreen in many meaningful ways provides a strong case for how the implementation of citizen science and community engagement programs like these may be an important innovation in the higher educational context around the world. This has transformative potential to lead the way for more socially engaged, critically thinking youth that participate in collaboration with organizational structures to achieve their localized version of *conscientização* that can lead to meaningful social engagement on their part. For example, other than the different ways in which BGreen is already growing as a participatory network, one of the important growth directions could be to develop alliance building across nations, both from global north and south. This would enable such participatory networks to exchange, compare and collaborate in transnational processes that hold the potential to bring about significant discursive shifts in the ways in which youth, academia and community organizations relate to one another and their relationship to non-human actants to facilitate social transformation.

As a researcher, I would be very interested in exploring the ways in which these academic–community partnerships play out in other unique, geo-political locations, since comparative cases provide the opportunity to really grapple with the nuances of narratives and discourses that are generated from specific origins. I would be interested in exploring south–south as well as more north–south collaborations, to investigate the ways in which these private-public, multi-institutional partnerships play out in diverse social, cultural, political and national contexts. Also, another project I am interested in exploring in the future, is an analysis on the non-human actors/actants in the process of developing networks exclusively, to emphasize the importance of these entities in making actor networks and participatory processes stable.

BGreen is showing promise of developing more goal-oriented educational-environmental youth projects, by taking advantage of non-human, new media actors/actants that are really addressing the youth's concerns about the gap in the educational system in the world today. With increased youth mobilization around this issue in both nations, there is always a potential for big change: one that may positively impact future national (and/or regional) policy-making around the issues of environment and climate change. The large community of people that have been and will be interacting together through a common goal brings forth a myriad of possibilities for further organization and action. The process itself is empowering and transformative, as it places importance in incorporating the voice of the core players who are actively engaged in knowledge and discourse creation— the youth. As Cammarota and Fine (2008) aptly write, "PAR treats young people as agents in ongoing, critical struggles . . . working with youth, in distinction, means seeing young people as partners in struggle, as resources to be drawn upon in common cause" (p. viii). The participatory network of BGreen has certainly been a transformative process for all actors/actants involved and hopes to be a contributing factor in the redefinition of the educational futures of global youth, building on their own, unique brand of social engagement and transformation.

Bibliography

Anzaldua, G. (1999). *Borderlands/La Frontera: The new mestiza*. San Francisco, CA: Aunt Lute Books.

Bergold, J. & Thomas, S. (2012). Participatory research methods: A methodological approach in motion. *Historical Social Research/Historische Sozialforschung*, *13*(1): 191–222.

Busch, L. & Juska, A. (1997). Beyond political economy: Actor networks and the globalization of agriculture. *Review of International Political Economy*, *4*(4): 688–708.

Cammarota, J. & Fine, M. (2008). *Revolutionizing education: Youth participatory action research in motion*. New York: Routledge.

Castree, N. & MacMillan, T. (2001). Dissolving dualisms: Actor-networks and the reimagination of nature. In N. Castree and B. Braun (eds) *Social nature: Theory, practice, and politics*. Malden, MA: Blackwell Publishers, pp. 208–224.

Fields, A. B. & Feinberg, W. (2014). *Education and democratic theory: Finding a place for community participation in public school reform*. Albany, NY: SUNY Press.

Gibson-Graham, J. K. (2006). *A postcapitalist politics*. Minneapolis, MN: University of Minnesota Press.

Giroux, H. A. (2013). *Youth in revolt: Reclaiming a democratic future*. Boulder, CO: Paradigm.

Haas, P. (2001). Policy knowledge: Epistemic communities. In N. J. Smelser & B. Baltes (eds.) *International encyclopedia of the social & behavioral sciences*. Amsterdam: Elsevier.

Hall, S. (1996). New ethnicities. In D. Morley & K.-H. Chen (eds) *Stuart Hall: Critical dialogues in cultural studies*. London: Routledge, pp. 441–449.

Harvey, B. (2014). Negotiating openness across science, ICTs, and participatory development: Lessons from the AfricaAdapt network, *Information Technologies and International Development*, *7*, 19.

Latour, B. (2004). *Politics of nature*. Cambridge, MA: Harvard University Press.

McAnany, E. G. (2012). *Saving the world: A brief history of communication for development and social change*. Champaign, IL: University of Illinois Press.

Sen, A. (2015). India: The stormy revival of an international university. *The New York Review of Books*, *62*(13): 1–12. Available at: http://www.nybooks.com/articles/2015/08/13/india-stormy-revival-nalanda-university/

Straubhaar, R. (2014). A place for organisational critical consciousness: Comparing two case studies of Freirean nonprofits. *Comparative Education*, *50*(4), 433–447.

Tol, R., Pielke, R. & Von Storch, H. (2010, January 25). Save the panel on climate change! *Spiegel Online*. Retrieved May 21, 2010, from http://www.spiegel.de/international/world/ 0,1518,673944,00.html

Tuck, E. (2009). Suspending damage: A letter to communities. *Harvard Educational Review*, *79*(3), 409–428.

http://www.thedailystar.net/star-weekend/shutterstories/no-vat-education-109981

Index

350.org 207, 208

academic–community networks 3, 7,
    8–13, 16, 18, 20, 21–2, 38, 44, 46,
    50, 53–7, 66, 68–9, 78, 79, 81, 83,
    179, 183–4, 187; networked
    architecture 86–113, *see also BGreen
    Project*
accountability 41
action research *see* participatory action
    research (PAR)
activism 81, 90, 91, 105, 143; online 143,
    144, 146–8, 150–3; Shahbagh
    Movement 42, 71, 146–9, 150, 163
actor network theory (ANT) 2, 4–7, 8, 9,
    11, 16, 18–19, 45–7, 49, 54, 83, 195,
    197, 203–7; building networks 38–42;
    history and application 28–33; multi-
    media amplification 114–17, 123, 127,
    129–30, 138, 141–2, 147, 155–65,
    169–72; networked architecture
    86–113; new media 184; political
    economy 37–8; Shahbagh Movement
    147; youth reflections 169–91
advocacy approach 118
Agamben, G. 26
agenda-setting theory 121
Ahmed, A. M. 117
Ahmed, S. Z. 143, 145, 164
Ake, 78
Alaldulal 146, 150, 163
Alhassan, A. 116
Amherst Media 101, 106, 120, 130, 131,
    157, 175, 182, 200

Amherst Public Access Television 182–3
Anderson, 5
anthropocentric approach 32
anti-functional approach 37
Anzaldua, G. 3, 23, 33, 36, 190, 193
Apple, M. 193
architecture of participation 2, 4, 5, 7–10,
    18, 20, 31, 43–4, 51, 128, 140, 142,
    149, 165, 195
architecture of unity 107–11
Arise for Social Justice 101, 106
Arizona State University 103
Arnaboldi, M. 93
autonomy 23, 126, 198–9, 201
Awami League 145

Bangladesh 1–2, 9–11, 12–13, 35–6, 38,
    42–4, 46–51, 52–6, 59–62, 192–209;
    multi-media amplification 114–68;
    networked architecture 86–113;
    transnational political economy 66–86;
    youth reflections 169–91, *see also
    BGreen Project*
Bangladesh Climate Justice Project 153
Bangladesh Youth Environmental Initiative
    (BYE) 104–5, 119–20, 123, 153
Bangladesh Youth Movement for Climate
    (BYMC) 104–5, 119–21, 123, 124,
    125, 126, 133–4, 153
banking model 26, 58, 80, 82, 90, 193
Barrett, M. 145
Battistoni, R. M. 86
'becoming' 26

Beltran, L. R. 22
Bennett, J. 187–8
Bergold, J. 45, 57, 171, 203
BGreeners 149, 158
BGreen Media Literacy Project 106, 120,
    131, 182–3, 184, 185, 189, 199–200
BGreen Mentorship Program 181, 189
BGreen Project 1–2, 4–5, 6–7, 8–9,
    11–13, 16, 18–19, 20, 21–2, 28–33,
    35, 38–9, 42–55, 58–60, 78, 80,
    82–3, 194–209; blog posts 123;
    growth and sustenance 169–91;
    multi-media amplification 114–68;
    networked architecture 86–113;
    pTA exercise 59–62; transnational
    political economy 66–85
binarism 31, 36–7, 72, 127, 149, 162,
    170, 178, 186, 197, 201–3
'black box' 30, 31, 40, 106, 110, 130,
    142, 147, 158
blog posts 123
Borda, O. E. 26
Bordenave, J. D. 22
borderlands 3, 23–4, 33–4, 36, 190, 193
bottom-up approach 102–3, 194;
    globalization from below 80, 89
Bradbury, H. 26
Brightbill, N. 41
Brown, M. B. 66, 80, 89
Brulle, 171
Brundtland report 69
Buckland, P. 9
Bunz, 146
Burr, V. 41
Busch, L. 3, 30, 37–8, 171, 206
Butler, 27

Callon, M. 5, 28, 29, 31, 39, 42, 111,
    127
Cameron, J. 26
Cammarota, J. 4, 18, 20–1, 34, 94, 173,
    193, 209
capitalism 67–8, 76, 78
capitalocentrism 25
Cardoso, F. 22
career-building opportunity 121
Carlisle, S. 86
Castleden, H 100

Castree, N. 5, 6, 8, 29, 32, 35, 39, 40,
    43, 111, 127, 162–3, 182, 202, 207
Cavalier, D. 7, 20, 60–1
cell-phone technology 144–5, 146, 150
Center for Sustainable Development
    (CSD) 99–102, 122, 164, 205–6
Choi, S. Y. 120, 121–2, 159, 160
Christens, B. D. 90, 105
citizen science 7, 8, 9, 13, 20, 21–2, 36,
    43, 51–2, 75, 78, 171–2; deliberation
    model 103–4, *see also BGreen Project*
civil society movement 80, 89
civil society organizations 89, 90
climate change 2, 56, 102, 105, 134, 196,
    209
collective action 17, 28, 31
Colombo, M. 41
colonialism 22, 72
commercialization of education 70
community economies 25–7
community-university partnerships *see*
    academic–community networks
comparative approach 12
complexity theory 4, 6, 28
consciousness 80, 107; three stages 139,
    see also critical consciousness
    (*conscientização*); magical consciousness;
    naïve consciousness
Consortium for Science and Policy
    Outcomes (CSPO) 59–60, 103–4,
    202
constructivism 4, 28, 110
Cooks, L. 2, 3, 33, 143–4, 147–8, 149
core and periphery 4, 7, 11, 22, 23–4,
    30, 35, 37, 43, 190
corporatization of education 79–80, 89
corruption 117
cost-benefit approach 74
Couldry, N. 37, 40, 62, 69, 127
Crawford, T. H. 4
Cressman, D. 8, 21, 28, 30, 32, 36, 41
critical consciousness (*conscientização*)
    2–13, 17–18, 20, 26, 42, 52, 54–5,
    58, 173, 193, 200, 208–9; journalism
    141; multi-media 128, 139, 143,
    161–2, 184; networked architecture
    90, 94–5; political economic realities
    66, 69, 70–1, 75, 78, 81, 83;

pTA exercise 60, 62, *see also* organizational *conscientização*
critical pedagogy 26
critical performative approach 26
Cropper, S. 86
cross-media 159
cultural context 66

The Daily Star 193
damage-centered perspective 3, 7, 11, 21, 27, 33–4, 193
Das, J. 115, 117, 118, 140
David Suzuki Foundation 207, 208
de–briefing 59, 177–8
decentralization 159, 162–3
decolonial research 27
decolonization 25
"deep" method 172
deliberation model 103–4
democracy 31, 32, 80, 81–2, 109–10, 117; educational 67–8, 193; horizontalizing of communities 147–8
Denzin, N. K. 40
dependency theory 22, 23–4, 25
de–peripheralizing of the youth 189–90
de–politicization 7, 79, 81, 82, 88
Dervin, 24
destabilization 7–8
development goals 56
Dhaka University 72, 81
dialogical approach 24
Digital Bangladesh 145–6, 150
Disaster Awareness and Response Association of Bangladesh (DARAB) 180–1, 185, 189
discursive turning point 128
distancing 187–8
Drayton, 152, 198
Duncan, A. 188

earth/green clubs 185–6
Edward Kennedy Center (EMK) 105–6, 206
Elahi, M. 117, 139
emergent networks 5, 18, 20, 28, 42, 44, 87, 96, 115, 119, 123, 201–2, 207, *see also BGreen Project*

enrollment 29, 87, 95, 125, 172
environment 21–2, 43, 55–9, 87–8; advocacy approach 118, *see also BGreen Project*
epistemic communities 18, 19–20, 31, 60, 61, 69, 140, 142, 150–1, 193, 196; distancing 187–8; power relations 176
Escobar, A. 24, 25, 26–7, 51
Espino, S. L. R. 86, 89
ethical community building 4, 21, 25
ethics 33–6, 41, 57
Etmanski, C. 86
Eurocentrism 22
experts 60, 176, 178, 196
Extended Structural Adjustment Facilities 73

Facebook 95, 140–2, 145, 149–65, 199, *see also* social media
Faust, K. 29
Feinberg, 67, 82, 193
feminism 25, 26–7
Fields, 67, 82, 193
Fine, M. 4, 18, 20–1, 34, 94, 173, 193, 209
Flanagan, C. A. 90, 105
focus groups 52
Foley, 56
Freire, P. 2–3, 4, 6, 8–9, 10, 11, 12, 17–18, 26, 42, 54–5, 58, 60, 62, 66, 69, 71, 75, 80, 90, 128, 139, 141, 143, 161–2, 173–4, 176, 208
Frisby, W. 4, 21
functionalism 37, 62, 69, 107, 149, 194, 195
funding 68, 73, 76, 78–9, 90, 93, 185, 193, 206

Ganim, M. A. M. 146
Geddes, H. 120, 121–2, 159, 160
genetically modified food 118
Gibson, R. J. 76
Gibson-Graham, J. K. 21, 24, 25–7, 39, 51, 188, 204
Giroux, H. A. 36, 67–8, 70, 74, 75, 76, 79, 80, 88, 90, 105, 109–10, 145, 188–9

global warming *see* climate change
globalization 27, 37, 70, 73, 90; from below 80, 89; political economy 37
goal-oriented projects 209
Google hangout 95–6

Haas, P. 18, 60, 140, 142–3, 193
Hall 194
Hanitzsch, 117
Harvey, B. 2, 5, 18, 20, 31, 33, 44, 142, 161, 164–5, 196, 201
Hassard, J. 28
Hemment, J. 26
Hicks, J. 27
historical analysis 52–4
historical overview 53
holistic approach 69
Holland, B. A. 3
horizontal participation 178
horizontalizing of communities 147–8
Huesca, 24, 26
Hussain, F. 144–5
hybridity 3, 29, 32, 38
hyper-capitalism 76, 78

imperialism 22
India 192
Information and Communication Technologies (ICT) 5, 145–6
informational science 30
infralanguage 4, 5, 6, 39, 42
interactive approach 58–9
inter-connectedness 57
interdependence 24, 25, 57
interdisciplinarity 9
interessement 29, 87, 95
Intergovernmental Panel on Climate Change (IPCC) 56, 196
international financial institutions (IFI) 73, 74, 78
International Monetary Fund (IMF) 68, 73, 201
Internet *see* online activism; online news portals; social media
intersectionality 4, 21

Jacobson, T. L. 22, 23, 25
Jahan, I. 143, 145, 164

journalism 122, 125–41, 155, 158, 204–5; co-writing 129; youth 114–19
Journeys for Climate Justice (JCJ) 101–3
Juska, A. 3, 30, 37–8, 171, 206

Kabir, A. H. 9, 69, 71, 72, 73, 74, 75, 76–82, 88, 89, 95, 109–10
Kamruzzaman, M. 146
Karim, L. 66, 80, 89
Kemmis, S. 41
Kepes, 144, 146
Khaleduzzaman, M. 88, 95
Knorr-Cetina, 140, 142
Kolkata University 72
Kolluri, S. 23, 25
Kountoupes, D. 21, 78
Krøvel, R. 118

Lamb, C. 100
Lassen, I. 51
Latour, B. 4, 28–33, 40, 60, 61, 172, 195–6, 197
Law, J. 28, 42
Lerner, D. 22
Lewis, D. 90
Lewis, L. A. 71
liberation theology 25
Lindlof, T. R. 48
linear model 8
literature research 52–3
local level 56
López, A. 151, 171, 186

McAnany, E. G. 198–9
McChesney, R. W. 37, 38
MacMillan, T. 5, 6, 8, 29, 32, 35, 39, 40, 43, 111, 127, 162–3, 182, 202, 207
McTaggart, R. 41
magical consciousness 2, 17, 44, 61, 71, 80, 107, 139, 149, 156, 170, 185, 200, 208
Malikhao, P. 23, 24
Manzo, L. C. 41
mappings 187
marginalized peoples 7
market-based solutions 73
market exchange 171
Marx, K. 37

Marxism 22, 23, 194–5
Maxwell, J. A. 48
Media Literacy Project 106, 120, 131, 182–3, 184, 185, 189, 199–200
media networks 11–12; BGreen strategy 123–5
media organizations 47
media technologies 90, 95–6, 102; multi-media amplification 114–68
Mehmet, O. 69
Mentorship Program 181, 189
micro and macro level 37
mobilization 29, 87, 125
modernity/coloniality/decoloniality (MCD) framework 25, 27–8
modernization 22, 23–4, 27
moral responsibility 139
Morgan, D. L. 45, 52
Morgan, S. S. 100
Mosco, V. 3, 37, 67
Mostert, 51
Muhammad, A. 9, 66, 80, 89
multi-actors 9, 30, 45, 95, 108, 179, 198
multi-dimensionality 37
multi-industries 9, 71
multi-institutions 43–4, 56, 69, 75, 93, 197–8
multi-media 184, 204–6; amplification 114–68; goals and strategies 119–22; networks 54–5
multimethod qualitative research 16, 45
multiplicity paradigm 24–5
mundialization 27
Murdoch, J. 40

naïve consciousness 2, 17, 44, 61, 71, 80, 107, 139, 149, 156, 170, 185, 200, 208
Nalanda Mahavihara 192
Nath, S. R. 66, 80, 89
neoliberalism 66, 67, 73, 74, 75, 76, 78, 81, 83, 89, 109, 185, 198, 205
neo-Marxism 23
network instability 29, 93, 95, 138, 154
network stability 2, 29, 96, 110, 114–15, 119, 157, 158, 182, 198, 201–2, 203–4
networked architecture 86–113

newspapers 126, 130–2
non-human actors/actants 31–3, 37, 39, 41, 42, 75, 83, 96, 111, 184–6; new media 141–2, 148, 156; Shahbagh Movement 147, *see also* social media; technology
non-profits 89–90
Nordtveit, B. H. 27, 69, 70, 73, 78–9, 90
North South University 74–5
nuclear power: plants 118; pTA exercise 60–2
Nuruzzaman, M. 75, 81

Oberhauser, K. 21, 78
obligatory points of passage (OPP) 34–5, 40, 49, 90, 93, 95, 96–7, 99, 108, 116, 126–7, 129, 131, 138, 156, 157, 165, 200, 202
Olssen, M. 75
One Degree 153
online activism 143, 144, 146–8, 150–3
online news portals 136–7
organizational *conscientização* 17, 42, 62, 71, 120, 128, 129, 143, 152, 207
organizational tunnel vision 8–9
Orr, D. 57, 186–7
Ovimot 73

Pachi, D. 145
Pakistan 72
Pant, M. 86
participatory action research (PAR) 1–2, 4–7, 9, 11–12, 16, 18, 45–7, 49–53, 54, 57–8, 195, 197, 198–9, 203–9; building networks 38–42; history and application 20–8; MCD 25; multi-media amplification 117, 123, 128–30, 132–8, 142, 147, 151–3, 155–9; networked architecture 86–113; political economy 38; youth reflections 169–91
participatory technology assessment (pTA) 59–62
Patuakhali Science and Technology University 180–1
peer-to-peer platforms 151
performative approach 26–7
Peters, M. A. 75

Pioneer Valley 48, 97
place 27
pluriversality 27–8, 195
political economy 2–3, 10, 11, 16,
    18–19, 53–5, 66–86, 127, 194–5,
    198, 205; complexity 36–8; feminist
    economic research 25; social media 149
politics 93–5; elections 94, 124–5;
    injustice 117; instability 96, 109, 111,
    117, 124–5, 151, 193, 208; journalism
    117–19; movements 71, *see also*
    political economy
"politics-free campuses" 77, 79
politics of the cave 28
Politics of Nature 28, 32
Postcapitalist politics 25
post-development 25
postmodernism 24
post-questionnaire 177–8
poststructuralism 24
power 53, 67, 72, 127, 178, 186, 197,
    201–3; binarism 31, 36–7;
    decentralization 162–3; OPP 34–5;
    relations 134–5, 171, 176, 178, 201;
    social media 149, 150; technology 33
praxis 8, 42, 69, 99, 128, 141, 195–7,
    202
Prebisch, R. 22
press release 124
print media 125–32
Private University Act 1992 74
privatization 10, 66, 68, 70, 74–5,
    76–83, 89, 109, 198, 205; funding 73;
    global 66; media 122, 139; policies
    52–3; tax 193
problematization 29, 87, 95, 123
profit maximization 68, 74–5, 76, 78, 79,
    82, 192, 193
public education 76–7, 109

Quddus, M. 71, 72, 74, 75, 77, 81
Quijano, A. 22

radical alterity 28
radio 120, 122, 129–30, 135–6, 145
Rahman, A. 116, 117, 118, 122, 140
Rahman, M. 68, 73, 75
Rajshahi University 72

Rashid, S. 71, 72, 74, 75, 77, 81
Reason, P. 26
reflexivity 41
Reid, C. 4, 21
relational dynamics 142
researcher's role 34
Roberts, 32
Roger, E. 22
Ross, E. W. 76

sampling 48–9
Sandmann, 89
Scharrer, E. 3
Schramm, W. 22
Science 32–3, 60–1, 195–7
Science, Policy and Citizenship (SPC)
    program 60
Sen, A. 192
Senegalese education 78–9
Servaes, J. 22, 23, 24–5, 26
session jams 77, 79
Shabazz, D. R. 2
Shahbagh Movement 42, 71, 146–9, 150,
    163
'shallow' method 172
Smith, 37
snowball sampling 48
Social Bakers 145
social class 116–17
social context 66
social control 72
social justice 118
social media 137, 138, 140–65, 179, 199,
    see also Facebook; Twitter
social transformation 66–85
sociology of translation 29
sociotechnical network 41
solution-building approach 171
Sparks, C. 24
Spicer, A. 111
Spiller, N. 93
Spinuzzi, 29
Sri-Lanka 103
Strategic Plan for Higher Education
    (SPHE) 74, 81
Straubhaar, R. 9, 17, 42, 71, 128, 129,
    207
structuralism 23

surveillance 34
survi-vance approach 35
sustainable development 1, 24, 27, 69–70
Suzuki, D. 56, 207–8
Swidler, 171
synergistic participatory networks 203–8

Tatnall, 161
tax on private education 193
Taylor, B. C. 48
technology 36, 90, 95–7, 102, 204; divide 144; innovations 31–2; multi-media amplification 114–68; power 33; pTA exercise 59–60
television 120, 122, 129–31, 132–5, 145; BGreen Media Literacy Project 106, 120, 131, 182–3, 184, 185, 189, 199–200; journalism 118
text messages 96
Thomas, S. 45, 57, 171, 203
Tol, R. 196
top-down approach 22, 26, 58–9, 70, 80, 89, 90, 97, 174, 194
translation 29–30, 47, 87, 96, 111, 115, 123, 125, 160–1, 172, 176, 201
transnational political economy 11, 16, 54, 66–86
transparency 92–3
Trickett, E. J. 86, 89
Tuck, E. 3, 4, 33, 34, 35, 174, 193
Twitter 140–2, 145, 149–65, *see also* social media

Ullah, M. S. 144–5
UMASS Amherst *see* University of Massachusetts (UMASS) Amherst
United Nations, climate treaty 56
United Nations Children's Fund (UNICEF) 146
United States 1–2, 9–11, 12–13, 35–6, 38, 42–4, 46–51, 52–6, 59–60, 192–209; Embassy 206; multi-media amplification 114–68; networked

architecture 86–113; transnational political economy 66–86; youth reflections 169–91, *see also BGreen Project*
University Grants Commission (UGC) 72, 74, 75, 82
University of Liberal Arts Bangladesh (ULAB) 99–102, 122, 164, 198, 205–6
University of Massachusetts (UMASS) Amherst 91, 99, 104

Varghese, N. V. 9, 73, 74, 75
video-conferencing 95
video narratives 159–60, 175, 182
Vision 2021 56
vital materiality 188
"vocationalizing" education 81–2

Wadsworth, Y. 34
Wallerstein, I. 4, 37
Wasserman, S. 29
Water Defense 94, 101, 107, 199
websites 153, 155, 199
Western approach 22
Whittle, A. 111
Wiest, R. 68
Wildemeersch, 22, 23, 24
World Bank 68, 73–4, 78–9, 89, 90, 201
World Commission on Environment and Development (WCED) 69
World Systems Theory 37
World Watch Forum 2010 186
World Wide Views (WWV) 101, 104, 120, 121–2, 207, 208
Worthington, R. 7, 20, 60–1
wrap-up documentaries 159–60, 182

Xuan Zang 192

Young Night 132–4

Ziegler, P. 150
Zohir, S. 89

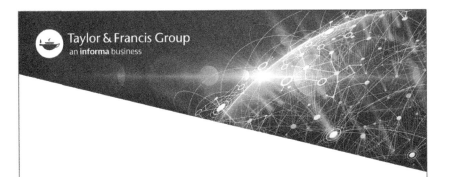

For Product Safety Concerns and Information please contact our EU representative GPSR@taylorandfrancis.com Taylor & Francis Verlag GmbH, Kaufingerstraße 24, 80331 München, Germany

Printed and bound by CPI Group (UK) Ltd, Croydon, CR0 4YY
01/05/2025
01858438-0004